WORLD WAR II LETTERS
AND NOTES
OF COLONEL
JAMES H. POLK
1944-1945

EDITED AND COMPILED BY

JAMES H. POLK, III

RED ANVIL PRESS

OAKLAND

RED ANVIL PRESS

1393 Old Homestead Drive, Second Floor
Oakland, Oregon 97462-9506.
E-MAIL: editor@elderberrypress.com
TEL/FAX: 541.459.6043
www.elderberrypress.com

Red Anvil books are available from your favorite bookstore, amazon.com, or from our 24 hour order line: 1.800.431.1579

Library of Congress Control Number: 2004115932
Publisher's Catalog-in-Publication Data
World War II Letters and Notes of Colonel James H. Polk/James H. Polk, III
ISBN 1932762191
1. Letters.
2. Military History.
3. George Patton.
4. WWII.
5. Tank Warfare.
I. Title
This book was written, printed and bound in the United States of America.

Front Cover: Oil portrait of Col. James H. Polk, C.O., 3rd Cavalry Group. Painted on a window shade by Mieczylaw Koscielniak in June 1945 at Gmunden, Austria. Koscielniak was liberated by the 3rd Cav. and was a survivor of both Auschwitz and Ebensee.

Map (p.6): Molly O'Halloran, Ltd, Austin, Texas

TABLE OF CONTENTS

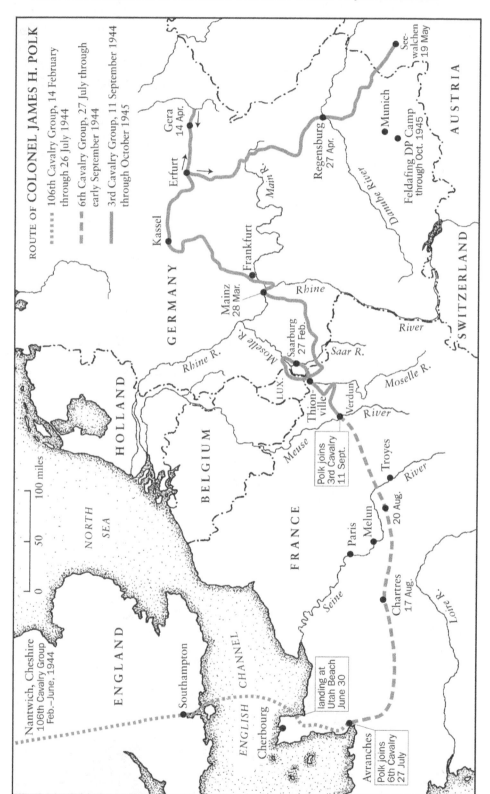

ROUTE of COLONEL JAMES H. POLK

•••••• 106th Cavalry Group, 14 February through 26 July 1944

– – – 6th Cavalry Group, 27 July through early September 1944

——— 3rd Cavalry Group, 11 September 1944 through October 1945

FOREWORD

In 1985 my father, General James H. Polk (U. S. Army, Ret.), living in El Paso, Texas, edited, transcribed and spiral-bound his letters written to my mother, Josephine L. "Joey" Polk, during World War II from the European Theater of Operations (E.T.O.). After reviewing various after-action reports and other sources, he also added his notes and recollections to the letters, plus a few photos. The period covered began on 14 February, 1944, upon his emotional farewell from his wife in Dallas, Texas and his departure for England. It ended on 23 May, 1945 following V-E Day, in Seewalchen, Austria, just to the east of Salzburg.

He titled this work *World War II Letters and Notes of James H. Polk*, which primarily covered his service as 32nd Colonel of the historic 3rd Cavalry Regiment, originally organized in 1846 at the start of The Mexican War. He was given command of this unit personally by Gen. George S. Patton, Jr. on 11 September, 1944, serving under Gen. Patton's 3rd Army and Gen. Walton Walker's XX Corps. The early part of the narrative also covered his proud service as Executive Officer of the 106th Cavalry Group under Col. Vennard Wilson, and very briefly as C.O. of the 6th Cavalry Group, in England, Normandy and across France.

Over the ensuing years until his death in 1992, he occasionally sent the loosely-bound letters to former comrades-in-arms, colleagues and family as an informal memoir of his service during WWII. Gradually, the work gathered a small following and became somewhat well-known in military circles as a first-hand, day-to-day and personal account of a cavalry commander in modern warfare. This was especially true among U. S. Army personnel serving in modern-day cavalry units, including, notably the 3rd Cavalry, which has served with distinction following WWII in the Cold War, the Persian Gulf War and currently in Iraq.

Following the end of World War II, the 3rd Cavalry Group was split up, some being redeployed back to the U.S. and others staying on in Germany as part of the Occupation. Col. Polk remained in Bavaria until late October, 1945 with remnants of the Regiment, serving in the notable effort to help remedy the terrible plight of the Holocaust survivors and to govern the devastated German people and their economy. This included the endeavor to administer the Displaced Persons (DP) Camp at Feldafing, about 30 miles south of Munich.

For reasons unknown, there are almost three months of missing, letters, and the twenty-plus surviving letters from this period were never transcribed by my father. Most probably this was the result of the unpleasant memories he had of the five months he spent in Bavaria following the war's end: longing to be reunited with his family; waiting to be re-deployed for the possible invasion of Japan; and confronting first-hand the horrors of the Holocaust and the effort to help survivors at the Feldafing DP Camp. The latter situation, with overriding humanitarian and political considerations, must have been extremely difficult where there was limited authority and resources, with ultimate accountability to higher command, and where a fighting regimental commander previously had enjoyed clear lines of authority with definite and straightforward objectives.

The occupation of Bavaria and the experiences with the Camp at Feldafing make a fitting Epilogue for the publication of my father's letters as we near the 60th anniversary of the end of WWII. I have taken the liberty of not deleting all of the "personal" statements from these final letters contained in Part IV (as he did in editing the first three Parts), since they importantly portray the deep and intimate love my parents had for each other throughout their 55-year marriage. After an absence of twenty months, Col. James H. Polk was finally reunited with his family in El Paso, Texas on November 7, 1945, my parent's ninth wedding anniversary.

I would like to extend deep thanks to my sister, Jody Polk Schwartz, and her husband, Jonathan, for working side-by-side with me and for their total support, guidance and encouragement in helping to publish these letters. In addition, special thanks to Paul Martin and Scott Hamric with the Third Cavalry Museum at Fort Carson, Colorado for their help in making available some hitherto unknown photographs and maps. Special thanks, also, to my father's former comrades and fellow officers in the 3rd Cavalry Group for their interesting insights and background facts: Col. Marshall Wallach, Warrenton, Virginia; Judge Aaron Cohn, Columbus, Georgia; and Col. Harry Sewell, Livonia, Georgia. Also, thanks to my friend James

Brooks at the School of American Research (SAR) Press in Santa Fe, for his encouragement. Finally, to my wife, Mary, and our daughters, Molly and Anne — I am grateful for their love and support.

James H. Polk, III
Santa Fe, New Mexico
March, 2005

ORIGINAL PREFACE

This narrative has been compiled primarily from letters to my wife and supplemented by official After-Action Reports, unit histories, newspaper clippings and the memories they evoke. It should be noted that our mail was heavily censored. We were not permitted to say where we were, what units were around us, what combat actions we were engaged in or use the names of senior people. Consequently, many letters are followed by an explanatory note. Also, some personal remarks have been deleted.

At the beginning of this narrative, I was a Lieutenant Colonel and Executive Officer of the 106th Mechanized Cavalry Group of the Illinois National Guard. We were a light armored brigade with our major mission that of reconnaissance and security, either leading or on the flanks of a larger force, generally a Corps of several Divisions. We were equipped with light tanks, armored cars, half- tracks and armored jeeps.

My wife, Joey, had joined me for my last three weeks at Fort Hood, Texas before shipping overseas. Since there were no quarters on the post and almost no apartments available off-post, she stayed part time in a hotel in Temple and part time with her cousin, HeilCampbell. Our two children, Jody and Jamie, remained behind in ElPaso with their grandmother, Mabel Leavell, because we could not find a place to live anywhere near Fort Hood. It was an emotional and difficult time for us — filled with promises and enduring love in the coming separation — faced by war.

The Group was ordered to Europe in January and I was detailed to lead a small advanced party to make arrangements for the arrival of the rest of the unit in England. After a very brief holiday with Joey in Dallas, I joined the rest of my party and we departed for the Army Port of Embarkation in New York harbor on February 12,1944.

General James H. Polk (U.S. Army, Ret.)
El Paso, Texas
1985

EXTRACT FROM
THE PATTON PAPERS
1940 -1945
By Martin Blumenson

PATTON'S FAMOUS SPEECH
Diary, May 17, 1944

"Made a talk. As in all my talks, I stressed fighting and killing."

It was probably about this time, a month or so before the invasion, that he began to give his famous speech to the troops. Since he spoke extemporaneously, there were several versions. But if the words were always somewhat different, the message was always the same: the necessity to fight, the necessity to kill the enemy viciously, the necessity for everyone, no matter what his job, to do his duty. The officers were usually uncomfortable with the profanity he used. The enlisted men loved it.

"Men, this stuff some sources sling around about American wanting to stay out of the war and not wanting to fight is a lot of baloney! Americans love to fight, traditionally. All real Americans love the sting and clash of battle. America loves a winner. America will not tolerate a loser. Americans despise a coward, Americans play to win. That's why America has never lost and never will lose a war.

"You are not all going to die. Only two percent of you, right here today, would be killed in a major battle. Death must not be feared. Death, in time, comes to all of us. And every man is scared in his first action. If he says he's not, he's a Goddam liar. Some men are cowards, yes, but they fight just the same, or get the hell slammed out of them. The real hero is the man who fights even though he's scared. Some get over their fright in a minute, under fire, others take an hour, for some it takes days, but a real man will never let the fear of death overpower his honor, his sense of duty, to his country and to his manhood.

"All through your Army careers, you've been bitching about what you call "chicken-shit drill." That, like everything else in the Army, has a definite purpose. That purpose is Instant Obedience to Orders and to create and maintain Constant Alertness. This must be bred into every soldier. A man must be alert all the time if he expects to stay alive. If not, some German son-of-a-bitch will sneak up behind him with a sock full o' shit! There are four hundred neatly marked graves somewhere in Sicily, all because ONE man went to sleep on his job ... but they are German graves, because WE caught the bastards asleep! An Army is a team, lives, sleeps, fights, and eats as a team. This individual hero stuff is a lot of horse-shit. The bilious bastards who write that kind of stuff for the Saturday Evening Post don't know any more about real fighting under fire than they know about ********!

"Every single man in the Army plays a vital role. Every man has his job to do and must do it. What if every truck driver decided that he didn't like the whine of a shell overhead, turned yellow and jumped headlong into a ditch? What if every man thought, "They won't miss me, just one in millions?" Where in Hell would we be now? Where would our country, our loved ones, our homes, even the world, be? No, thank God, Americans don't think like that. Every man does his job, serves the whole. Ordnance men supply and maintain the guns and vast machinery of this war, to keep us rolling. Quartermasters bring up clothes and food, for where we're going there isn't a hell of a lot to steal. Every last man on K.P. has a job to do, even the guy who boils the water to keep us from getting the G.I. shits!

"Remember, men, you don't know I'm here. No mention of that is to be made in any letters. The U.S.A. is supposed to be wondering what the Hell has happened to me. I'm not supposed to be commanding this Army, I'm not supposed even to be in England. Let the first bastards to find out be the Goddam Germans. I want them to look up and howl, "ACH, IT'S THE GODDAM THIRD ARMY AND THAT SON-OF-A-BITCH PATTON AGAIN!"

"We want to get this thing over and get the hell out of here, and get at those purple-pissin' Japs!!! The shortest road home is through Berlin and Tokyo! We'll win this war, but we'll win it only by showing the enemy we have more guts than they have or ever will have!

"There's one great thing you men can say when it's all over and you're home once more. You can thank God that twenty years from now, when you're sitting around the fireside with your grandson on your knee and he asks you what you did in the war, you won't have to shift him to the other knee, cough, and say, "I shoveled shit in Louisiana."

PART I

Departure for England and Invasion Preparations
14 February — 28 June, 1944

14 February, 1944

Dearest One,

It was terrible to leave you at the station. I shall never forget it -the heartache and your bravery. You are an adorable person and I shall never forget your expression all mixed up in love and sorrow and bravery as the train pulled out.

It was a fun few days in Dallas with you, even if you did lose all your hats. Let me know if you ever get them back. Also, I think Kate was a dear to come to Dallas and I'm so thankful that she was with you. It made me feel so much easier in my mind about your return trip to El Paso.

And now you're home again with the babies back in the old housekeeping chores and the problems of raising children. My one regret is that I didn't get to see them before I left. I'm certainly going to miss a lot in not seeing those little squirts grow up in the next years.

We had an uneventful trip and arrived on time. Since our arrival, we have been very busy but did have time to send you that wire about my new APO address. You'll probably soon get a card with a different APO written from Camp Hood. Do not use it — but use the one I wired you.

I have some time off and can get out tonight so I think I'll try and get hold of Ruth Devereux and shall also try and phone you as I'm anxious to know if you got home alright.

Good night, dear one, and kiss those little punks for me.

Your loving husband,
Jimmy

NOTE: We were put up at Fort Hamilton on Long Island which was a transient billet for officers while we were awaiting a sailing date. My reference to Ruth Devereux was to tell Joey I was in New York City.

16 February, 1944

My Dearest One,

Got in town for a while to do some shopping and was able to get a very nice trench coat. I couldn't get one at any of the Exchanges and tried a lot of stores and finally found one at Abercrombie and Fitch that was expensive but very good. It will stand me in good stead in the days ahead. I had them send my overcoat home to you.

I also bought you a parting gift — absolutely the only one like it in this town as I shopped all over for it. I hope you like it and I think you will. Now you guess what it is.

Saw a wonderful movie at the Post last night — "The Miracle of Morgan Creek." One of the funniest I've ever seen. I would love to take you to it as I just roared. You must see it. People were turning around looking at me, I was laughing so hard.

I really don't have to do the income tax now as we are allowed to wait until I come back from overseas. However, I think it much better to get it all cleared up now and over with, as it would be very hard to settle later. I will have to make out the blanks after I get the information I asked you for and send it all to you for your signature, so don't delay.

I have been hoping to hear from you but as yet haven't. I guess there is some delay in getting through the censor.

There is much of interest here that I wish I could tell you about. However, I'm allowed to say little or nothing. My life is full and busy, but I miss my loved ones. But most of all I miss you, my adorable one.

Your loving husband,
Jimmy

NOTE: We were kept busy doing loading plans for units, equipment and individuals on the "Queen Mary" which was due to sail in a few days. However, she arrived in port with the bridge stove in and all plans were thrown out the window as she had to be repaired. Then we were slated to go overseas on the "Aquitania" and started the work all over again.

22 February, 1944

Dearest One,

We put to sea yesterday and are now rocking along with a storm on the way — which everyone says is good news as the submarines can't operate. Am on a famous old boat that creaks and groans with every move. There are eight of us in a state-room built for two. So we are comfortable but very cramped. Fortunately the others are out to supper so I have enough room to spread out and write you.

This is an English boat so all the crew sound very Cockney. Also, they make a surprising effort to keep us comfortable. We have a cabin steward who makes our beds and does what he can to help. We only have two meals a day, breakfast and supper. But they are big and good and the officers eat in the main dining room with waiters, tables, silver, linen and all the proper accoutrements. There isn't a lot to do so I've been reading detective stories furnished by the army and doing some gambling. We also have boat drill and exercise periods and aside from that, our time is our own.

I am reminded all the time of you because of your talk of your trip to Europe so often. And I can see you running around the deck and playing shuffleboard and all those nice things, dancing, being gay and so forth. While my trip is very grim with little or no fun on board but all serious business. I wish it was a pleasure cruise with you instead of what it is today. I feel so remote from you already. Every day takes me further away. Hold on to your sweet happy self, my precious wife.

Your man,
Jimmy

NOTE: We left New York Harbor early in the morning on the "Aquitania," an old ship that could do 20 knots, and we had about ten thousand on board as it had been converted to a troop-ship. I looked at the rafts and life boats and figured that only five thousand could possibly stay afloat so I just about gave up my life to God and figured I wouldn't survive if we were torpedoed. We left the harbor with a cruiser in front of us, a destroyer on each side and a blimp overhead. In the late afternoon, on the cold sea, they all honked their horns and blew their whistles and fired a gun or two and turned around, and we were on the open sea with no escort and doing 20 knots which they said was faster than the German submarines could run.

AT SEA

Dearest one,

We have been at sea three days now and it hasn't been too bad. They announced they had a lot of mail for delivery and I was so in hopes of getting a letter — but no luck. I can't understand the great time lag.

I managed to catch a nice cold but have been doctoring myself and feel a bit better this morning. Our cabin is hard to ventilate with so many in it, and the deck is cold and windy. I suppose the frequent changes got to me. Don't worry though, I have nothing to do but doctor myself and I have two doctors in my cabin so I am getting a lot of good advice.

I suppose the children are all over the colds you mentioned in our last phone conversation and probably have new ones by now. Please write me all about them and how they develop, copies of report cards and such, and don't forget to keep your own diary.

It gets harder to be away from you with every day and every mile that separates us. I realize how much you mean to me and how important you are to me. I pray that all of this will soon pass and that we can resume our beautiful life together soon again.

Your loving Jimmy

AT SEA

Dearest One,

This cold of mine still has me feeling very punk and I think I shall take to my bed for a day in the hope of getting over it. Everyone is getting awfully bored with the boat by now. There are practically no diversions and we are packed in so someone is always in your way. Writing a letter in the cabin is out of the question most of the day with all the people stirring around. It boils down to the fact that I am good and tired with this phase of the trip by now and am ready to get there. Nothing exciting has happened. The water is as calm as a mill-pond. All the seasick people seem to have recovered.

Darling, I miss you and simply hate to be cut off from your letters. It is terrible not to hear from you at all. I would so much rather get a letter a day than a whole raft of them at once. But it ought to straighten out when we reach our destination.

All my love,
Your own Jimmy

NOTE: It was pretty spooky sailing along in that big troop-ship full of people and nothing in sight. About one day out of the U.K., a British bomber came and circled over us for a while and we were mighty glad to see him. Then coming into Glasgow harbor, we had about five destroyers to take us in. And we really felt truly safe at last. They pushed us up to the dock and there was a Scottish pipe band marching up and down, and I tell you they got us ready to fight. So, we made our crossing safely and we were mighty glad to do it.

2 March, 1944

My Dearest One,

I haven't written in several days as we have been on the move the whole time. At last today I was glad to send you one of those standard cables which didn't make much sense, but I guess you got the idea. We still haven't settled in our final location and probably won't for a week yet.

I want to emphasize how well we were received and how well everyone treats us here and God bless the American Red Cross. They are really angels of mercy getting us coffee, doughnuts, candy, cigarettes, lunches when we really need them. They are tireless workers. They appear at stations along the route at all hours of the night. I hope you give them a good donation because you can be sure it is a good cause and a lot of it will come back to me.

We are quartered at present in wood and corrugated iron type barracks. It is quite comfortable but we keep stoves going overtime, as the weather has been cold with rain and light snow alternating. The countryside is very pretty, very neat and well kept, green. And we are near a small town that I am told has little or nothing in the way of entertainment. We went for a walk today and walked along a canal that had barges pulled by horses and real swans swimming around. Also went into a chapel where I contributed to the organ fund and walked among the gravestones. This country is a strange mixture of quaint and new. Planes overhead always, motorcycles racing by, firing on various ranges, tanks going past and then sheep and swans and horse-drawn barges and donkey carts.

I want to emphasize that I am absolutely in no danger now. There isn't a thing to worry about now that the trip is over, and there probably won't be for some time to come. I'm really a good long way from seeing any Germans. I still haven't heard a word from you and really don't expect to for another week until we get to our permanent location. It really is maddening but can't be helped. When I can't write often, I'll write long.

Your loving man,
Jimmy

4 March, 1944

My Darling Wife,

I have been on the go for two days and am getting well acquainted with the railroads of this country. It was a most interesting trip and I met a lot of old friends, which helped.

It's cold all the time over here. Not much coal or wood available. But I purchased some long woolen underwear and wear it all the time. Baths are a great problem which I solved by getting a bucket of hot water from the mess and taking a sponge bath. Not very satisfactory. But I can't get the nerve to take an ice-cold shower. It you want to send me a present, send me some of those ski pajamas — nice warm material. It would be a great luxury. However, wait until I give you my permanent APO address before you mail them.

I haven't gotten a single letter so far, but I understand one load of unit mail is in so I have hopes. Everyone says to write one or more V-mail letters once a week because they are much faster, but seem quite unsatisfactory as they are so short.

I wonder so much about the children, if they are well and prospering and how they are developing. It is a great comfort to know you are at home surrounded by so many loved ones. Send me all or any pictures you can get. I treasure my folder and it is always with me in my shirt pocket as you and the children are ever in my heart.

Much love,
Jimmy

NOTE: We were very busy at this time running around middle England, arranging for the reception of the regiment; that is, going to ammunition depots, equipment depots, post offices, camps, everything where we needed to draw the supplies that we would soon need, as well as going to target ranges and arranging dates for us to shoot.

7 March 1944

My Dearest Love,

We reached our final home late last night after much long and tiring travel. I was certainly glad to get here. And there was a hot meal awaiting us, and warm beds. Today, I've been stirring about getting settled and we are quite comfortable. We live in a barracks with coal stoves to warm us and have bunks and mattresses. The bathrooms are a bit on the primitive side but adequate, and plenty of hot water. Tonight I just finished doing my laundry and must admit that I have much to learn on that subject. However, I couldn't detect any tattletale gray and hung them out to dry. I shall have another inspection in the morning. Then I took a hot shower and rushed back to my barracks and hopped in bed so here I am. I feel very fit now. The cold is gone. The food so far has been awfully good and I have been eating like a horse. We have three large meals a day. No snack at lunch, but a big meal. I really ought to gain weight on the menu and the amount I put away. Eating seems to be the chief amusement and routine of the day. And breakfast isn't like the good old routine we had at home but I'm getting used to it.

Something else you can send me — very important — toilet paper. Not in rolls, but the flat packets like they have in hotels. The local product is terrible and rough. Also Kleenex if you can buy it — I think you can get it at the Fort Bliss PX. I wish I could share all these new sights and sounds and experiences with you. I miss you so. It's terrible not to have you around to discuss the affairs of the day. I worship you and love you. Keep fit and well.

Your man,
Jimmy

P.S. I wish I could have just one letter from you.

NOTE: Our permanent camp was in Cheshire in a little town called Nant-wich. We were located on the estate of Sir Giles Broughton who was quite famous in England because he had killed his wife and a white hunter with one bullet on a camping trip in Kenya. He was found "not guilty" and was not fined or punished.

9 March, 1944

My Darling,

My permanent APO is now 403. My permanent cable address is AMIMBU. You can send me one of those canned messages for about 60c. and, of course, a regular message costs a lot more. I hope you send me a canned cable when you receive this that you are all well, 'cause I still haven't heard a single word from you. The mail ought to be much better soon now that I have a permanent APO address. I certainly hope so. Because this huge time lag is driving me crazy.

I can at last tell you that I am in England which I suppose you guessed long ago. I spoke of a trip in which you'd be interested. Well, I got two days leave and went into London. It was lots of fun and I got to sleep in a clean soft bed and have a hot tub bath. I saw lots of old friends and find that I have forty-five classmates over here in England. Dave Wagstaff showed me all around town to see the usual sights that you saw as a tourist. We also went night-clubbing without females but it was only fair fun as we talked about you and Bea and our old Fort Myer days. Also, saw Gordon Bartlett and just missed seeing Joe Haskell. There were no air raids while I was there and I was sorry, as I wanted to see a mild one. Everything was completely blacked out so it was very difficult to get around, but it doesn't seem to bother anyone. But I was glad I had a guide. The natives are wonderful, the way they have borne all the blitzes and just keep right on trucking. It is an amazing sight to see them all sleeping in the subways — little children and everything. I really missed you there. I begrudge every minute and every mile that separates us.

Your loving husband,
Jimmy

13 March, 1944

Dearest Wife,

The mail has arrived. Such joy, such happiness. I am really excited by it. I got six letters all at once from you. Also, one from Mother and one from Fred Devereux which I will enclose. It's funny. I read the first two very quickly. Then I didn't want to finish them but rather hoard them like candy so I have been opening them one at a time about every half hour because I couldn't wait any longer. The first one is written February 21st and they are all air mail, so I guess that's the fastest. I think we better start numbering our letters so that we can keep them straight. I will call this one number one.

So much you say intrigues me. Funny Jamie walking and laughing and Jody's remarks. None of your letters were opened by the censors so our thoughts are not shared by anyone, not that I care as the censor has gotten to be a very impersonal thing to me. He has so much to read that I'm sure he isn't interested. I'm glad that you got the dressing case, have Mitch saddle-soap it. It was terribly hard to find. About the only one left in New York. Also I got the income tax and it's just what I need. I will forward it for your signature later and you can send it on in.

I adore your letters. They are my life.

Your loving husband, Jimmy

15 March, 1944

Dearest Love,

Have been busy all day today. Not on anything mysterious, but just routine work in my regular job. The CO, Vennard Wilson, doesn't seem to feel too well but won't admit it. So I have been trying to take most of the load off his shoulders and let him relax some. I don't like doing all this petty detail work, but it is my job. Haven't had any time for any exercise for almost a week now.

I went down to the PX to draw my week's rations and it consisted of the following: seven packages of cigarettes, one bar of soap, two bars of candy, two razor blades and one package of gum. That is all we get but is sufficient except for soap and you provide me with plenty of that. I give the candy to the local children who are always hanging around our camp as they only get six ounces of chocolate every month. Also the cigarettes are enough as I shouldn't smoke more than that anyway. I'll start sending money home every month as soon as I have far more than I need or can spend. Always hard to get to any place to send it.

I think of you always.

Your Jimmy

NOTE: *The 106th Cavalry Group had arrived on station at the camp by this time and we were busy drawing equipment, vehicles and ammunition and getting ready to start some more serious training.*

18 March, 1944

My Darling Wife,

For about the first time since my arrival I am alone in the barracks and it is an actual pleasure. It is a Saturday night and all the officers have taken off for the neighboring town. I did go into the neighboring town last night. All blacked out. We got in about eight and went to a pub, Frank Oliver and I. You can't buy whiskey but only English beer which tastes like a refined home brew. We watched a bunch of old men throw darts and they are really wizards. They have a league much like one of our bowling leagues in the U.S. and they go every night to the public house to play. They also have a ladies' room full of old scrub-women who come in and ask for a "pint of bitter". The movies in town are over by 9:30 p.m. and the pubs close at ten, so night life in the English town is non-existent. It's very eerie to walk along the streets as it's really black. No sidewalk is straight, so you are continually falling off the curb or bumping a lamp post.

I have been looking for a present for you, but everything is terribly high and they add 100% luxury tax on silver or china. But furthermore, there is little in stock to choose from. However, Col. Wilson and I plan to go to an auction nearby when we can get the chance, so maybe I can do some good there. I've gotten to like Col. Wilson more each day. He's really a fine man. Also he has a dry sense of humor and comes up with some very droll remarks now and then. He said he'd spent a lot of money as a bachelor learning to play poker. Then he got married and has never had a chance to cash in on his experience.

We haven't been gambling since the boat as no one has the time. We work all day and then have schools at night. The rest of the evening is usually spent doing laundry, writing and other odd jobs.

I am well and healthy and am still a long, long way from the "Jerries", as the British say.

Your loving man,
Jimmie

20 March, 1944

My Precious Wife,

(There is a discussion of family finances which is omitted from this letter.) My life here has been filled with detail work and I have been busy day and night. It is also still cold and mean. Everyone has sort of an incipient cold but very little sickness in the units. I guess the weather agrees with us but we still don't like it. It makes for good-looking complexions but it surely does chap the women's bare legs. All the women are poorly dressed, but then they can buy only about one dress every six months.

There is a good army store near us, like a well-stocked PX, where you can buy anything in the military line. Also, we've gotten someone to do our laundry and dry cleaning, so I'm through with that chore for awhile.

I do wish I could see Jamie walking about. Does he try and say anything yet? How many teeth does he have? And that sweet Jody — tell her Daddy loves her and misses her, and I love her remark. Tell her I will be careful and not hurt my leg.

Much love.
Love you completely,
Jimmy

22 March, 1944

Dearest One,

Today we had a visit from our new Commander. But I had little or no time to talk to him. However, he is most cordial and said he was glad to see that I had finished teaching school. (What he meant was that I wasn't stationed at West Point any longer.) I didn't have a chance to ask about Ruth Ellen or Bea. He gave the usual type lecture to the troops and was off in a flash. A very busy man, I suppose.

I have been buried in work as Col. Wilson leaves practically all the detail work to me and they are many. You will remember that I asked Charlie Dodge what he as Col. Wilson's Exec. did, and he said that I would soon find myself running the Group. That's just about the score now but I am just as glad.

Paul Kendell is over here at a nearby camp, but I haven't had a chance to see him yet. He has quite an important job in the QM and should be a General soon.

You mentioned sending me various things, but I really don't need them except for the articles I asked for, ski pajamas, Kleenex and toilet paper. Also candy bars would be nice. Rich ones like Baby Ruth and Hersheys. That's plenty for me as I never used to eat candy but it is strictly rationed and what we get here is very poor. I sort of crave it, as do we all, I guess because of the cold weather and the lack of an ice box to raid or anything to ever eat between meals.

I am developing a few dislikes for food — never again after this business is over, will I ever touch turnips or Brussels sprouts. The whole of England is concentrated on growing those two horrible vegetables. Also, we get lots of cocoa made with water — I never did like it but this is definitely the end. We have parted company for life.

Please have as much fun as you possibly can without my help — but not too much. I adore you.

Your Jimmy

NOTE: *The reference to the new commander was, of course, to Gen. Patton. He gave us one of his horrible "blood and guts" speeches with lots of profanity and phrases like, "I didn't come here to get killed, I came to kill Germans" and "The best maneuver is to hold the enemy by the nose and kick him in the ass". The speech in my opinion alienated about 20% of the command as it was distasteful to see a senior officer using such profanity. However, he was very pleased with himself, and I heard it two more times in the next year.*

24 March, 1944

My Adorable One,

No mail now for five days, but the boat must be due soon. I live for your letters. Col. Wilson is away and will be for some days. It does add to my responsibility and to my work. But tonight I have time to read a mystery novel for a while and last night we even played black-jack for shillings — about the same as a dime, I guess, I'm never quite sure.

As soon as the money order man comes around, I will send you some money. I didn't win it either, I saved it; although it isn't very hard. It is really hard to spend money here.

Today is really the first pretty day we have had in England. I went for a walk to get my exercise and it was truly beautiful. You would never know there was a war on, except for the constant formations of airplanes passing overhead. However, I would take New York, Virginia or especially Texas anytime. Everything is so small, so old, so much like a park. And you have that shut-in feeling all the time. It would be fun though to bicycle through this country with you — but to live in it, never. We could stop at inns together at night, cycling down the road. Sharing it all with you would be Heaven. Sharing anything with you would be Heaven so that is what I want to do — share my life and my love with you forever.

Your devoted husband,
Jimmy

26 March, 1944

My Darling Wife,

Today I got four wonderful letters after almost a week of hearing nothing. And those adorable pictures — I have looked and looked at them. You look so cute and adorable and happy with the children. The one of Jamie about to fall over is a real scream. Darling, I adore your letters and look for them, even if they do all arrive together. Please, please keep on writing me often because I have already read the whole lot over four times and I've only had them about four hours.

I hope I wasn't careless in that letter about the Red Cross. We are asked to tell our families not to have our letters published. And if I talked too much about our trip, it might get me in Dutch. Please don't publish any more of my letters, at least over my signature. I don't mind your reading them to people, but don't publish them.

You certainly did as I said when I asked you to be generous to the Red Cross, but I'm glad because what I said was true.

As I wrote earlier, I'm saving money and will send some home to you as soon as I can contact the money order man. I'm glad that we both agree that this is our golden opportunity to save. But please don't be tight with your Mother or anything. In other words, save wisely but still have fun.

Last night, Saturday, Frank Oliver and I went into a neighboring town for dinner. And it was fun. We had a couple of martinis, a good meal, beautifully served with wine, and finished off with brandy and coffee. It was a delightful old place called "The Crown," an old English inn. The furniture and china around the walls were very old. They also had some very old hunting prints like ours. All were small rooms with dark panelling and fireplaces. It was off the beaten track so it wasn't crowded and we dawdled over the meal for two hours. We think we will make it a regular affair. We came home in the most awful fog — just like that night we drove from New York with Fred Devereux, but here the roads are crooked, unmarked and we go blacked out. It took us an hour to get six miles. We ran into the ditch once but not a scratch. These blackouts in the fog are a real experience. I'm glad you weren't with me on that one as you would have been a nervous wreck.

All my love, my Precious One,
Jimmy

3, April 1944

My Darling Wife,

I haven't written you for a few days except for V-mail last night, as I got back yesterday from quite a long trip inspecting and so forth, and it was impossible to write in route. It was an interesting trip and I saw a lot of friends. I will summarize as follows:

1) Jess Hawkins — Fat and pink and completely unchanged. We ate supper in a local town. He really seemed to know everyone so we got good service and two real drinks of Scotch. He had marvelous tales to tell of Sicily which lost nothing in the telling, I'm sure. All about governing the city and living in a palace with a full staff of servants. I guess I had changed more than he has.

2) Dick Nelson — He has changed a great deal — looks older and worries all the time. He sure takes his war hard and we aren't even in yet, and I have no intention of letting it change me.

3) Peewee Collier — Looks badly as he has had some teeth pulled and is run down. However, he was lots of fun. Spent an evening with him, and he produced a bottle of Sicilian brandy for the occasion. His wife is in Dallas and the child is completely well, so he says.

I got to see a lot of the English countryside, but it was a terrifying drive with a reckless soldier driver and the roads full of troops, trucks and inhabitants all on bicycles. We spent three hours in Oxford looking at all the old colleges, now full of Royal Air Force people. Lots of our soldiers there on leave. I like it better than any English town I've seen, as the shops are modern and yet a half block off the main streets — you're in the middle of the 17th century. It's really amazing how nice all the English are to our soldiers who must worry the hell out of them running in and out of colleges, cathedrals and restaurants. And it's real funny how American soldiers talk about these foreigners, referring to the English. Also, we went by Stratford-on-Avon, which I felt was a big disappointment.

I sent you a cable for Easter which I hope you got on time. Also, I sent one to Mother and wrote her a letter. I'm sorry I couldn't send a present but I haven't seen anything worth buying as yet.

I adore you, love you and miss you like blazes all the time.

Your James

NOTE: *I had been down to the Salisbury Plain, which is a tank training area in Southern England, arranging for our outfit to go down and train later on. The 2nd. Armored Division was in training and Jess was the G2; Dick, a Tank Battalion Commander; and Peewee was the Division Brigadier.*

9 April, 1944 Easter Sunday

My Beloved One:

I have thought of you so much all of today. It's always such a fun day in our house with the new hat and the spring clothes and the egg hunt and the little presents on the table. I know you had fun at your Mother's home showing off your new outfit and all the dear Easter doings. And I was completely with you all day long.

My day started with a funny little sunrise service that the Chaplain had out under a tree. He bought a squeaky organ for $16.00 and had rehearsed a little choir. There were about a hundred of us there and it wasn't pretty or noble, but all the same it was real and earnest. It did me good.

The rest of the day has been tough. I have just been given a very important job that will keep me extra busy for the next ten days; plain old detail work and lots of it, and I don't look forward to the prospect at all.

Just got two letters from you written on the 22nd and 24th of March telling me about your stay at Charles's. Sounds to me like you were the honored guest rather than the housekeeper.

It seems silly to write about your poisoning in Juarez as it is now almost a month old. You must be quite well by now. That is one of the meanest things I hate about this life. I am so damn utterly remote from you.

Darling, I am troubled that you haven't gotten mail in so long. You ought to have gotten a flood by now. I thought I had been awfully good. I do love and adore and worship you. Goodnight my wonderful one.

Jimmy

NOTE: I had just been put in charge of a detail with about half of the regiment to prepare camp for the arrival of the 83rd Division, which was to be stationed within 3-4 miles of us. So it was a lot of work — putting up tents, and mess halls and hard stands and all that kind of thing, and cots with hay mattresses and all that.

12 April, 1944
V-Mail

Dearest Joey,

I have been seeing a lot of the country today in my rounds but I have been too busy or worrying too much to enjoy it. I went by my camp and picked up two wonderful letters from you that I read going down the road. Also one from your Mother that was grand because it praised my children and said that you were gaining weight. I'll have a chance to write you a decent letter tomorrow. This is difficult as I am writing with a flickering light and am very weary. I do wish for you so you could see all the blossoms and the green country.

Much love,
Jimmy

13 April, 1944

My Dearest,

Tonight for the first time in England, I am occupying a room all to myself. It's a big old high ceiling room with dark panelling on the walls — UGLY! I have a coal fire burning in the grate, sitting on a rickety chair and writing on the bed. I have just closed the blackout curtains so no lights will show forth, as it is 9:00 p.m. There is a little lake out below my window and I have been watching two swans swim around in it. This place is really a hall owned by some type of gentleman with apparently lots of house and no money. Must have been quite a showplace in its day, as at least fifty officers eat in the dining room with no trouble. I guess all Americans write home that they are living in a castle and they practically are. But it really isn't any bargain. Each camp is a group of huts or tents clustered around some old castle or hall in the country. There are hundreds of them scattered all over England and I presume the owners are glad to rent them out at any price. They will probably sue the good old U.S.A. for all the damage we allegedly do to the place, and then build themselves a decent house with the money they collect.

The bathing and toilet facilities over here are really awful. All the johns are strange. You always pull a chain and then nothing happens. Then you release the chain and there is a great flood of water. As for the baths, I've come to the realization that the English just don't take them. However, this room is unique in that I have a great tub with real hot water so I shall shortly go swimming in it.

I will probably be here about a week more but don't stay here much on my present job. I'm out all day touring camps and working on my job that I can't tell you about and some days like last night I didn't even get back at all. My life is so simple, no frills, no dates, no parties, occasional suppers in town, no real friends, wearing rough clothes and long underwear and seldom sleeping with sheets.

I guess I miss having my friends next to missing you. Vennard is really my closest companion and he is a good deal older than I am. I like Frank Oliver but our jobs keep us separate much of the time. Most of the others are much younger or don't interest me. In other words, I hope we get on with the damn war soon and get it over. Bless you and goodnight.

Your adoring husband,
Jimmy

NOTE: *What I was describing was the 83rd. Division's camp that I had been told to set up. The room I was living in it was to be the room of the Commanding General when he arrives.*

18 April, 1944

My Darling One:

I'm sitting down in the main room of the old hall writing on a table near a nice big roaring fire. My job that has kept me so busy is beginning to wind down and so far it has been most successful. I was on the go all day yesterday and most of the night, but managed to get in about three hours sleep this afternoon and am feeling pretty spry now. I called on the General and he gave me two drinks and a cigar so I now have that contented, well fed, warm feeling of well being. You know the job is working out okay and I am rather pleased with our accomplishments. I will go back to my regular outfit in a day or so.

I have a soldier driver who has driven me over most of England in the past month named Barber. I am most fortunate as he is a wonderful jeep driver and has no bad habits. He is always there when I need him at any hour of the day or night, doesn't drink, smoke or cuss. He is an orphan who was raised by an uncle in the mountains of Kentucky. However, the wonderful thing about him is his remarks on the English and their customs. Most of them are completely unprintable but his remarks on the women are just priceless. Also, he has a great disgust for English farmers as they go to work in a suit with a white shirt and a tie. He also said that if he gets a chance, he'll make me better beer than what they serve here. He said he could make whiskey but says there is no use as you have to let it sit for too long. In his words, "This three-day moonshine is dangerous." He's also a great whittler and can spit hard enough to drive a nail. My best friend and constant companion in the British Isles, Private Barber.

When I return, it will be wrong to meet you in El Paso, I think. Instead, on the happy day that I land, I can wire you and we'll meet someplace and spend a few days together in some swanky hotel. Wouldn't that be fun. I love you dear one.

Your devoted,
Jimmy

20 April, 1944

My Darling,

Well, I really had a fascinating day today. I got the afternoon off as I had worked through Sunday and was up about half the night for the past ten days. I arranged to go through a fine china pottery factory, expecting to spend about an hour there and winding up with spending the whole afternoon. We, a Major Calloway and myself, saw the whole process from the original ingredients of crushed bone, clay and granite to the beautifully finished product. We watched them mold and then fire it in a tremendously hot oven. Then they put on a glaze and fire it again. Finally they start to decorate it and it may be baked as many as five more times before it is finally finished, depending on the amount of decoration that goes on the cover plate or what have you.

Many things about the plant amaze me. One was that little boys, as young as ten, were apprentices there and were working and doing hard manual labor. Another was to see the artists decorate the plates with a brush — real craftsmen. The buildings of the factory were indescribable; old, dirty, rambling stone buildings, all with bad lighting and what looked like the most primitive machinery. Why they don't all put their eyes out I don't know, as the light was horrible. The craftsmen have worked there for generations, father and son, and really know their business. But it is all hand craft with the most primitive equipment.

The plant is producing very little as compared to the old days because many of the craftsmen are in the army. Also, they are not allowed to sell the fine china to the English customers, but it is all for export. We saw china marked for Tiffany's and other expensive stores in New York, Mexico City, Toronto and other places.

Well, we finally got to the showroom, a dusty dark warehouse with beautiful china all over the place, on the floors, on the shelves, on packing cases scattered all over helter skelter. You would have gone absolutely crazy. I wished so for you and Mabie. The teacups would have driven her wild.

There was such an array that you would be stopped cold.

Now you want to know, did I buy anything. Well, Punkin, I did. I just couldn't resist it. It was too much. Also, we were allowed to send home gifts duty-free if they cost less than $100.00. It was such a bargain to get English hand-painted china at factory prices with no duty that I bought a dozen dessert plates. God knows you don't need them as you have eight Spode ones, but I figured dessert plates don't need to match anything else and could be used for tea and so forth. I never wanted you so much in my life — really and truly so that you could select what you wanted. But I had to make a choice so I did. They are sort of a white center with buff sides that are scalloped with hand-painted flowers in the center — each one a different set of flowers and all signed by the artist's name with a gold bank around the edge. Reading the above, they sound awful, but they really are beautiful. I hope and pray you like them, but if you don't give them away as a wedding present. They are made by Minton, which I never heard of but which everyone here says are one of the tops in the line. Wedgewood and Spode are in the same town, but will not sell as they have agents in New York who have import rights. They have exclusive rights in America. I'm told the English prefer Minton which is not advertised, as are Spode and Wedgewood, but are supposed to be better.

As a matter of interest to me, when they arrive, take one down to a store and see what it would cost in the U.S., just so I can brag about my bargain.

I also enclosed a small present for Mabie in the box. It is being packed and I will ship them in about a week. It will probably take a month more to get there. I hope they come through all right.

Darling, if you had only been here. As I said, I may not be long in the vicinity so I had to select. So they are sent with all my love as a souvenir and as a present to the beautiful woman that I love and adore.

Thy Jimmy

23 April, 1944

My Lovely Wife,

You seem to be worried about my safety, but I think it is needless. Of course, I have my own idea of when the invasion will come, but I'm not even allowed to speculate when it will be. Remember before I left that I told you what part we will play in the invasion. Well I have no reason to change my ideas yet. In other words, when the headline breaks announcing the invasion, don't picture me on some beach with someone shooting at me as I won't be near the first wave. We will go in considerably later.

Last night, Col Wilson and I were invited to a dance at the nearby British airfield. It was their big to-do of the year and we were the only Americans present except for a few nurses. Everyone was in evening dress and they had a lovely club. They must have skimped on their rations for months, as they had a large table groaning with sandwiches, sausage patties and so forth. Also they had plenty of Scotch, which was a treat, so it was a most successful party. More like a tea dance at home than a regular dance, except that it was at night. Very interesting to see that their flyers come from all over the world. The women try hard to look well but the dresses are rather old- fashioned and their hair is, in general, messy. They are very sensitive about it. They took pains to tell us that there was hardly a beauty shop anywhere in the vicinity. I found the English very friendly, and they certainly were last night.

There was a much-decorated youngster who had trained in San Antonio, so we Texans by adoption had a lot of fun talking about milkshakes and barbeque sandwiches. It really did my morale good to see everyone all dressed up and hear good music. But no one reminded me of you in even a remote way. They just don't look like American girls. I danced a couple of dances but it was hard going. They are very stiff and our styles just don't mesh so I gave it up.

Prince Bernhardt, the consort to Princess Juliana, was there sitting in the balcony. Col. Wilson got to talk to him and he seemed like an ordinary man, very easy to talk to and spoke perfect English. One of the New Zealanders called him the "Dutch Stallion."

Please don't worry about my safety, my darling. Danger is a long way from me and I want so to come home to you that I'll be careful. Of course, I will do my duty also. Bless you my lovely.

Your Jimmy

22 April, 1944

My Dearest One,

Last night we had a rather extensive officers' school which lasted about three hours. I then intended to write you but had some trouble with my little white clock so Col. Wilson proceeded to take it apart and fix it for me. He took some hours with my able assistance to complete the job; hence no letter.

Col. Wilson has bought some very interesting clocks about 200 years old that only have one hand, all made of brass and signed with the maker's name. They are real authentic antiques so he spends his late evenings tinkering with them, cleaning them up and so forth; but so far, has yet to get one to run properly. However, it keeps him happy and Ruth is going to be flooded with a deluge of old brass. Also, he's paid a pretty fancy price for his junk but will have something when he gets them all repaired and cases made for them. I'm afraid such work is beyond me.

My temporary job is all wound up now, and I'm back with the old outfit. I'm glad the chore is over as it was an awful lot of work but everyone concerned was most complimentary.

How are you getting along in the big house without the Moores? It must be odd not to have them around and I bet you miss them. I hope you get a nice boarder, but don't get some young, handsome fellow or I'll be jealous.

Here is what our Corps Commander wrote and I think it is worth saving. "Your organization will be as good as you are. It will be no better and no worse. It will follow you through hell and high water and it will freeze to the ground or run away if you do. You are soon to find that you can gauge your ability as a leader by the action of your own men. When dangers arrive, they will turn to you. If you are what you should be, have no fear for what they will do. They will do as you do — nothing more, nothing less."

I love you, dearest.
Your devoted Jimmy

26 April, 1944

Dearest One,

I have just written a page and some and said something I shouldn't have, so now I have to start over again. It is very difficult to write of a day of my work, as there is so much we can't mention. My whole day from 8 to often 11 at night is taken up with solving various problems. Most of them very small but requiring thought and judgment. So much of executives' work is getting along with people. I can't issue orders quickly as I must reflect the will of Col. Wilson. So I have to put myself in his place and think what he would wish. He is away so much that I have plenty to do.

We also have a very extensive physical training program. I have to run a mile in 8 minutes with a pack and personal weapon every day. We have been doing it now for two weeks and it just about killed me at first, but I'm getting better now. It was actually hot today and the sweat really poured off me at the finish, but we all do it. I'm really more fit than I have been in a long time and feel just fine.

I loved your long letter about Easter and the party for Fred and the crazy hat and all your other activities. Your letters are so clear that I can almost see our children grow. I have a picture as well of your daily life. How I envy you that life. How jealous I am of all the people that share it with you.

Shall I picture my daily life for you? — Up at 7:00 in a cold Nissen hut from my cot, a quick shave in a crowded washroom, also cold, but with hot water and breakfast. In my office by 7:45. My office shared with Col. W is the walled-off end of another Nissen hut. My desk, a rough table with a folding chair, maps on the wall, clerks in the next room. Most of the morning taken up with visitors, American and British, from higher or lower headquarters. Reports, training for the coming week, decisions about people and their troubles, schools, petty crimes or equipment, or ranges to shoot on, or any of a million other things. Lunch — and our food is good and often appetizing. Then I usually get out in the afternoon to see some phase of training. Retreat is at 5:45 and then supper. Then four nights a week we either have schools or night exercises of some sort. Other nights I often have to work to catch up and sometimes go out for a walk as it is still light by 9:30 p.m. By 10:00 p.m. I'm usually in the hut again and write you or read a little or just flop in bed.

It's a busy life, often interesting, sometimes maddening, but through it all runs the current of you. You are with me always just back of my conscious mind ready to pop out at any time. I love you and adore you and miss you like hell.

NOTE: Letters of 27 April and 30 April are omitted as containing nothing of real substance.

2 May, 1944

My Dearest One,

These weekdays are busy ones indeed. It is late and we are just finishing officers' school. Now I have a few minutes to write you before I tumble into bed. Last night I had to represent the Regiment at a Home Guard gathering that was really brutal. Three officers, all British, from the last war and I sat down to work out a small maneuver with the Home Guard. But of course, they couldn't get right down to work. First we had to eat a British boiled dinner, very tasteless and have some half-coffee, half-milk and nothing to drink. Then we went into the lobby of this little hotel where we had eaten and beat around the bush some more. They tried so hard to be pleasant and so did I, but they were all rather provincial, all junior to me in rank and all about twenty years older than I am, so it was very hard going. We finally did get the job done. One of them promised to give me a real Cheddar cheese. So, if I get it, I will send it home. I don't have the ration points to buy one.

I wish you wouldn't worry about me in the invasion. I assure you and I really mean it, that it will be many days after the invasion begins before I go into it. And I won't be in the front line by a long-shot.

I am continually amazed by what a rambunctious child our Jamie seems to be growing into. I can see you trying to be a daddy to him and making him tough and strong. I think you are a wonderful Mother to pillow fight and ride him on your back and all, but I know that if you do it with him, you must also do it with Jody. So don't overdo your life, but keep yourself strong and fit as I do.

And don't be stingy with your Mother and the household expenses. She is really giving you more than money can buy and the expenses will be greater with the Moores gone. So do your part well. I don't often send my love to your Mother, but she is so often in my thoughts and I shall write her soon. I certainly thank God you have such a beautiful home to go back to, but you must remember that it is her home so don't forget she's the boss. She is a wonderful person. I will be forever greatful for all she is doing for me and for my family.

Your devoted husband,
Jimmy

6 May, 1944
(Saturday)

Darling Joey:

The box came yesterday and I was delighted to get it. The pajamas are beautiful and there have been many sassy remarks about my night attire as hardly anyone else wears them. Thanks my Love, they are nice and warm and remind me of you so they make me very happy. Also the T. paper, knife and hankies are appreciated.

I'm all set for this bad climate as I have long underwear, sweaters, fur-lined gloves, wool clothing, heavy water-resistant combat jacket and outer trousers, my lined trench-coat and para-trooper boots — not to mention my knitted cap for my helmet and my warm pajamas and sleeping bag for the night. I certainly ought to be warm if nothing else.

Your life sounds fun at times. I'd so love to go to a country club dance with you and that nice crowd. Go on to the Chinaman's later and finally wind up at home with you. Charles and Shirley are certainly wonderful to you. Would you like me to send them something like I sent you? If you do, say the word and I will go after it.

To answer some of your questions; yes, Col. Wilson is still with me and I'm still his assistant. I think I'll remain there. I was offered another job, perhaps a bit more dangerous, but turned it down as he said he needed me and it didn't mean a promotion. In fact, I don't know enough to be promoted yet and don't want to be.

I live with the regimental staff, all junior to me, eleven officers in a tin hut with a cement floor. It does not have a thatched roof. In fact, I've never gotten back to London since that first leave and don't expect that I will.

Life is full of ups and downs. It's a strange world. Yesterday, I got a really very fine letter of commendation for the job I told you I was on the special task. It really made me feel very proud of myself and put all right with the world. Now today, the outfit gets a hell of a dirty dig that is really unjustified — no reflection on me personally, but any reflection on the outfit is also a reflection on me. Oh hell. Someone is always taking the joy out of life. I guess the good Lord made most staff officers stupid, and we shall just have to put up with them and try to like it. In other words, I'm a bit blue tonight, it being Saturday evening and everyone has put off for town and a night out. I can't get up much enthusiasm myself. There isn't anyone to see that I want to see. I want to see you if you want the plain truth. I want a good meal and a good drink and most of all good company. But I guess instead, I will go for a walk as it is still light although 9:00 and try to work it off. But while I'm out walking, I shall be thinking of you and wishing for you.

Your own,
Jimmy

7 May, 1944

My Dearest Woman,

Just got your letter about poor Jamie's bout of fever (we get mail on Sundays) and was worried but it really isn't much use because it was nine days ago and he is surely well by now. The poor little guy! I pray all is well now and that he is out in the sunshine playing about — but shall be anxious until I get your next letter.

I have missed you today. We worked this morning, but this afternoon my friend, Col. Emberton of the British Home Guard invited Vennard and I over to tea. He is the man who gave me the Cheshire cheese and who had me to the grim meeting I mentioned earlier. However, he has turned out to be an extremely nice old guy and most hospitable. It was the first time I have been invited to an Englishman's home and it was fascinating. Mrs. Emberton was most gracious and friendly. A woman about 45 dressed in tweeds and wearing her hair much like Susie Cherry used to wear her hair in a bun. We really had a sort of supper about 5:30 with a small glass of sherry before.

Very small portions of food were served but it was quite good. And they had coffee instead of tea in our honor. You would have loved the house, spotlessly clean and many old pieces of brass, all shined up. They had a bed warmer, brass candlesticks, various copper bowls and vases and some lovely old furniture — a desk and a grandfather clock that I particularly admired. They also had a gate of wrought iron that was priceless. Part of the house dates back to the seventeenth century. The roof had a bad sag in it but the owner assured me that it was sound. They also had a lovely old garden, all flagstones and rock garden and apple blossoms and spring flowers that are now out in bloom. They have invited you and me to come and stay with them when all of this is over. It would be fun as they live reasonably near our camp and I could show you where I lived and worked and where I took my walks and all. In other words, they were most kind and hospitable and are the only people that have made me feel at home in England.

I also met another crazy chap yesterday, a fellow in the R.A.F. to whom I gave a lift. So I swapped him five cigars for a dozen eggs. They were wonderful. We feasted on them at breakfast today. I had them fried because the only way that dried eggs can be served is scrambled, and I'm sick of them.

So I think I'm a fried-egg man from now on. Please send me more cigars, as he will trade me eggs for more cigars.

Vennard is a wise old man with WWI experience. He said, "If we can break in without too many casualties the first few days, we will be a great outfit." I think he is right and I hope we are lucky.

I love you forever and ever.

Your Jimmy

12 May, 1944

My Precious One,

Here it is Friday and I haven't written you since about Monday. But I've really been buried in work and going day and night. Night problems or night schools or something of the like all the time. Also, I had planned to cable you and Mother on Mothers' Day but they have stopped all cables for us, for security reasons I suppose. But anyway, I'm sorry. Don't think I had forgotten you on your little day, its just that I didn't think of it soon enough.

I do hope and pray the kids don't get those measles. It seems a cinch they will. So I expect at this very minute, you are battling the horrid stuff. But with their shots and all, you ought to get by okay. You really are such a good mother that I don't worry about the children. I know you have an eye on them all the time. I guess you only write me about the good things, but from your letters, it sounds as if they are developing into wonderful fine children. I am so proud of them and of you, my love.

The weather has been perfect and it's fortunate, as we have been outdoors all week. Two nights under the stars. They always make you seem so close to me when I sleep out and get out of the hut. They are never as bright as the stars in Texas and the North Star is higher in the Heavens. But they are the same stars that look down on you. I do miss you dear.

Your devoted husband
Jimmy

13 May, 1944

My Darling Joey,

I want to explain to you how we live in our camp here. We have a Nissen hut. It has no walls and roof as such, but is round and made of tin. The floor is concrete and it has some windows and doors. It looks sort of like a small airplane hangar. There are 14 men in our hut. In addition, there is a radio, 3 little coke stoves and a barrel of beer and one table to write letters on. Doesn't it sound crowded and nasty?

It is a rather cold and drafty place because we can't light good fires. There is such a coal and coke shortage that we can only use these coke stoves to fire our hot water boilers. It is better than a pup tent and I have an iron cot and a mattress filled with straw, two blankets and a sleeping bag. So I sleep nice and warm at least. I use the big bath house and it has no heat in it. Taking a bath requires a lot of courage and with me is rather a speedy affair.

Our mess hall has six plain wood tables and some wooden benches. We built a screen to separate us from the soldiers and eat on regular heavy British army china and silverware. The men have to use mess kits, but I'm thankful that we don't. We have a private who waits on our table and is very good. Garnishes our plates with little patches of lettuce and so forth. But the helpings are on the generous side. Our meals are good but lacking fresh articles and rich food. I eat huge quantities except at breakfast when we usually have French toast or scrambled eggs made from powdered eggs. So I'm getting a bit fed up with both.

Well Darling, that just about covers how I live and it's about the same as at any temporary camp. The only trouble is that it isn't just for only 2-3 weeks that this foolishness goes on. Rather, it seems to go on and on. It's been three months now, longer than we have ever been separated before in the last eight years. And I don't see any prospect of getting home soon. But it all has to end sooner or later. I can't wait for the ending. I love you.

Your devoted husband,
Jimmy

Wednesday, 17 May

My Darling One,

Our days and nights are really full now. I just got in from three days in the field and they were miserable ones indeed. Wet and cold and windy — this is really a stinking climate. Make no mistake about it. I was dressed for it but I don't care what you put on, it still gets through to you. And living in a wet pup tent with rain dripping off your steel helmet and your mess kit is not conducive to happiness.

However, the training was very good and realistic and I'm really getting enthusiastic about this outfit. And boy, can these boys shoot. As a matter of fact, two sheep were killed on the range the other day, each with one bullet from 250 yards. The British range officer certainly did raise hell. But as I out-ranked him, he had to do it in a nice way.

As a matter of fact, the British are crazy as far as safety regulations go. There are always cattle and sheep roaming all over the target range, and I don't know why we don't kill more. Farmers calmly plow their fields right in the danger area with ricochets flying all around them. It worried us at first, but they all know they are in the danger area and are warned to stay out. So to hell with them. We just go on shooting and they go on plowing.

Did I tell you that I bought a pair of English tank boots? They are very nice and waterproof up to my calf. But they cost six whole pounds. That's $30.00. So that's why I'm broke. I don't spend money for much but these spelled comfort so I bought them. Good old Mr. Peale made them. I ordered them when I was in London and they just got here.

I am so tired and sleepy that this is a very rambling letter, what with being warm for the first time in three days. My face is all burned from the wind, for an armored car is a very wet and cold place to ride with the wind blowing in your face at 30 mph. I'm just living on creature comforts, warm feet and a good meal under my belt now and a feeling of work well done.

God bless you and keep you safe and happy and well and the children the same.

Your own,
Jimmy

22 May, 1944

My Adorable One,

I have been continuously in the field living in a pup tent and going on all sorts of field problems. It's been a miserable period and still cold and rainy. My writing paper got soaked the very first day, as did all my baggage, as our baggage truck turned over and dumped everything into a creek. I never did get my bedding really dry the whole period.

We have been in a very sparsely settled region that in some respects reminds me of Kansas or New Mexico. This is really an amazing country. We were never more than 20 miles from a city almost the size of El Paso, yet we had the feeling of being out in the wilds. Yet I am healthy and free from any sign of a cold.

The problems were interesting and very well done. I am so often impressed with the spirit and the determination of the American soldier. Under the most difficult and most uncomfortable weather conditions, these kids show a drive that is amazing. I am proud to go to war with them.

I also saw a man the other day who gave me some wonderful news. Pidge's husband Van (Col. William Van Nostrand) is not a prisoner and is doing some very wonderful work out in the jungle. He will be a famous man some day when this is all over and if he survives.

I had a funny experience the other day. Our mail was delivered in the field and I got a wonderful looking package. All the officers clustered around my offer of cigars and candy which I thought was what was going to be in it. It was going to be a great feast in that cold and sodden meadow. So I opened it up and what was it but toilet paper. What a roar went up. You funny lovable woman. We all laughed until we were sick. When I ask for something, you really send it. However, all the headquarters officers are most grateful, and we are all revelling in the softness of our imported American luxury. I had to give most of it away for such reams of it would have taken up half my baggage, as I only go into the field with a small musette bag. All my love and it is for you and you alone that I shall be fighting.

Your Jimmy

30 May, 1944

Dearest One,

From our papers over here, it seems that everyone in the U.S. is all excited about D-Day and making all kinds of preparations for it. I think the closer one gets to it the calmer everyone is. The English are not at all excited, nor are we. We have no idea when it will occur. Our job is to be fit and ready, which we are. But we are certainly not sitting around waiting for the big day. Instead we are training like all get out. And everyone is so busy that they don't have time to speculate about it. When we get called out for the big show it will be so routine that no one will turn a hair. Just another exercise, except that it will be for keeps this time.

Now I haven't the slightest qualms about this outfit. I did have some considerable qualms at Fort Hood, but now that I have seen them work under real combat conditions, I am very proud to go to war with them. They are a good lot and will acquit themselves with distinction. And by George, they really look after me, God bless them.

I am glad that the carving set finally arrived. It certainly took long enough. Please have Mabie try it out and see if it is really good. Good steel should be used so don't put it away. The salesman bent the blade all over the place to show me how good the steel was.

Your devoted husband,
Jimmy

2 June, 1944

Dearest Punkin,

I got the most adorable letter from you today telling me about Jamie's new shoes and how he talks and how Jody misses me. Tell the sweet thing that her old daddy sure does miss her too all the time and hates to be away while she is growing up.

Last night, Frank Oliver and I took our R.A.F. friends out to supper, the Hamiltons and Litchfields, both in the R.A.F. and stationed nearby. Flight Lieutenant Hamilton is so typically British that Frank and I are rude — we laugh at him so much. He really is just like a P. G. Wodehouse book. His wife is just plain dull. Mrs. Litchfield is very gracious and charming but Squadron Leader Litchfield is the real gem of the crowd. He's kind of fat and bald but loads of fun with a keen wit. He looks about forty but he's only thirty-one. We spend our time kidding each other about the funny customs of each other's country.

We ate supper at sort of a roadhouse and pub combined, much like one of those Howard Johnson places in the States. It was called "The Raven." We had a good supper with some cocktails beforehand and a couple of liquors afterwards. No whiskey or gin as they were not allowed as is the usual way around here. It was good fun though to sit down at a nice table with linen on it with ladies and gentlemen about you and feel civilized and waited on. We certainly paid through the nose for it. I can't afford to attend such to-do's very often.

I miss you so terribly on occasions like that. And if we ever come back here, I will take you to supper at "The Raven" and then the next day at "The Cat and Fiddle" and then the next day at "The Crown." And you will love it.

My life is in sort of a state of suspended animation right now waiting for action. I want to get on with this damn war for I know it will be okay for me and the sooner it happens the better, because the sooner we invade the sooner I get my chance to come home.

All my love, my dearest one,
Your Jimmy

7 June, 1944

Dearest One,

From the radio, it sounds as if the whole invasion show came off quite well. At least the initial landing is off to a good start and that is the big thing. I don't imagine that we hear half as much news as you do, as the British Broadcasting Corporation is the only one in England. And in my opinion, their newscasts are lousy. All filled up with Sir Hoople's remarks or all about the British troops and very little about our own American troops. But I guess our papers barely mention the British, so that makes us even.

I think of you so much and will try and write a short note every day just to keep you from worrying. I can't say much about our work except we are very busy and that the outfit is in fine shape. I am completely yours.

Your Jimmy

10 June, 1944

My Darling One,

Take the enclosed check for $70.00 and get Tom (my youngest brother, Tom Polk) a nice wedding present. You shouldn't need all of it by a long shot for that, so buy yourself a nice present also. It is amazing how cheaply I live over here because I think I wrote you that I sent Mother $40.00 the other day to help her out on her trip. I would like to increase your paycheck but I'm afraid to fool with it as it takes several months to change and you might have none in the meantime. So I will continue to send you money whenever I get near a post office.

We have been hanging on the radio as I suppose you have, listening to all the news broadcasts of the invasion. However, it is rather maddening to us as the newscasters never go into details enough to suit our military minds. It is interesting to listen to the German broadcasts. They tell much more and their stations come in as strong as the local ones. However, much of it is clever lies, as they are obviously fishing for information. The show seems to be going well from all accounts but I imagine the worst is over now that they are through the beach defenses. I hope you aren't worried about me. I am still a long ways from it.

It is Saturday night, but for some reason there are some 5-6 officers in the barracks, contrary to custom. Therefore this letter is somewhat disjointed as the radio is going and there is a black-jack game on and a lot of conversation and speculation flying back and forth as to what is going to happen to us. I am rather sorry as I miss my Saturday evenings being alone. There are too many people in my life that I don't care a damn about. I am forever yours.

Your Jimmy

NOTE: About this time, four of us in the regiment were what was called Bigoted. That means that we were briefed on what our missions were to be when we got on shore on the Coast of France. There were four of us, the C.O., Col. Wilson, myself and the two squadron commanders. We were told where we would land and on what beach, although we were shown only a small portion of the area so we didn't know too much. We were told the date and the time. We were given our ship and we were told to make out our shipping lists and then were told our mission once we got ashore. It was pretty scary because our mission was to cut straight across the Normandy and Brittany Peninsulas, right through enemy lines, and make a stab at capturing the port of Nantes at the mouth of the Loire River. It looked like a suicide mission to us, but fortunately, we never had to do it because the mission had changed considerably by the time we got ashore in France.

13 June, 1944

Dearest Only Love,

We're still waiting around for orders and have nothing yet. But I spent a very interesting day today. Col. Wilson and I went on a business trip and stopped off in a very famous old English town. (It was Chester.) We spent the afternoon there. It was the most interesting place I have been in all of England. Very old and full of antiquity, so the antique shops abounded. We went shopping all over the place and saw the most fascinating shops you've ever been in. You would have been completely mad. I saw two sets of hunting prints that I'd have given anything for, $160 the set each. All the most wonderful antique furniture you ever saw — some of it dating back to Queen Elizabeth. Clocks with brass dials and cat-gut weights, Chippendale desks, Charles II chairs, a duelling sword he wanted $120.00 for. I almost bought it. A real rapier with a silver chain wound around the handle. If I hadn't sent you the money yesterday, it would have been on the way. So maybe it is just as well. Really is one of the places we shall visit on our return trip. Suits of armor, old china and glass, old prints and paintings, antique furniture and silver. But with a price on it that was horrible. These English really drive a hard bargain.

And then tonight as you have no doubt guessed by now, I went out to supper at a British castle and have drunk all the famous vintages for the last decade. We started off with Scotch and pleasant conversation, while I was shown around the place. Then went on to famous old Bordeaux wine and supper. Not bad at all and wound up with a famous port and dessert. To top it all off, we had more Scotch and more pleasant conversation. You'd have loved the place. A big castle with a view over the lake and all the laurel in bloom around it, red, pink and purple. Was quite a formation and I rather think the British are fine people in spite of their weather.

You would really have gotten a thrill going over the drawbridge and through the gate with modern British soldiers on guard, popping to attention and rendering a salute. I felt like the Duke of Whoozit with all the ceremony that ushered me in. I really missed you at the castle and love you.

Your devoted husband,
Jimmy

NOTE: It was the castle of Sir Giles Broughton and it was the first time we had been admitted to the castle since our arrival. Sir Giles was not there and it was occupied by a British Officers' School.

NOTE: Several letters have been omitted simply because they just speak of boredom waiting for our orders to go in and sitting around. We were initially ordered to go in on D+6, on June 12th., but our orders were delayed because of the heavy fighting in the hedgerows and the requirement for more infantry than had been originally planned. Therefore, we were set back and the infantry were moved up. We now expected to go in about D+16.

24 June, 1944
(D + 18)

My Dearest One,

I'm so glad that the plates have finally arrived as I had begun to worry about them. I presume that none of them were broken or you would have mentioned it. Do you really like them? Tell me how you plan to use them.

There is a severe water shortage over here so our camp is rationed on the amount of water we can use. It's really ridiculous, because it seems to rain all the time. Bathing is most difficult but there is an army bathing and delousing unit near that we can go to every three days. So far, I've been able to stay out of the delousing department. I hope my luck holds as I hear it is rather rugged. We are also issued louse powder to keep the little visitors away.

I saw Paul Kendall yesterday and had a most pleasant but short visit with him. We had a drink and a steak supper at his mess. I think I wrote you that he lives with a British family in a very lovely home and is really in good shape.

Also, I had an unexpected letter from Mollie (my sister, Mollie Polk Wilson) telling me about getting Mother off on her trip. She said she finally prevailed on Mother to get some colorful clothes and a couple of new hats, and that she looked quite stylish. I'm certainly glad that she is out of that dreadful mourning habit. She said that Tom's wedding is to be July 13th., so I hope you have gotten off a nice present. She also said that Tom was assigned to the battleship "Colorado" in the Pacific. That puts all the Polk boys but me over that way. But then I can tell lies that none of them can check me up on. I love you, my very own.

Your Jimmy

25 June, 1944 (D + 19)
(Sunday — England)

My Dearest One,

Today started out as a beautiful day so with not much on the calendar, Col. W. and I went out for a walk after our morning pancakes. We did about 8 miles of cross country and I managed to raise a small blister on one toe chiefly because this last week I have been too preoccupied to do my usual running or walking. The countryside was beautiful and I wish so that you'd have been along instead of the old man. We spent most of our hours circling a big estate that is enclosed by an 8' stone wall, very un-American of them; so we had to peek in at every gate or break in the wall to see just what the owner had that he was so anxious to hide.

Over here, none of the beautiful homes or big estates are visible from the road. They do love their privacy. So they always have a great thick hedge or stone or brick wall around the place and the houses sit well back in a grove. In most of the village, on the other hand, the doorstep is right on the road and they have a small garden in the rear. I'm really getting to know rural England quite well and though much of it is most attractive, old and quaint, I would certainly hate to live there. Give me the wide open spaces. Talk about feeling enclosed — you really are over here. There is always a fence or a hedge around you.

Due to the water shortage, I spent most of the afternoon getting a bath and doing my laundry. And after all my labors of washing underwear and socks, I dropped them by mistake on the ground and got dirt all over them. However, it is clean dirt and not body dirt so I shall probably wear them that way.

This afternoon we had the inevitable drizzle, which doesn't seem to relieve the water shortage. It's very queer.

Goodnight my love. I adore you.

Your Jim

P.S. As you see, I am still in England, well and healthy and missing you. JHP

NOTE : We got our orders to proceed to Southampton on the 27th., waterproof our vehicles on the 28th., and sail on the 29th. of June for Normandy. It was all very exciting.

28 June, 1944
(England)

Dearest,

It is terribly difficult to write as I can tell you nothing. I know you are worried about where I am but you will just have to be content and I will tell you as soon as I am allowed to do so. You must just accept the fact that I am well and healthy and in no danger as yet.

I don't know if I have gained weight or not as I have no opportunity to weigh, but I imagine I weigh about as much as I ever have, as I eat like a horse and the food has been wonderful of late. They are really feeding us. As I knock on wood when I say that I haven't had a cold in a long time, I guess it's the healthy life I lead. Much love as always.

Your devoted husband
Jimmy

NOTE: This letter was written at Southampton where we were in a temporary camp. We were employed in waterproofing our vehicles and loading combat ammunition and checking our loading plans and in storing away our foot-lockers with the personal objects and clothing that we would not need in the combat zone. The next day, on the 29th., we loaded and sailed at dark for Utah Beach in Normandy. The LST (Landing Ship Tank) carrying the headquarters troop of the 106th. Squadron hit a mine not too far out and was beached, two men killed and a total loss of all their vehicles and equipment.

NOTE: There are no letters from June 29 until July 21st. Probably I wrote very few as this was our first combat.

NOTE: On landing at Utah Beach on the morning of June 30, the sea was littered with sunken ships while ashore there were broken gliders, burned-out tanks and vehicles, and some German bodies and dead animal stock. There was also much activity of other troops landing and big dumps of supplies and evacuation of the wounded. We assembled around a small village, Veau le Viscont, near La Hay du Puits, de-waterproofed the vehicles, checked weapons and set our new combat radio frequencies. The 90th. Division was in a violent attack near us. We could hear heavy cannonading, and we awaited our new mission with considerable trepidation. I took temporary command of the 106th. Squadron, pending the arrival of Frank Oliver and his re-equipped Headquarters Troop.

Our first job wasn't too difficult; one Squadron to connect between the 83rd. and 79th. Divisions, the other between the 79th. and the 90th. We didn't have to attack frontally, but just slid forward in their wake. The 79th. gave us artillery support, which we used quite frequently.

On the 10th. of July, upon the arrival of another division, we were pulled out and directed to clear and defend the area from the 90th. Div. west to the Atlantic Ocean near Lessay, thus closing the neck of the Normandy Peninsula. We encountered little resistance, picking up stragglers including some of our own paratroopers, cleaned the area in two days, and began to feel like combat veterans. Oliver returned and I reverted to Group Exec.

The 106th. stayed in this position, mainly occupied with patrolling and artillery fire, until the St. Lo breakout. During this time, we took a direct hit on our primary radio van, destroying it and killing two officers and three enlisted radio operators. After that, we all slept in slit trenches below ground level.

PART II

Normandy, Across France and the Moselle River
21 July -13 November, 1944

21 July, 1944
(Friday)

My Dearest One,

Today it is pouring rain. The war is in a bit of a lull and I am seizing a chance to get off a letter. Someone will surely come in and bother with me with decisions or orders, but I have hopes of really writing you a letter.

A hard rain is a blessing in some ways even if my bedding got all soaked this morning. But it gives us a pause and the Jerries don't like it any better than we do.

I've hopes of getting my name in the Chicago paper and someone will relay it to you. Yesterday, we had a visit from some war correspondents on our particular front. So the story may help you know where I am. However, it will probably sound very dangerous as the dumb reporters all walked to my observation post in a big herd. And I knew damn well it would draw fire. I had no more than finished giving them hell about it and here it came. I really had plenty of company in my hole. They nearly trampled me to death jumping on top of me. It was the only fire we had had in that position all day but they thought it was continuous. And after taking my name and thinking me a very brave man, they got the hell out. It really was funny. They also took my picture and I look just like a complete pirate.

As a matter of fact, there has been no heavy fighting here so we can get eggs and onions and potatoes, and I found a peasant who would do my laundry so I am in fine shape. We also swept the area of the beach clean of mines and I got to swim in the ocean — my only bath in three weeks. You might say it is an interesting sector without being too dangerous. We just get nibbled now and then.

The refugees here are a terrific problem. Nearly all of them are destitute and it is very hard to eat when they watch with hungry eyes, particularly the children. All of our soldiers give away some of their food. A lot of the refugees sneak through the lines at night and of course some get shot or step on a mine. The others just shrug and say "C'est la guerre". They really don't give a damn. When they finally get with Americans, even the men are prone to embrace the nearest soldier and kiss him on both cheeks, very embarrassing.

I did not send my trunk home as I thought I might be here awhile so I put it in storage. However, you are right as I sent a box of my good blouse and some other items. I can get a GI one over here.

NOTE: Letter ends — apparently there is a lost page.

At this point, Col. Joe Ficket, the Commanding Officer of the 6th Cavalry broke his leg and I was pulled from Executive Officer of the 106th to command the 6th Cavalry. This was just about the time the 3rd Army broke out near Avranches and started the race across France. So, I took command of the 6th Cavalry almost on the run. I was told that I had to command for three months before I could be promoted to Colonel, so I was commanding as a Lieutenant Colonel. There was no ceremony, I just walked in the C.P. and said, "I am your new Commanding Officer."

NOTE: The 6th Cavalry Group was a most unusual outfit as they were an old line Regular Army Unit, long stationed at Fort Oglethorpe, Georgia and went from horse cavalry to porte cavalry (horses transported in large vans) to armored cavalry with the same organization and personnel. They were never cadred, as was almost the entire Regular Army, since they were earmarked for the North African invasion in 1942. However, on arriving in Northern Ireland, there wasn't sufficient shipping to transport them to North Africa, so they remained in Ireland and England for two years, training and honing their skills.

The 6th was very sharp and snappy with beautiful equipment and experienced men and officers. Their mechanics, cooks, armorers and particularly their radio operators were as a group the best in our rapidly expanded Army, without question. The troop radio nets operated on an 18 word per minute basis with a key, while from troop to squadron and above, the operators used a bug and got up to 30 words per minute in flawless transmissions.

When 3rd Army became operational, the Signal Bn. serving that headquarters simply did not have the radio skills required for that fast-moving and far-flung command, so the 6th Squadron of the 6th Cavalry was given the job, much like the British Army's Ferret System. With a Recon. platoon at each Division Headquarter, a Company at each Corps Headquarter and the Squadron Headquarters at Army, we were a special information service working directly for General Patton. We reported events as we knew them but had to be careful, as some of the Divisions initially regarded us as spies.

I had a front row seat at 3rd Army Headquarters, attending morning briefings which were fascinating. I actually sat in on the famous meeting where Gen. Patton told Lt. Gen. Wyland that it was up to the 17th Air Force to guard his totally open and vulnerable right (south) flank as he didn't have the troops for the job.

The other Squadron (the 46th) was used as security for the Army C.P. and a sort of rear-area security system, cleaning out pockets of bypassed German units and soldiers, sweeping woods and villages, clearing mines and protecting supply convoys. It wasn't very arduous or exciting but watching Third Army operations in its race across France was a rare experience.

27 July, 1944

My Beloved One,

I have again changed jobs, address and APO. I am in an entirely new outfit and am the Commanding Officer! Do you realize what that means! My new address is:

Lt. Col. J. H. Polk
Headquarters 6th Cavalry Group
APO 403
c/o Postmaster
New York, New York

The number 6 seems to be following me around this year, and I'm about sold on the idea that it's my lucky number. Naturally, I am excited and thrilled by it all. It means, however, a whole new load of responsibilities and duties, with no one to guide me. I pray that I am up to the job and will certainly do my best.

I cannot tell you my new location. You can make a good guess but please don't discuss it with anyone. It's sufficient to say that I am as safe as if I was at home in bed. My sleeping is undisturbed by night noises and I am eating great quantities of fresh food and I have access to a shower-bath, and am now completely cleaned up and bathed — my first shower in three weeks. All rested up and well fed. It's amazing the importance that cleanliness takes on when it is impossible to obtain it.

I'm crazy about my new outfit, as I am back in the regular Army at last. It is a veteran outfit with a glorious history. Old NCO's who have grown up with the regiment -experienced officers. I am amazed to get it, as there are many officers far senior to me floating around looking for just such a job. Ruth Ellen's daddy (this is a reference to Gen. Patton) was very complimentary when I was assigned and said I was picked personally as the best man for the job. His is a grand headquarters to work for, and I have many old friends up there and they really know their business.

My lucky assignments since I left West Point last fall have really been amazing. If I lined up and ordered my own assignments and training schedule, it couldn't have been worked out any nicer. I am only sorry that you aren't here to be the First Lady of the Group. Wouldn't that be something? And wouldn't you feel old? I have become an old man overnight with all sorts of service and all sorts of comfort, like a canvas cot and a chair, a large tent all my own, an armored car and a jeep at my beck and call, the seat at the head of the table, first crack at the food and so forth. However, there is much to be done, new training, new names and personnel to learn, new policies to put into effect, new examples or standards to set. My job will be much safer because I will be farther back behind the lines, so you can rest easier on that score. Also my standards of living and comfort will be much greater. So I would say that your worries about my safety and health should greatly decrease and perhaps your worries about my abilities should increase.

Of course this means that mail will again be thrown into a complete tailspin and that your letters, Life, Time and the Army/Navy Journal will again begin the dizzy merry-go-round trying to locate me. It can't be helped. But maybe this time I have a permanent home for a while. I certainly hope so, as I would almost be content to keep this same job for the rest of my service — with you along, of course. Maybe we can arrange it if the Jerries would just realize it and quit their futile efforts. But no one here can see any indication that the recent turmoil in Germany has affected the Jerries' fighting ability or courage.

About every two weeks, I would like you to send me the following:

1) A dozen or more cigars
2) Two bars of laundry soap
3) Package of razor blades
4) Assorted candy bars

Do not send me a whole lot of anything as I cannot carry it.

It is much better to send me small amounts more often. Also, I still crave pictures of you badly. Please send me pictures of you.

> Your devoted husband
> and excited man,
> Jimmy

NOTE: *The reference to the recent turmoil in Germany refers to the plot to assassinate Hitler.*

29 July, 1944

My Beloved One,

Here it is Saturday night. Things have slowed down a bit and I am sitting in my command post thinking of home and you. I've just finished my chores of cleaning my gun and oiling my boots. I don't trust my striker for that specific operation, after having spent a very busy day, most of it out with the troops.

Just before supper tonight, I had all my staff over for a drink as one of my officers was able to procure a bottle of brandy, so I made a little occasion of it. They are a very fine group. All of them are young but able and enthusiastic about their jobs. Most of them are from the South and many from V.M.I or the Univ. of Georgia, with a good sprinkling of gentlemen in the crowd. As a group, they are way above the headquarters that I was just with in the 106th. You might remember my new Executive Officer, Sam Goodwin, whose father was in the 7th Cavalry with Dad. The others you wouldn't know.

Everything is quiet and peaceful here. I still am no where near any danger, not even from the flying bombs which are hitting the people in London. We occasionally see planes go over and the area is filled with troops, but otherwise, it is just like maneuvers in the States. I sleep peacefully all night long and am getting some fresh meat for a change, and actually today got some white bread.

You poor Darling. You've been carrying a load with that big house and no help. But I suppose it is all cleared up by now with your Mother back home a long time by the time you get this. And maybe you're getting ready for your trip to the East by now. Do you ever hear from Heil Brown and Temple? I often remember how nice she was to us and when we take Paris, I shall try and get her a dirty picture or something as she loves them so. One of my favorite stories is about her idiotic car dummy.

I'm fit and well and forever yours. Bless you.

Your adoring,
Jimmy

PS: Now I can tell you that while I was in England, we were camped at Daddington Park in Cheshire. It was near Nantwich and about 15 miles from Newcastle-under-Lyme, where the big pottery works were and where we got the plates. The city where all the wonderful shops and antiques were located was Chester itself. Truly a fascinating place that you would really love. Col. Emberton lives at Audlum and Wing Commander Litchfield lives at Market Drayton. I liked Nantwich and The Castle Hotel was where we occasionally ate supper. However, I really like France much better, the people, the climate, the countryside and the weather has been just wonderful. The towns simply go crazy when we go through. Some of the people seem to spend their day waving to us, throwing flowers, offering wine and so forth. Thank God this world of kill-or-be-killed in the Normandy hedgerows is over and we have them on the run.

I think of you always and carry your pictures with me always, the Kodaks in my little case, the bigger ones in my map case. I'm always showing them to people. Today Jim Sneed came by my C.P. and I trotted them out. He also has two children slightly younger than ours. It is a strange life we lead. The intervals or moments that we meet old friends and recall our old lives, stand out like jewels. All the rest of it is hectic activity, little sleep and hurried food. Not that I am not in good physical shape for I am. But I assure you all the passion is burned out of me. I do love you though and hope all is well with you.

Your devoted husband,
Jimmy

NOTE: *Above, I am describing the 3rd Army's race across France in July/ August of 1944.*

8 August, 1944

My Dearest One,

This crazy campaign has been whooping along at such a rate that I have no idea when I wrote you last. I only know the date because I signed so many messages. But I haven't the vaguest idea of what day of the week it is. I have been tearing around the country. We are on the move everyday so as a consequence, I have gotten no mail for at least ten days. I have lost most of my baggage and have been living on K-rations plus eggs and potatoes that we get from the French. I did get paid a couple of days ago and sent you a check for $80.00. It will probably be about a month in coming.

I've had no one shoot at me since I came to this new command. And I'm leading a very safe life. We are not on combat duty as such but on a special task. A fascinating job but we hope to get to the front as a unit fairly soon. We do have an almost nightly bombing, not too close to us but really has us all well underground at night. I have some of the fastest and deepest diggers in the world. It is quite a sight to see or rather hear the planes come over and drop flares, make it as light as day and all the red streaks of tracer bullets going up and then comes the crump of their bombs. No one in the whole outfit has been hurt from it as the Jerries are in an awful hurry to get out of there.

It is really an awesome sight to see what our air has done to them in the last few days. The roads are littered with German tanks, trucks, guns and all the trash that men throw away when they are retreating. There are times when I think we are on our way to a quick victory and soon. They simply cannot move in daylight in any strength or our air will get them. So we go like hell in daylight and have trapped them by the thousands. All their stragglers seem glad to quit. I don't see how it can last past this fall. In addition, the Free French have really given the Germans hell behind their own lines. They never know when they'll get a shot in the back. I would hate to be a German today, but don't mistake me. I emphatically do not feel sorry for them. It all makes me happy to see the end in sight.

I passed a beautiful sight the other day -a regular fairy castle built on a giant rock in the sands. So symmetrical and beautiful and un-touched by war. It has been mentioned in a popular mystery story or rather spy story. (The reference here is to Mont San-Michel.)

Your devoted,
Jimmy

11 August, 1944
(Somewhere in France)

My Dearest One,

Today is a hot sunshiny day and we are drinking it up. Today has been easy. We have been more or less resting and I had a hot shower this morning in the most ingenious contraption. The boys captured or scrounged a German trailer and boiler and they rigged up a fire under it, stole some hose and a pump and we have a wonderful shower that follows us wherever we go. The Germans must think it is a secret weapon because bed-check Charlie, our nightly visitor, was apparently taking pictures of it last night. We move again tomorrow and begin the mad rat race again. But we are clean and rested and ready for it.

I've been much saddened by the death of two good friends, both from those damnable mines and booby traps. Those hateful Huns. I think how you used to think they were a decent race. I know that you no longer do and tell anyone who thinks so to look at the casualty list, knowing at least half of them, the deaths I mean, are from sneaky things. I'm not allowed to mention any deaths for a month but will tell you then. (I have reference here to Jess Hawkins and Frank Oliver.)

My old outfit is doing marvelously well. They are really the top people in the game over here and sometimes I miss them a lot. It's different being a commanding officer. I'm like the captain of a ship. Almost live alone. I'm proud of my new regiment and we are doing a difficult job very well. No heroics and the minimum danger. But difficult none the less. The war is really going to town but it is not the pushover that you hear on occasional broadcasts. I haven't seen any newspapers in weeks. But if the paper writes it's a pushover, they're nuts.

Yesterday, I got five letters from you, all of them were a month old but heart-warming and gladdening to my soul. You have no idea how they give me courage to go on and the determination to return to you safe and well. I love you always.

Your devoted,
Jimmy

16 August, 1944

My Dearest One:

We are in a new bivouac and things are slow for a little so I will write you hurriedly. Please write Mother for me, as I have had no chance to write her for almost a month, and tell her that I am well and safe and not really in any danger unless it is from speeding trucks on the highways and reckless driving by the Yanks and French which is really a serious nuisance.

We are camped in the grounds of a French chateau. The house itself was occupied by the Germans and they burned it down when they left so it is only a burned heap now. But the grounds are lovely with beautiful lawns and trees, statues scattered about and a formal garden that is going to pot. It is not one of the show places of some count but rather the home of a wealthy merchant or businessman. There is a lovely river running by the camp, quite deep and about 100' wide, all lined with poplar trees. The weather has been lovely with lots of sunshine and dust on the roads. But this part of France looks like what I had imagined France would be like. We have gone through it so fast that even the bigger towns are almost undamaged. Terrific celebrations everywhere we go. All the French immediately get tight and proceed to block the road. Much kissing and the old men are particularly dangerous in that respect. The French resistance groups beg us for guns and rush out to clean up any small groups of Germans. They are a great help in telling us where the enemy is, but more talk than any real action and any kind of an honest fight.

This letter was just interrupted by a sentry bringing in three German prisoners. The prisoners have been hiding in the woods nearby. One captain with an Iron Cross and two soldiers — all very glad to surrender. The Jerries have retreated so fast and the air has harried them so hard that we pick them up all the time. But they are afraid to surrender to the French who often shoot them or, at least, beat the devil out of them.

In a nearby town yesterday, I didn't see it but some of my officers did, the French were parading two naked French women up and down the street. Their heads were shaved and ropes were around their necks because they had been sleeping with Germans. They had also tattooed swastikas on their behinds and everyone was hooting and throwing garbage at them — some business.

I will probably be able to tell you about Paris soon, at the rate the old blood and guts army is going. As a matter of fact, I am eaten up with jealousy as we have an unconfirmed report that my old outfit (the 106th) is now in the outskirts of Paris, way ahead of anyone else. That outfit has really been rolling.

We have been hanging on a little portable radio listening to the accounts of the landing of Southern France. Apparently it came off wonderfully well and they ought to be rolling North to meet us soon. It is strange how out of touch we are with the rest of the world. All my news of you is over a month old and for such a magazine as Time or Life is unheard of. I try and imagine what you are doing now — perhaps you and the kids are up at Ruidoso right this minute. That wonderful place. How I would like to be with you and recreate our trip of last fall all over again.

All my love, my precious one. Don't worry about me. I am fine.

Your adoring husband
Jimmy

17 August, 1944

My Dearest One,

Today we are all standing by rather idly but have indications that we shall be snorting off again tomorrow in the same kind of job with no danger involved. I shall miss our little bivouac by the river and my daily swim, although I haven't gone in today as I have been busy with troublesome details. Lots of times it's easier to be in a fight than be embroiled in the paper administration war that soon catches up to you when you halt the forward rush.

Today, great stacks of mail arrived for everyone but me. And I felt so lonesome and blue. As I have been here almost a month in this job now, I ought to start getting mail direct instead of through my old outfit. That is what is delaying my mail at present and I will probably get it all in one great lump again.

I am enclosing some invasion francs for the scrapbook, also the label off a cognac bottle that I think is very interesting. You will note that it is made for the German army, over-printed on the label. One of my platoons captured a whole warehouse full of it and each officer was given a bottle. As a matter of fact, one division nearby took away 16 truckloads and I don't think it even made a dent in the stock. However, you need not worry about my drinking, as I have too much trouble with soldiers, no officers as yet, but I expect it. The French are very generous and give them all they want to drink of a foul applejack called Calvados. We're not in the grape country as yet and I shall be glad when we arrive. But the Germans certainly left in a hurry, to leave that warehouse full.

Our food has been very poor but we live almost completely on K-rations supplemented occasionally by bread or canned vegetables. It has been very dry here so all the vegetables grown locally aren't ready yet. We do manage to have eggs for breakfast quite often. But lunch and supper come right out of the can. We got some potatoes yesterday and are having onions tonight. It's a rare treat. I haven't had any fresh meat of any description since we left England. The Jerries killed most of the beef and depleted most of the livestock, so none of the farmers want to butcher what they have left. We are negotiating for a goose at present to supplement the can-fare.

I suppose you have been reading about the 3rd Army's accomplishments which we're all very proud of. Gen. Patton is really a great general even if he has his odd quirks that we know so well. He is daring and bold and all the men are proud of him and love him, even if the citizens of the United States don't think so much of him.

You are my love and my life.

Your devoted,
Jimmy

Monday, 20 August, 1944

Dearest,

The day has been most disagreeable as I have been having officer trouble. I had to reclassify a young officer, which is always difficult as hell. Sent him back to the United States in disgrace. I know I am right and I feel I must do it, as men's lives depend on it. But it takes everything out of me. I miss you terribly at times like this when I need reassuring. However, last night was wonderful. I walked into my command post and found 8 letters awaiting me. Seven of them quite old, but wonderful nonetheless, and one that came direct to me at my new address. So now I have hopes that the mail will be coming to me regularly once again. I loved them all and the pictures are great, the stories that you tell, the tales of the children and your love for me lift me up above all of this and make me a very happy man indeed.

The war is going great and I am well and healthy. The weather has been wonderful for two weeks so all I need to restore me is some sleep which I will get and then be happy again.

Thy James

NOTE: We were located at this time near Chartres about midway between the Seine and the Loire Rivers and short of Paris.

The officer I relieved was a troop commander, a fine captain with a good record. He simply would not do what I told him to do. I gave him orders three different times. On the third time, when he didn't follow my orders and my directions were perfectly specific, so I relieved him on the spot. I think the whole regiment was shocked as he was popular, but apparently this young man thought he knew better than I did and was going to do it his way. I think the regiment paid attention to me after this incident.

Monday, 21 August, 1944

My Darling Wife,

Today has been a good day. I feel I have accomplished much. For the first time I feel that the outfit is really with me and working for me all out. There is always that transition period in a new outfit when you feel like the strange cat in the litter. You aren't sure of anyone's name and you feel you are without a friend in the world. That is all over now. We are all a team and I hope we can stay together for a while as I'm tired of this jaunting about from outfit to outfit. I want to bring this one home with me and let you be the First Lady for a while. You will like them all, I feel sure.

In answer to some of your questions — Yes, I should be made a full Colonel but probably not very soon, as policy is that you must prove yourself and your ability to command in combat. Give me a couple of months or so. A Cavalry Group is the same as a Regiment, the only difference is that it's a more flexible organization. It may have any number of Squadrons. I have two at this point. I am not at liberty to tell you the number of men, but I imagine you can make a good guess. I cannot tell you our status. We are not out of the war nor are we in the front lines. Elements are in and out, put it that way. As for myself, I seldom have a chance to get forward of the line of Major Generals. I don't have time. But I'm constantly on the move, mainly organizing and directing. Not a lot of glory, but on the other hand, people have been most complimentary. It's a cavalry job, but not such a thing as guarding prisoners or the like. I can say no more.

You should see me. I look like a real pirate now — a steel helmet with a camouflage net, a scarf of parachute silk, a combat jacket, web belt with pistol, compass and knife, a carbine slung over my shoulder, muddy trousers and muddier tank boots, my fingernails broken and dirty, usually in need of a shave, and burned by the sun and the wind. But I feel great and am thriving. Fall in bed at night and have to be shaken awake. A soldier made me the most beautiful knife, about a seven-inch blade and the handle made of English pennies and plexiglass from a shot down German plane. It is very handy as I can open cans, cut brush and clean my boots with it. I hope I can bring it home, as it really is a beauty.

We are camped in a beautiful woods tonight on the estate of the Marquis of Blanche. He is quite a distinguished old gent and came to call on me tonight, but I was out. I shall return the call if I have time as, he lives in a very interesting-looking sort of run-down castle with towers and a moat and a wall. Most of it is old ruins, but he has apparently rebuilt part of it and he lives there with six daughters, ages 6-12. I don't know just where the marquis is on the social scale, but an officer in the mess said he was about the lowest in the line of nobility.

This is all a great deal about me and might sound conceited, but I try and let you see how I live and look and tell you some of my troubles. It's all because I want to share my life with you.

Your devoted husband,
Jimmy

NOTE: The war is starting to go faster now and 3rd Army Troops have closed up on the Seine River below Paris between Melun and Troyes and we (the 3rd Army C.P.) are about 30 miles behind them.

26 August, 1944
(Saturday)

Dearest One,

I've been out on the road visiting parts of my unit, it seems all over France. It's amazing to me. We are now out of the hedgerow country and the 1st Army has actually taken Paris. However, I don't expect to get in there as we are threatened with arrest for visiting the place. Much of the country looks like Iowa, wheat fields, wire fences, fruit trees and perfectly flat, level ground. It is interesting but very tiring as the roads are dusty and filled with American trucks and French children.

I captured six prisoners the other day. We were zipping down a road in my jeep way behind the front when a Frenchman rode by on a bicycle making frantic gestures and screaming "Boche", "Boche". We pulled up and looked down the side road where he pointed and there were six Germans. So Abbot trained his machine gun on them and they threw away their guns and marched in with their hands up, very happy to surrender. I couldn't take care of them so I turned them over to the French, who by this time had acquired their guns. The French were delighted and the Germans most unhappy as the French have a habit of killing all the isolated Germans they can catch.

I see Paul Harkins frequently, also John McDonald, Holly Mattox and others. Part of my outfit guards them. The other part is on entirely different work so I lead a divided life.

I'm now going down to have a bath in our secret weapon as I have just been informed that the water is hot. My first bath in over a week.

Thy James

NOTE: *In mentioning the names of those Cavalry Colonels whom Joey and I both knew, I am trying to tell her that one of my Squadrons is assigned the duty of guarding the 3rd Army Headquarters, that is, George Patton's Headquarters.*

29 August, 1944

Dearest One,

It is raining hard outside the tent and the world is rather drab and miserable. However, I shouldn't complain as this is the first hard rain we've had in over a month. The weather has been really perfect for a long spell. It is the end of August and I hate to think of the end of summer with winter coming on us. Maybe we should be inside a nice comfortable chateau before it gets too cold. We have a couple of months yet to end this damn thing and maybe we can. A lot of people seem to think so, but I'm beginning to doubt it.

I can now tell you that Jess Hawkins, Frank Oliver and Dick Nelson all were killed over a month ago. And John Ribold is missing in action. It's very sad for me, particularly Frank Oliver, as I'd grown awfully fond of him. Another one of those damnable booby traps. Also, he had two children and never got to see his wife when he went through New York. My old unit, the 106th, has suffered some very heavy casualties, but Vennard is still full of pep and doing great things.

This is a dull letter, but it's been a dull day. However, yesterday I discovered I have to hold down my job for three months before I can be promoted. It's a new Army regulation. It is becoming increasingly more difficult to become a Colonel as the Army already has too many of these fuddy-duddy types and they don't know what to do with them.

I'll write you soon again, but we are on the move tomorrow. Never am I near a place where I can cable you. Damn the rain. I'm in a horrible humor and shouldn't mail this. You see, I really need you now to make me happy and buck me up. I adore you.

Your own,
Jimmy

3 Sept., 1944

My Dearest One,

It is wonderful being back in closer touch with you again. I came in after a long day on the road and found a letter only two weeks old awaiting me. It gave such a good feeling. Are my letters to you getting better now?

My trip was long and tiring and we went through a lot of rain. Most of the day, I was soaking wet in my jeep. But this living outdoors does have its advantages. No one ever has a cold. Our food isn't much to brag about and will probably get worse before it gets better at the rate we are moving away from the coast and our base of supplies.

However, all this talk about the French being starved and the children under-nourished is pure bunk. They are way fed and healthy. It is true that you don't see many fat people, but they all eat far better than did the English. And in fact, the children in England are uniformly thin and anemic looking, but not the French. It just goes to show what bunk a lot of stuff is in our newspapers. And the French women are far better turned out than the English in a lot of respects except for shoes. It is true that almost all French men and woman wear wooden shoes or rope sandals, and they pull the shoes off dead German soldiers before they are even cold. Other items that the French lack are chocolate, tobacco and soap. They don't want our money for eggs or vegetables. They want one of the three above. Also, I think I wrote you about how all the little French kids want cigarettes. In all the towns along the route you see kids of 5 and on smoking cigarettes. I am much impressed though with the French children. You seldom see one dirty or doing badly. They are always polite and friendly and a great contrast to the nasty little scrubby children of England. I much prefer the French to the English and the feeling is mutual.

I had an officer come back from Paris the other day. He had seen the French Armored Division take the city as was in all the papers. He said it really was a riot. And he was right in the middle of it. The French Army wears U.S. uniforms so they really can't tell the difference at first glance. So all the people thought he was French: he saw as much kissing, hugging, drinking, and yelling as you ever saw, medium tanks running up and down the streets shooting German snipers with girls inside of them. He said the whole town was drunk and on a terrific spree, the cafes open, shooting in the streets and people watching, shaving and stripping women who had gone out with the Germans, bands playing, flags flying and right in the middle of an impromptu parade, a whole company turned out of line to get a batch of snipers. I wish I could have seen it. It really sounds terrific.

There are rumors that I may get a new job. I am a bit depressed by it all as the old C.O., Ficket, who had broken his leg, is about well and the powers above think he should get his command back. Everyone is most complimentary about my work, but it looks like I will get command of still another Cavalry Group. It is damn tiresome. Just as I am getting everyone's name correct and their confidence, I have to move on to somewhere else. And the mail situation will get all screwed up again. Damn, I wish I could stay on someplace permanently; it may not happen but I like this crowd I own now. So hope for the best. I will be the most travelled cavalryman in the E.T.O. before this war is over. But I am a good soldier and will do as I am told. It always seems to work out for the best anyway.

> Goodnight, my precious.
> Your Jimmy

5 Sept., 1944

Dearest One,

This is the first time in a long while that I have had absolute privacy to write you. The new C.O., who is also the old C.O. who broke his leg, Joe Ficket, has come back today and is in the process of taking over his old outfit. I hate like all hell to lose it. I really had them working my way and had gotten to know and like many of them and now am on my travels again. I will send you my new A.P.O. by cable as soon as I know the number. I am to command John Ribold's old outfit, the 14th Cavalry. So it still means a promotion. However it means all the hard work of getting to know everyone all over again, raising hell about my pet hobbies, and the extra difficulty of taking over a new command that is in rather violent combat.

I don't know just exactly what my new Group is doing, but they are engaged in rather a tough fight, so that part of it does give me a boost. Uncle George is sending me tomorrow in his private plane. It will be a long flight and it reminds me of your shapely chest. (I am referring here to say that I am going out to the fight around Brest). It ought to be fun as I understand the plane is done inside in pastel colors, has easy chairs and a well-stocked ice box. I'll write you the details later.

Everyone has been extravagantly complimentary about what I have done here. General Gay has been particularly nice. I think he furnishes the brains and George the drive. It has been a great show and I hate to leave it for what might be a stinko. Anyway, I am certainly seeing plenty of this damn war from almost the start to what I hope is a quick finish.

I am sending you another package today and I also hope it gets through to you. It consists of a lot of German parachute silk. I have a suggestion for a Christmas present. Make scarves of it for all the men in the family. I think it would make a beautiful present and any serviceman who has been over here will recognize it at once. It was captured by one of my platoons. I don't know just how good the silk is, but believe it is excellent and is a mild pastel shade of green and grey.

NOTE: The last page is missing. At this point, the 3rd Army Headquarters was moving into Verdun and the Divisions were bucking up to the Moselle River.

11 Sept., 1944

My Adorable One,

This is being written in Georgie's private plane about 5000' above France. It is a clear beautiful day and the countryside is lovely below — all green fields, little towns and the sea coast. We passed over Mont San-Michel which I mentioned earlier in a guarded sort of way. It is, even from the air, one of the most beautiful spots I've ever seen. I wonder if you saw it when you were over here.

The plane is a C-47, one of the medium sized transport planes, especially outfitted with a desk, an easy chair and a sofa, all done in green leather. The inside walls are pastel green and grey. We are sailing along about 200 miles an hour and will shortly land on the field near Paris to re-gas and then go on to the Brittany Peninsula.

I know you are confused about me and I am myself. I went out about a week ago to take over John Ribold's outfit and had no more than gotten settled in a private war of my own when I am jerked out again and on my way back, this time to command still another outfit of the same type. The Commander, Fred Drury, is missing in action and they need somebody at once. So again they sent the plane for me. I hope all this attention I am getting doesn't get me a swelled head. As a matter of fact, I hope I live up to all their high expectations as this war is still plenty rough, at least as far as the Cavalry is concerned. And the Germans apparently intend to make a stand along the Siegfried Line that will make it rougher on the people who have to punch through it. I guess the next month will tell the tale. This ought to be over about November 1st., is my personal guess.

I have not found it hard to be personally brave. It is really easy as everyone expects it of me, so I am. What I do find hard and terribly hard, is to order men in to do a thing in which I know some will be killed. To see the looks on their faces, to see the sometimes terrific heroism that they nonchalantly display, makes you proud and humble all at once. It is tough to be nonchalant and impersonal at such times. Pray for me my dear, that I will be smart and courageous and ready to command, for it is a hard job. It is so difficult to write even of love and home and soft things for my life now is so unlike that.

We are coming down lower now and the plane is bouncing about more so it is hard to write. My new address will be:

3rd Armored Cavalry Group
APO 403 New York

Tell other people as I don't have time to write. I love you.

Your Jimmy

NOTE: I was really happy to be recalled from command of the 14th Cavalry Group because I thought they were really a screwed up outfit. John Ribold, we all knew, was kind of crazy and it would have been an awful chore for me to get hold of that outfit and straighten it out. Actually, the whole Corps at Brest was being transferred to another Army and that was the reason that Gen. Patton brought me back. I was very happy about the whole affair.

About this time, my mother, Mrs. Harding Polk, got a letter from Mrs. Beatrice Patton (Gen. Patton's wife). It said the following: "This is what Georgie wrote about Jimmy's assignment. Jimmy Polk has just gotten a Regiment. He earned it having done a wonderful job. He is 32, I was a Col. at 31 but when I looked at Jimmy I wondered if I ever looked as young. He did, Esther. And you must be very proud that your son Jimmy is that kind of man. I am proud too and I cannot help but feel that the war with Germany is rushing to its close. Your affectionate friend, Beatrice Patton."

NOTE: The old and famous 3rd Horse Cavalry of pre-war days and stationed at Ft. Myer, Virginia, was unhorsed, moved to Ft. Benning and turned into three Tank Bns. of the 10th Armored Division. Hence, my 3rd Cavalry Group (Mecz.) bore no relation to the old outfit, except for its name, and wasn't even activated until about June of 1943. We did inherit the colors and assumed the traditions of the old Indian-fighting regiment.

The new 3rd Cavalry began with a cadre from many outfits and a large number of draftees, largely from northern New York and Western Pennsylvania, about half and half farm boys or factory workers with a large number of first-generation Poles and others from Eastern Europe. When I took command, they had nothing like the skills of the 6th Cavalry, but were a bunch of tough, resourceful, rough and ready men, not strong on discipline, but knowledgable of the Germans and knowing them as their natural enemies. Each troop had soldiers who between them could speak almost every central European language including Yiddish, but excluding French, so translation or prisoner interrogation was no problem. They could move, shoot and in some degree communicate, made natural soldiers and quickly learned combat skills, in this latter regard, far superior to the 6th Cavalry men. They took naturally to living in woods or beat-up villages, were by and large hunters and snipers, and had a keen sense of dominating the combat environment. They treated me with respect; we admired each other and I came to love them.

When I got back into Verdun, I went in to get my official orders and was told to report to Gen. Patton personally. He asked me how old I was and I said 32. He said that seems awfully young for a Command and I was being kind of brash and I said, "Sir, as I remember, you were 31 when you were Col." and he said, "That's correct" and laughed. Then he said to me, "Are you lucky?" and I said, "Yes sir, I think I am lucky". And he said, "Well, you're going to need it." Then he said, "Now I want to be serious for a minute. I want you to know I will not put up with a beaten Commander. So if you're ever overrun or your outfit is ever overrun and badly beaten up, you're going to be relieved. If it's the fault of some bad orders and you were doing things you weren't trained to be doing, on account of a higher command decision, I'll get you a job some place, but you'll still be relieved. And if it's your fault, I never want to see you again — you understand?" I said, "Yes sir", saluted and left.

Next, I reported into XX Corps as that was the higher headquarters to which the 3rd Cavalry was assigned and reported to Gen. Walton H. Walker, the Corps Commander. The Corps Headquarters was in a muddy woods in a place called Conflans and in a tent city. Gen. Walker was very grim and I had never known him before. Said he was glad to have me. He said he thought the 3rd Cavalry was doing well, but he didn't know what they were doing or where they were. He never got any messages from them. The communication with them was terrible, and he wanted me to straighten it out at once. I said, "Yes sir, anything else?" And he said, "No. Good Luck. Thank you. That's all."

15 Sept., 1944

Dearest,

Life has been very busy. I have been here about four days now, again busy getting acquainted and getting the troops to working my way. I have been in so many outfits lately that I hardly know where my home is. After the letter written on the airplane, I rushed right up here and into the thick of it. The outfit is battle-wise and already I am beginning to feel proud of it. However, it is very rough and ready, not nearly the expertise of the 6th Cavalry. However, we are doing well and have been given good cavalry missions throughout my first few days.

I have a lot of friends in the Corps Headquarters that I am working for, but not nearly the close or as influential friends that I had in the 3rd Army Headquarters.

My brain is sort of numb tonight but I feel I must write you. There are seven of us in a small C.P. tent with a flickering light. All of the poor guys are working but me but I can't be bothered.

It's funny how hard it is for me to write at times like this. The emotions are all drained out of me. The captured German food is adequate. The weather is generally good. I don't get enough sleep and I haven't had a bath in the last ten days. I really shouldn't send this because it sounds awful. Actually, I am having the time of my life running this outfit and you catch me at the end of the day when I am tired out and there is a big crowd around me. I am allowed now to write my battle experiences after they are fourteen days old so later on I can go into detail about some of the things we have been doing for the past four days. Also, I can tell you more about my trip in a few days.

The war is really going damn well. The fighting is hard and fierce. Germans will readily surrender when you get the drop on them. But inside a pill-box, a 4-F is a pretty good fighting man. Also the fact that we are about to enter their own homeland seems to make a difference.

I do wish I could write oftener and I also feel that I have been neglecting you. However, I just can't do better.

Your devoted husband,
Jimmy

NOTE: *When I took Command, the two Squadrons were separated. The*

43rd Squadron was above Thionville along the Moselle River North of the 5th Division and the Germans had several bridgeheads across the river. Since the 43rd had some 23 miles they had to cover with only three reconnaisance troops, it was very much a cat and mouse game. Very aggressive patrolling from both sides and ambushes were to be expected anyplace. The 3rd Squadron was South of the 5th Division and attached to them and was bucked up generally against Fort Driant in the Fortress System of Metz. I didn't like this at all and was determined to get my two Squadrons together and get us on a better mission than that we had. The 43rd Squadron's action was sort of characterized by fluidity. Aggressive German patrols of up to 20 men were frequently encountered and the enemy's actions were such that they infiltrated the river towns and laid in wait in the surrounding woods for our troops. Also, the Germans strengthened their position by addition of numerous mortar and artillery pieces which opened fire on us whenever we appeared in the forward slopes of the high ground overlooking the Moselle. Nevertheless, effective and aggressive patrol action continually jabbed the enemy's defenses, scattering his local patrols so that at no time was he able to assume any offensive action.

17 Sept., 1944 (Sunday)

Dearest My Love,

It has been a cold day with really hard rain and we have been rather miserable as we are now out on a wind swept hill for our camp. The war sort of stops on a day like this except for the artillery which keeps on slamming it out. I got good and wet on the outside while inspecting some of my troops. I was dressed for it, so suffered no ill effects.

I can now tell you that I was out at Brest two weeks ago. The 14th Cavalry had enveloped the enemy lines as they were supposed to do, had punched into their outpost line or the main German line of resistance and had taken a lot of casualties. When I left, they were waiting for the infantry to take over. However, I was not impressed with the outfit. They seemed awfully ragged. In some respects it was rugged as there were a lot of big guns there that made your nights simply miserable. They would slam over a big baby about every fifteen minutes and you just knew it was heading straight for you. It sounded just like a freight train coming down the track. However, the line was manned by Russians and Poles, as we learned. They were forced into the German Army so that every night some would come over and surrender. They were all packed up with their toilet articles and blankets. Much more would have surrendered but the German officers watched them very closely and they will fight like hell on occasion. This is a strange war.

Parts of my new unit are working over old battlefields as all this part of France has been fought over hundreds of times I guess. It is a bit gruesome to see all the monuments and military cemetery. We have been eating lots of German captured rations lately and they are a big help. Some very good cheese in heavy tin foil, wonderful green beans canned in Hamburg and good coffee. Mighty little doubt about it, all good wholesome food. So we think they are not starving in Germany, as American reports seem to have it. The radio reports that we hear make most of us quite irritated. It sounds as if the war is over and we are having a pushover. It's bad psychology as it is plenty tough here now. Units fighting all day and maybe making a hundred yards. And the Germans are not surrendering around here. I guess they feel they are fighting to keep us from their homeland. However, the overall picture is still good and we pray we will finish this up this fall.

I would just like to take some of those radio commentators to a bridge I crossed over today. With the artillery fire we got, it would change their story. Well, you stick up for my side when the argument comes up and ask any of them if they have had to live on Spam and K-rations for three months.

I adore you, my lovely one. Write me often.

Your Jimmy

20 Sept. 1944

Dearest:

When I tell some of the tales of this business when all of this is over, the present situation will be just unbelievable. I have command of the damnedest army that has ever gotten together, as I have had a lot of extra units added to my outfit. I do wish I could tell you about it, as it is absolutely crazy. Right now I am sitting in a little forward command post about 1000 yards from the Germans, waiting for some officers to show up. I want to adjust some artillery fire. It is very peaceful and quiet and no one ever would guess there is a war on. We are going to have at them in a few minutes.

I have my headquarters in the most wonderful chateau in France -no kidding. We have just moved in last night and the luxury of it un-nerves me. We actually have electricity, hot and cold running water and real beds with sheets on them. Last night I took a hot bath in my private bathroom and climbed into bed ...real linen sheets and down pillow. All very modern, even the bath fixtures. And what looks like a special bowl for females. I've never seen anything quite like it but the consensus of opinion is that it is intended for females only. (This is our first encounter with a bidet.) The place is untouched and in perfect shape. It was used as some sort of German rest camp. It is only about a mile behind the front and the lines are very thin. But I assure you we will fight like hell to hold on to this place. We may get a Jerry raid in there anytime, but we intend to enjoy it while we can. It even has a few servants, but I don't know what they will do for us so far, and a wine cellar with red wine that tastes about like that bad port we got at Ft. Leavenworth. We also have some chickens and a nice vegetable garden, so I'll ask no questions if they show up at our table.

The war is going very slow along the Moselle and our front right now. It seems to be going fast in other places but we are more or less in the doldrums for which I am thankful. The weather has been perfectly rotten, so that no air can get up and we have been wet and miserable until we got into the chateau. Now I'd just as soon stay here for awhile. (Note: The reference is to Chateau Bettange just outside of Thionville that belonged to the Count de Mitry.)

My command is shaping up very well now that we are getting to know each other. I have two very capable squadron commanders who know their business. But it is confusing to try and write you with all the traffic so I will stop and continue sometime later.

Bless you my love.

Your Jimmy

22, Sept. 1944

More time has passed than I had realized. But I have been surrounded with work. Uncle George (this means Gen. Patton) came to visit my headquarters yesterday and caused quite a turmoil among the troops. I took him up to the front and he saw some of the units. He seemed very pleased with all he saw and was most complimentary. It was the first time that I had a chance to really talk to him as he is generally surrounded by other people and a lot of aides.

I also had a newspaperman named Donald Grant with me for a few days. He writes for the Des Moines Register. So tell Mother to watch for his stuff. He will probably write some pretty lurid things as we have some real characters in the outfit. Particularly he might mention a couple of girls who work with two of my platoons. He will probably give it a big spread. I didn't even know about it until he told me, as the officers in that troop kept them undercover whenever I came around. According to Grant, they are of real use and are not sleeping with anyone but really out killing or helping to kill Germans.

I must investigate it further and let you know. What an outfit — you will never know.

Bless you my love.
Your Jimmy

NOTE: On the 20th of Sept., my 3rd Cavalry Group became officially known as Task Force Polk. This is the first of any "task force" named down the line; but in a month or two it would become very fashionable. However, I do want to repeat that I was the first.

The reason we were designated "Task Force Polk" was that we (my two squadrons) had attached to us the 15th Engineer Combat Battalion, a Detachment from the 6th Cavalry of two tank companies and two assault gun troops and the 1st Battalion of the 1st Regiment of Paris. This latter Force, a bunch of crazy communists, were intent on killing Germans and DeGaulle didn't want them in Paris so nominated them to come up and join the fight. No one else wanted them so they were forced down our 3rd Cavalry throat. They were ill-equipped, ill-trained but a bunch of really crazy guys. I will tell more about them later.

Right after I had written this letter, Gen. Gay called me from 3rd Army Headquarters and asked me if I had seen the Stars and Stripes. I said no, I had not, and he said, "Well, I understand that the modern Joan of Arc is *riding with B Troop of the 43rd Cavalry. Is that correct?" I said that I had just heard about it from a war correspondent named Grant. He continued, "Well, I'll tell you something. The modern Joan of Arc will be back in Orleans tonight and you will call me up in the morning and tell me that she has safely reached her hometown again. Do you understand?" And I said, "Yes Sir, she'll be on her way!" Actually, these two girls would get on their bicycles and ride into French towns (one girl was American, the other was French) ahead of the troops and ask the French if there were any Germans around. Any number of times, they helped us avoid getting into some sort of ambush. We never heard of them again. But we were very grateful to these two. The 3rd Cavalry got famous for a lot of funny things, but that was one I didn't really care for.*

About this time, I asked that the 3rd Cavalry colors be displayed and everybody looked very sheepish. It turns out that they had been lost in this fashion. Major John (Johnny) Logan, the S-4, had the 3rd Cavalry colors in a safe in his C&R car and they were ambushed about the 5th of Sept., before I took command of the outfit. Johnny and the driver got out safely into a ditch and crawled away. The third man in the C&R car was killed or captured. But in any event, the car was burned and the safe was captured so we didn't have any Regimental colors. As a matter of fact, we didn't recover them until way late in 1948. However, we put in for colors, saying they had gotten moth-eaten and wet and please ship us another set. As a matter of fact, they never did arrive all through the whole war.

23 Sept. 1944

My Beloved One,

I am still installed in this marvelous chateau with the clean linen sheets on the bed. My private room has two large French windows, a day bed, a quilted double bed that is too short for me, a beautiful inlaid wood desk that I am writing from, tables, easy chairs, vases, lamps, drapes, etc. and a private modern bathroom as I told you. It has a marvelous view of a gentle grassy slope running down to the river all picturesque and beautiful, but punctuated by occasional gun fire. So far we haven't any coming in on us so I keep my fingers crossed and keep all men and vehicles away from the front of the chateau.

However, it has been nerve-racking and wearing on me in this my first real command in combat and we are sitting on a powder keg, my whole unit I mean. And I am constantly on the go, either visiting units or making decisions that may mean men's lives. I am thankful for the rest this place gives me as I need it -not that I don't like responsibility or fear for my abilities, but it is a constant state of tension. I guess it wears on me a bit as I am taken to having horrible nightmares and fighting battles all night long.

Please send me, if you can find them, fur-lined gloves, sheep-skin vest, cigars and maybe sheep-skin slippers and a picture of you. I love you.

Your Jimmy

NOTE: At this point, the 3rd Squadron was deployed in front of Fort Driant and attached to the 5th Infantry Division. They were acting as infantry entrenched in the woods and I didn't like it at all, as it was a bad mis-use of our armored cavalry. However, I was so new to the Corps that I really didn't dare complain vehemently about it.

Up in our area on both sides of Thionville we had the 1st and now the 2nd French Battalion which had joined us deployed south of the town around Garche. The 43rd Squadron with the Engineers and one battalion of field artillery was deployed to the north covering some 20 miles of river front and by no means did we hold the river. There were several places where the Germans were on our side of the river and the situation was really (as I mentioned in my letter) quite touch and go.

Action in this area was characterized by constant enemy patrols either crossing the river or coming out of their little bridgeheads and seeking information on our order of battle. No German patrols were particularly successful and we captured several of them, in one case, taking one prisoner and killing another man; and in another case, catching several German soldiers changing into civilian clothes. The enemy never did attempt to cross in strength in this zone, for which I was duly grateful.

27 Sept. 1944

Dearest One,

My private Army is expanding everyday. Right now, I really have a Brigadier General command and job. Not that it will stay that way at all, for it will not. But it keeps me busy as all get out for right now running this big show. It really is funny how I fell into this job. It has sort of been like a snowball rolling downhill, getting bigger all the time. It drives me mad that I can't write about it.

My chateau is getting to be quite famous in this area and we have a constant stream of visitors, all anxious to take a bath in hot water and spend the night in a comfortable bed. We are going to have to start charging rates before very long in order to manage the overhead, particularly to war correspondents who cannot resist our comforts. We even had a photographer come to take a picture of one of my platoon leaders and his famous female interpreter and spy that has now gone back to Orleans. What a war! I am still sitting on the powder keg and keeping my fingers crossed.

We have gotten a fancy officers' mess organized. The food is cooked in our regular mess truck outside, but we have cleaned up the servants to serve it inside. We use German china and silverware, served by French maids and eat off the Count's linen. It is too good to last and the first General that gets his eyes on it is going to throw us out into the damp world. Incidentally, the French maids are not what the name implies, but two giggly girls, the daughters of the gardener, and I think they are more used to digging than to serving meals.

I have just been looking out the window. I had to turn off the lights first because of blackout. Out over the beautiful valley in front of me, the stars and the quarter moon are out and the Germans side is covered with a haze. It is an altogether peaceful and beautiful scene with an occasional brilliant flare shot up in the air like a Roman candle where our patrols and the enemy are operating. It seems impossible that men are crouching down there with guns in their hands waiting to kill one another, watching and listening for the slightest sound on the other side of the river.

This phase or our war isn't exciting for me really, it is just a matter of worry and decide and dispose troops to the best advantage and my nights are calm and comfortable.

I love you with a deep and complete and everlasting love.

Your Jimmy

NOTE: On this date I was further reinforced by the 807th Tank Destroyer Battalion, and I parcelled them out among my troops. By this time, we had closed up to the river and were in strong contact with the 83rd Division on the North and the 90th Division on the South and covered about 25 miles of the Moselle River. We had also cleaned out all of the bridgeheads on our side of the river with the exception of one which I shall mention later.

1 October, 1944

My Adorable Wife,

I'm afraid no one will believe me when all this is over. It really is too utterly fantastic to hope to convince anyone of its truth. In addition to my regular command, I have the most unusual additions to my local Army that one could imagine. Actually, my command is now approaching that of a Maj. Gen. I almost have a Division. And I could write a wonderful play about it. It goes like this.

Scene: Command Post

A large room with French windows and brown drapes; bookcases on the three walls with doors entering from each wall; a grand piano in the corner of the room; various tables, chairs, maps on the wall, telephone, switchboard and so forth.

Time: 1900 (about 7:00pm)

Shades are drawn, lights are on.

In one corner, there is a clerk typing and another working a switchboard, several Lt. Colonels, a couple of Majors are having a conference. The phone rings. Officers come in to consult on a matter. A French officer in very splendid uniform answers the phone. Shells are going overhead. Everything is calm and businesslike. Someone is always talking on the phone. Orders are issued. People constantly come and go. A soldier brings in coffee, thick tobacco smoke in the room. Motorcycles go by outside. A general comes in and everyone comes to attention. He has an aide who lisps. He looks at the map, says a few words and departs. (Note: We seldom had Generals visit us at the front. The rest of it is pretty authentic.) A messenger comes in with a large envelope. It is opened and amid much groaning and catty remarks about the stupidity of other staff officers in higher headquarters, the order is read and orders are then issued for the next day's operations. Remarks are passed about how tomorrow's job doesn't look too tough.

An officer comes in and repeats the information we have just gotten out of the last batch of prisoners. Another officer comes in and reports that he lost a tank and five men and where in the hell is his weekly supply of cigarettes. An Officer announces that he has gotten enough eggs for everyone to have two for breakfast, amid cheers. The tension begins to drop off, the shells are fewer, the conversation turns from food to mail to home. An airplane is overhead and someone casually remarks that "Bed Check Charlie" is a little late tonight. Some bombs drop off in the distance. Officers gradually go out until only about three are left. There is a machine gun in the distance. The final reports for the night are dictated. Someone telephones that the shooting was just a small raid — one man hurt and three prisoners. A sleepy looking officer comes in to take over the graveyard shift and a sleepy looking soldier comes in to take over the switchboard.

The Col. gets up (that's me) and stretches. He gives orders to be called if anything happens. Suddenly there is a hell of a lot of shelling outdoors and dirt comes off the ceiling and out of the floors and everyone curses the Jerries. The Col. goes out, the duty officer gets out an old magazine and looks through it in a bored manner. The switchboard operator says, "Jaybird calling Blackbird -priority for fire mission — clear the line". All is quiet. The lights go down. The officer yawns and says, "Another day, another dollar". There is shelling in the distance and the curtain falls.

Wouldn't that make a good play? I know all the dialogue. I know all the actors and sound effects. All I need is some kind of a story to tie it all together and I've almost got that. I suppose I should have to be the hero.

A friend of mine is going to Paris, so I told him to get me some lingerie for you — something slinky and seductive. I have gotten no mail at my new address. It is still forwarded from the old outfit (the 6th Cavalry) and takes about 25 days to get here. I am way out of date on your doings. I will be glad when it starts coming direct again. How is the Red Cross and your driving ambulances doing? Have you gotten a uniform? How is the Jr. League and what is your job this year? I want to hear all about you. What do you weigh? Do you play the piano often? I miss you every minute of every day.

Your man,
Jimmy

NOTE: It was not this dramatic in my command post in the evening all the time, but sometimes it was. The 3rd Squadron was still down in front of Fort Driant in the woods and acting as a connecting link between the 90th Infantry Division and the 5th Infantry Division. I still couldn't get them out and up with the outfit. I simply hated to see them deployed in the woods as infantry, sitting there taking mortar and artillery fire and not doing an ounce of good.

About this time, I realized that what Gen. Walker had told me on taking command was true and that he really didn't know what we were doing because we were some distance from his command post. The common radio *nets were unsatisfactory and the land line, when the Corps crew brought it in, was unsatisfactory because people stole the wire or tanks ran over it or so forth. High-powered radio was the only answer. I therefore set up our two high- powered radios, our SCR 399's on trucks, one with a liaison Detachment at XX Corps and one at my headquarters, staffed with high-speed radio operators and intelligence officers. We therefore pumped our information to our liaison detachment at Corps who promptly went into operations and told them what we were doing. It worked both ways as any orders from Corps were promptly relayed to us. I think actually, if I hadn't done that, my reputation wouldn't have been nearly as good as it was because, with this set up, the Corps Commander knew more about 3rd Cavalry operations and intelligence than he knew about any of his Divisions. And I have frequently told armored cavalry units since that time that they must do this.*

2 October, 1944

My Dearest One,

The weather is really getting brisk around here. We get temperatures in the 40's at night and it never gets much above 65 degrees in the daytime. Also, we have had almost daily rain or drizzles and I suppose it will get a lot worse before it gets any better.

Today I saw several amazing sights. There are such incongruous things in this war that never fail to amaze me. For one, I was up in one of our sniper posts overlooking the Moselle River where a soldier was quietly watching through field glasses with his rifle and telescopic sight beside him, looking for a target. In the same room — I am not exaggerating, actually in the same room and in imminent danger of death — was a woman and her two small sons eating lunch. Also, they fed the soldier. Nothing you can do can make some of these people leave their homes.

In a hotel on the top floor, there is an artillery observation post in operation, complete, and on the next floor down, people are living. I actually saw a trolley car filled with people, running its regular route within a mile of the actual front line. Yesterday, we caught some kids putting up hot air balloons for fun, near the front and kids from all around come to see our batteries of artillery fire. One got killed the other day, but it doesn't seem to make a damn. We haven't enough soldiers to chase them off.

We have been living here for some time now and suddenly discovered tonight that they have a whole cellar full of beer. So I am now enjoying German beer as I write you. Also, some of the boys brought in one of the most beautiful and complete ship models you have ever seen, captured in a German naval rest camp. It is so big we can't keep it. We are thinking of sending it to the President with the compliments of the 3rd Cavalry.

With all the above foolishness, I still have plenty of responsibilities and plenty to worry about. It is very hard for me to relax and I know at times that I am too irritable and too tough on my soldiers and my officers. I really so need someone to talk to. All these lads are nice, but I am senior to them and can't get on any personal basis with any of them.

Your devoted husband,
Jimmy

NOTE: During this period, we were deployed along the Moselle River from Haute Kontz on the North in contact with the 83rd Infantry Division and to Uckange on the south, maintaining contact with the 90th Infantry Division. There was a good bit of artillery fire and mortar fire up and down the line, some engagements on the river, some patrolling into our area and some of our patrols into theirs. But during the month of September, we had rather light casualties. Perhaps the outfit that suffered most was the Assault Gun Troop of the 43rd Squadron which was heavily shelled, disabling several of our artillery pieces. They lost most of their equipment with very severe casualties. Also during this period, the 2nd Regiment de Paris of some 750 men and a Battalion Freddie of 480 men were assigned, so that the French forces of this strange Task Force kept on building up and now totalled about 2600 people under a Col. Fabian. Later in the war, a subway station in Paris was named for him. They were a crazy lot, well versed in ambushing, guerilla warfare and underground activities, but not at all qualified to do well in a front line position.

7 October, 1944 (8:00pm)

My Dearest One,

Just a note to let you know that I am still getting along okay and to tell you that whoever wrote that article about mail from home and how people act when it arrives certainly had the right dope. It is an actual fact that the war practically comes to a dead standstill when mail arrives. Everyone loses interest in all else.

My cold has gotten a bit worse if anything, you know, a complete head full. But I am taking care of myself and have some sulfa pills which I am taking religiously. There is no use to worry about it as by the time you get this letter, it will be completely cured.

My private part of the war is rocking along in pretty good shape, sort of a sniper, patrolling and artillery war at present. And we are still managing to live quite comfortably.

Last night, the Countess de Mitry who owns this particular place came to call. It was obvious that she wanted to move right back in but I refused to be chased off. The Germans had had this place for four years, so she wandered all over the house to see how it was doing. They had taken most of her nice furniture, but had installed a lot of modern plumbing which pleased her. Also, we are keeping it nice and clean so she was quite happy about that. She was a charming woman, spoke good English and in some ways reminded me of your Mother. I was amazed at her figure as she is supposed to have had 12 children, according to the servants. She is very well dressed, but no airs or graces about her that you generally associate with a Countess. She told me of the liberation of Paris and her whole face lit up as she spoke of it. It was really a great day for the French when their own French Armored Division took the town.

I am tired and worn out and going to bed. I adore you.

Your Jimmy

6 October, 1944 (10:00pm)

My Dear Joey:

Received two letters today, one dated 11 Sept., the other 21 Sept. They were a large boost to my morale. You had apparently received my letter when I was on my way to Brest over a month ago, but didn't know of my still newer location with my 3rd Cavalry Group. I certainly will be glad when I start getting mail direct to this, my newest and I hope permanent outfit. It is a nuisance to get letters all out of order and way late.

Here the weather is getting quite bitter. I wear practically all of my clothes already. I don't know what I will do when winter actually comes. I was at a higher headquarters today (the reference is to Headquarters 83rd Division on my North) and had supper with them in a steam- heated building, then got frozen coming home in my jeep which didn't help my cold any.

These trips in the night are always nerve racking as we go tearing along tree-lined roads, completely blacked out, and there is some danger — not so much from Germans as from a nervous American sentry who may shoot at you without much as a challenge. I'm usually about done in after such a trip and last night was one of the meaner ones. There was also the strong possibility of running over stray Frenchmen or dogs or pigs, etc., that seem to be all over the highway. I really loathe these night trips and only take them when it is necessary.

God bless you, my love.

Your Jimmy

NOTE: My driver, Icekant, was really a superb driver and I hoped to keep him the rest of the war. He never put me wrong and had the most marvelous night eyes — far better than mine. Also, my high-speed radio operator and gunner, Sabu, who rode the rear seat of the jeep, was a marvelous young man, a perfect radio operator who could put the key on his knee as we bounced along the road sending messages, telling people that I was coming in or going out or where we were and so forth. I treasured both of them. They didn't look after me very well, but they sure protected me and saved my life at least twice.

9 Oct., 1944 (Monday)

Dearest One,

There has been quite a rash of colds and flu in the command lately and I think it is for two reasons: 1) bad weather, and 2) lack of fresh foods. It would be a good idea if you sent me some vitamin pills. Also, I would like a couple pairs of those Cooper's long drawers if you can get them. You know, light weight, cotton, size 32. I expect several boxes are following me around France and will catch up with me eventually. I hope the cigars catch up to me soon as I am down to smoking German cigars and they are simply horrible.

It is strange how remote in the world we are here. I never see a newspaper or hear a radio. I have no idea what the world is doing, except for an occasional Time that arrives about two months late. All I know is my own sector and I know it well, and a bit about the units on each side of me. I really think that our chief interest, aside from our job, is food, and not much fresh food at that.

We had a Red Cross Clubmobile up to our Headquarters yesterday for the first time. The three girls stayed for supper, but they weren't very charming as they wore pants and were as dirty as we are, their hair, their fingernails and so forth, and talked just like men about the Corps Sector of the front. They lead a hard life for women and show it. But they are certainly appreciated by the men and are doing good work.

Life is rather routine of late, not much excitement and we haven't been moving forward so all the administration paperwork and red tape and discipline problems seem to take up a lot of my time, although I have a very fine Executive Officer who takes a lot of it off my shoulders. When we were tearing across France so fast, everyone thought Germany would tumble over and die immediately. Now it doesn't quite look that way. We still have a hard fight in front of us so I guess everyone is suffering from the reaction. I still have my big command with all its attendant responsibilities and worries.

I also heard that my papers went in yesterday to make me a full Colonel. But it takes at least a month to go through, so it will be sometime yet before I am promoted. In other words, they consider I have proven my ability in combat and now the paperwork starts.

Bless you my love and those darling kids.

Your Jimmy

NOTE: *I was being very reassuring in this letter, but actually, there was some pretty fierce artillery and mortar fire going on back and forth across the Moselle River. Any sort of movement in daylight would draw fire from the Germans. At night, the Germans had been very aggressive in crossing the Moselle River and we were so thin, we couldn't keep them from it. We were stretched out over more than 20 miles. There were some fierce little fire fights as they would come over in a patrol of anywhere from 2-20 men and we usually would beat them off and get a prisoner or two. Our casualties were fairly light in all this, however.*

10 Oct., 1944

My Dearest One,

Today my Corps Commander called me in and complimented me on the work I have been doing (that's Gen. Walton H. Walker) and told me that he had sent in my recommendation to be a full Colonel "for superior and proven ability as a combat commander". I told you in my letter last night that it had gone in but it was praise indeed, and I was afraid I would have to wait three months in this new job before I would be promoted. But such is not the case, as this is a battlefield promotion over the last months. Please pardon me if I seem to brag, but I know you would like to know and in addition, I am damn proud of it.

Also, Gens. George Marshall and Patton were visiting today. Gen. Marshall remembered me from the Ft. Myer days which is good of him, I think, and Gen. Patton put his arm around me and said, "This boy is doing damn good work. He will be the youngest Colonel in my Army soon, about my age in the last war when I was a Colonel, but God damn, doesn't he look young"! So all in all, it was a mighty big day for your husband. If I had a drink, I would drink it. Take one for me.

For God's sake, don't spread this around now, as this is a private letter and you do understand me and know how I value my professional reputation. So you know how proud I am and why I want to share it all with you.

Your Jimmy

NOTE: *Generals Marshall and Patton were visiting the 90th Division Headquarters to my south and I was told to come down. I stood in line behind the Generals and the four infantry and artillery Colonels of the 90th Division. Gen. Marshall went down the line; he apparently didn't know any of them, shook hands with them in a very cursory and cold sort of way. He finally came to me and said, "Well, Jimmy, goodness sakes, what are you doing here? How are you? How's your mother? I'm sorry to hear about your father's death. How is this Division treating you?" And I said, "They treat me just fine, Sir. I like to be with this Division." And he said, "Well, let me know if they give you any trouble, will you?" And believe me, from then on, I was a very special person. Gen. James A. VanFleet, the Division Commander, asked me where I had known Gen. Marshall and I answered I*

*had played tennis with him when my father was Commandant of V.M.I. He
had come back from China after having lost his wife and spent a month in
Lexington. Also, when he was Chief of Staff of the Army, we were stationed
at Ft. Myer and lived just a few doors down from him, so we had known him
then. Anyway, this really was a big day for me and I will never forget it.
The 3rd Squadron finally was relieved from the woods in front of Ft. Driant
and came up and joined the Task Force. We did a good bit of repositioning
and consolidating, and we were a lot thicker along the river, our 20 mile
sector, than we had been before and felt a good bit more secure about it.
I decided that we had to be more aggressive about these German patrols
and that we had to start patrolling on their side of the river. Therefore, we
started putting patrols over, protected by artillery barrages and gave the
Jerries some problems. One of the funny things that happened was that the
French were told to patrol and they sent two patrols out on the night of 8
Oct. One reported they were fired on and the other reported they had fired
on some enemy. And what we thought was, one fired on the other and there
was no Germans involved in it at all.*

13 Oct., 1944

Dearest One,

I have been here in this command a month already and I have yet to get a letter direct to my new address. My private army has been undergoing a change that has involved a lot of work and shifting around, but in a day or so, it ought to be all smoothed out. And then it should be plain sailing. But right at present, I am still sitting on the old powder keg.

Don't worry about me writing bad things about George Patton. I don't know why I should as he has been wonderful to me — simply wonderful. I wrote you the other day of the nice things he said. I couldn't ask for better leaders all along the line above me. I really feel I am among friends and I am getting along just okay.

Your clipping telling about the war lasting until the Spring over here seems about the right dope to me. Of course, we often get examples of the very low morale in the German Army but this is not always the rule. Yesterday, we got a real fire-eater, a Hitler Youth and SS prisoner, who said they would soon win the war as their secret weapons would be ready and that they would massacre us. He really believed it, having been raised on that sort of stuff, even though he fully expected to be shot. German officers tell all their soldiers we shoot our prisoners just to keep them from surrendering.

Today I saw Johnny Thimer. He said that his wife also was living in El Paso, so if you get together with her and compare notes, you might be able to figure out a few things between you about what we are doing.

I still have to see a single one of your letters censored, but you said some of mine were. We hear that a lot of officers' mail is being censored, as there has been a rash of security violations. Also, it was odd you mentioned Johnny Thimer in your letter as he is in the outfit next to mine in the line. He does not command as I do, but is quite close to me and we met purely on business, then renewed our old acquaintance. Also, Jim Boswell is in the same outfit with him and Jim Skinner who was with us at Myer (they were all in the 90th Division to my south).

I am all yours.

Your devoted,
Jimmy

NOTE: On this date, the French Regiment de Paris was ordered south to Colmar to join the 1st French Armored Division and we were rather glad to be rid of them, as they were really more trouble than worth. Also, with the 3rd Squadron coming up, we had to do a lot of shifting around which I referred to in the letter, but once we all got together, we were much firmer and stronger and more confident than we had been.

On the 13th, we witnessed an extraordinary event. Lt. Robert Downs, one of our finest platoon leaders, and just a kid, went to his Squadron Commander and said that he was sure that the Germans slept during noontime and so he asked permission to row across the river in broad daylight, grab a prisoner and row back. He said he had been watching them through his field glasses and he was sure they were all asleep. His Squadron Commander agreed and Lt. Downs and a Sergeant rowed across the Moselle River, stopped next to a fox-hole, jerked a German out of it, rowed back across the river and got within ten feet of our shore before somebody finally shot at him. Naturally, we had him protected with all the artillery and mortars we could arrange, so all hell broke lose and he walked into the Headquarters with his Sergeant and the prisoner and not a scratch on him. It was so bold and so courageous that he was put in for the Distinguished Service Cross, and Down's barracks at Fulda was subsequently named for him.

We also learned from prisoners captured at that time that the 19th Infantry Division which had been across from us had been replaced by the 416th Volks Grenadier Division. We really didn't know quite what this meant except the Volks Divisions are supposed to be a little less active and not as well trained as the lower-numbered divisions.

We had the 664th Medical Clearing Company and a Signal Detachment attached to us on this date. The Medical Clearing Company stayed with us almost the rest of the war. We loved them, but there were no female nurses and no nonsense in that outfit.

18 Oct., 1944

My Precious One,

This will be just a short note as it is late and I am tired. It has been a busy day, out in the rain most of the time, but I have recovered from my cold and feel fine now. We had the most wonderful supper tonight, actually steak (a bit tough as a cow was hit by a shell) and french fries and a salad. You don't know what that means — and I really ate it up.

Our position remains unchanged and I continue to occupy my chateau with the river view. We are still careful to use only the back entrance and so far all is well. We have never been shelled. I managed to get a bunch of postcards of the place which shows it off to great advantage. But I can't send them until we move on at least 25 miles from the chateau. Then I will be allowed to forward them and you can see what a lovely place it is.

At the next party, propose a toast to the "Brave Rifles" the next time the crowd gets together. You should have some of my old 3rd Cavalry insignia someplace — it hasn't changed. You remember the sort of green knot with the bugle and the Brave Rifles written under it. Those were great days at Myer. The polo, horse shows, parades and our friends. It is not the same crowd but certainly has the same old drive and esprit.

All my love,
Jimmy

NOTE: We became convinced about this time that Count de Mitry had a number of friends and kinfolk across the line and in Germany and we noticed that his steel mill at Uckange and his chateau behind Thionville were never shelled. We felt pretty sure that this was cousins looking after cousins.

20 Oct., 1944

Dearest,

Sorry I haven't written for a few days but life has been very busy for me with much to do, much to think about and much to order. The going has been a bit rough and yesterday I lost a couple of damn fine officers and lost a few more people in trying to get them out of it. This cat and mouse game we play puts an awful premium on leadership and we all take a certain amount of risks. Once in a while, the law of averages catches up on someone. The really sad part of it is that the real leaders and the good men and the outstanding men are the ones that get hurt.

I am not blue tonight, just good and tired and ready for bed. But I did want to write you this note to tell you that you are with me always and that every danger, you share with me.

Bless you my dear.

Your Jimmy

NOTE: On this date in the late afternoon, Troop C of the 43rd Squadron sent out a patrol led by Lt. Robert Downs who was mentioned earlier. The patrol was accompanied by Lt. Col. Leslie Cross, the commanding officer of the 43rd Squadron and by Captain Nelson who was the commanding officer of Troop C. The patrol was near Gavisse, along the riverbank of the Moselle. The three officers were ambushed by a German patrol at an old ferry site. Lt. Downs got away while the other two were wounded and trapped. The three enlisted men also got away; so the four of them went back and rushed down again with a couple of armored cars to try to rescue their officers. Lt. Downs was shot through the head, several other enlisted men were killed and the two senior officers were captured. I felt very badly about it, but I had been stressing that we had to be front-runners and this is just the chance you take. I lost two fine men. I put Major Preston Utterbach, the executive officer, in command of the 43rd Squadron as of that date, and he was a great one.

Also on that date, a young officer from the tank destroyer battalion hit a mine in his jeep, tipped over and it killed him. It was a bad day altogether.

22 Oct. 1944 (Sunday)

Dearly Beloved,

Today has been quiet and rather uneventful. Most of my day has been taken up with conferences with some high-paid help. I got off with it all right. Now the usual night noises are going on, machine gunning, cannon fire going on in the distance. But I don't think anyone is getting hit; just pecking away at each other for the hell of it. They shell places they think we are and we shell places we think they are and once in awhile, somebody catches it right in the neck. My nerves are quite adjusted to it and I have a good ear — just like the book says, you very soon learn that when one is coming close you hit the ditch fast. When the occasion demands, I can really move. However the poor guys up close who have to stay in there and take it often get terribly nervous. You never can tell who it is going to affect or how it is going to affect anyone when they are exposed to it for some period of time. I must say too that size and physical strength don't seem to have any bearing on the matter. Some puny little guys are terrific and really get the job done and some of the big ones do also, but some don't know it is the mind, not the muscle.

I have been expecting to see Hank Cherry and Frank Britton, but haven't managed yet. Is Suzanne in El Paso, as you have never mentioned her? I suppose Hank will be having mail trouble, as will all the new arrivals. I can go see them and act like a real veteran. (I am trying to tell her that the 10th Armored Division has arrived in my sector.) Dave Wagstaff isn't too far away, but right now I can't do too much visiting as there is too much going on in my own private war.

The weather is really getting miserable over here. All the side roads are a sea of mud and all the bivouacs are muddy and dirty. I wear almost all the clothes I own now and still have the cashmere sweater in reserve.

I hope you aren't worrying about me too much. My sector has been pretty quiet (knock wood) and I don't take needless risks. It's just that I get blue when unfortunate accidents like the other day happen and my responsibilities sometimes weigh pretty heavily on me.

Your letter written Sept. 5th just arrived with Dorothy Parker's article in it and it certainly is food for thought. I don't agree with her, however. I don't think I will be violently changed and I know I will never feel that a great gulf separates us, the way she says. Of course, I will be older and so will you. We have both had greater responsibilities and different experiences, but we are still one, even more than before. Dorothy Parker is all wet. The more I think of it the more I know this is true. Every man and woman grows and develops and matures as God intended. The process is going on for both of us in this separation. But our more than seven years together, and our early training and associates long ago formed our characters. We are what we always are. And we shall resume where we left off. We shall resume our life together with a more complete awareness of each other and a more complete respect for each other. Don't fear. And I love you.

Your own,
Jimmy

NOTE: On this date, Fred Hughes, a Lt. Col. commanding the 244th field artillery and attached in support of us, activated what came to be known as Battery Thionville. At this point in time, we were very severely limited on the ammunition we could fire. It had to be a very serious problem to allow our 155mm or 105mm battalions to shoot at all. Battery Thionville was composed of six guns in steel turrets on a big hill behind Thionville and dated back to the war of 1871. The guns were about 90mm, made in 1871, the ammunition was made in 1914, the fuses and gun powder were made after World War I, somewhere about 1920. Fred Hughes figured out a firing table for them and of course, it was perfectly safe to fire under all that steel, so it came to be quite a visitor's mecca. On one occasion when Gen. Patton came up, we stood there and tried to find some German soldier across the Moselle River. Finally we saw one. Gen. Patton laid one gun on him, the other five were laid parallel, and on his command, we fired. He was simply delighted with the results. But the shells were so old and so slow, you could actually see them going through the air. The German ducked and I'm sure we didn't hurt him, but we must have scared the hell out of him. We had a lot of fun with this Battery Thionville and knocked things down across the river for no good reason at all. Fred Hughes was a very great man. I was terribly fond of him. He later commanded SETAF (Southern European Task Force) in 1970 and was killed in an airplane accident while I was commanding in Europe — a really great loss.

25 Oct., 1944

My Darling Beloved,

Life is rocking along okay and the weather continues cold and miserable. I had a good day yesterday though, inspecting my troops. They really look fine and their morale and pride in their accomplishments are tops. They are real seasoned troops now and are most condescending to the new arrivals. I suppose I am also. Our main diversion is telling the new people horror stories and our close escapes. (Herein, I am referring to our friends in the 10th Armored Division, many of whom left the 3rd Cavalry at Myer to form that Division and got into action much later than we did.)

Last night, we rocked with laughter for almost an hour, listening to the war experiences of a Captain who commands 200 Negroes in a labor company behind us. This Captain looked like Rudy Valle and spoke like him. He could pass for his double. He really had troubles. I didn't know what trouble was until I listened to him.

He told us about censoring the mail and from the general description they're much like what Sugar Lee (an old black maid) used to get. He also said that after reading about all the Germans each one of his soldiers has heroically killed or captured, he wondered if that could possibly be his own company. And to top it all off, he said he never gave them any ammunition, (right behind us in a combat zone) because after dark they would shoot at anything that moved and he valued his life too highly. He was a fine man though. Stuck up for his soldiers and told us their good qualities. I'm sure they love him. He has four black officers in the company. He says they all know two French words, "cognac" and "zig zig", and that's all they need. And his biggest single headache is they can't get hair oil over here and they pester the hell out of him about it.

You see some funny things in this world. There was an utterly deserted and ruined little French town yesterday, right down on the Moselle, in the front lines, and held by one of my troops. Well, in the middle of the town square, in a little grassy plot, there were four dirty American soldiers armed to the teeth with grenades, pistols, carbines slung over their shoulders and what have you; and they were solemnly playing a game of croquet. It is so utterly incongruous but gives you a good idea of the typical American soldier and of the high morale of my men.

In the Stars and Stripes, our only newspaper, they ran an editorial about hating Germans, which we all do. But the article went on about being friendly with the children. It said we must be careful never to give any German children any candy or gum or ever be friendly with them. The article evoked a storm of protest. Knowing my men, I know it would be impossible to keep them from giving things to the kids. We would still have a real hate for the Hun and give it to them without mercy whenever the chance presents itself. But this is typically American and we won't hate the children.

I still think we have a reasonable chance of cleaning up the German Army before Christmas. As far as the cleaning up of Germany, I don't think anyone can say. It will be mean if they go in for guerilla warfare; but I don't believe the Germans who will be left will have the guts to do it. It takes a very brave man to be an isolated sniper. So maybe it won't be too long before I see you. Let's meet in New York. I think that the best place to meet of any will be "under the clock" at the Biltmore Hotel some happy day at 6:00 pm, where we have met before so often.

Your devoted husband,
Jimmy

NOTE: During this period, there was very active patrolling by both sides with frequent clashes between small patrols, often at very close quarters, although our casualties were quite light. The civilian problem in the Task Force zone was also a very major one at this time. We occupied a thickly populated and highly industrialized sector of France that contained a civilian population which we estimated as about 75% pro-German. Incidents of cutting our wire, sniping, flashing signal lights and reports of civilians informing German soldiers of our locations or helping their patrols were rather numerous. It was impractical to evacuate the front line river towns, since the ability to take care of these people was limited.

Consequently, the troops in the front line towns enforced very stringent regulations as to civilian movement, curfews, restricted areas and so forth. With this strong hand, our problems in this area began to become less troublesome.

26 Oct. 1944
(Thursday)

Dearest punkin,

My chunk of river has been reasonably quiet the last few days. We are just doing our job and getting along okay. I did have one unusual thing that could only happen in this modern Army — I now have been assigned a full Col. under my command. He is very reasonable about it, but it makes it rather embarrassing and somewhat difficult to give him orders. I wish to hell my promotion would come through, then it wouldn't be so bad. But I don't expect it for at least a month yet. (This reference is to Col. Cooney, who commanded the two field artillery battalions with a group headquarters and, incidentally, was my earlier drawing instructor when I was a cadet at West Point.)

We got a captured German radio working, so have been hanging on it listening to news of the great naval battle in the Philippines and the Russian front. Maybe someday soon, we will cut loose and not stop until we shake hands with the Russians. That would really be in the news.

All our thoughts are on victory here. We really are a victorious Army and everyone feels it. We are, as one man, anxious to get on with it. To get the damn Germans beaten so we can get into the next phase of occupying Germany and getting ready to come home. I have been away almost nine months now and in most respects, it seems an age longer than that. In many ways, it has been interesting and broadening and educational. I have learned rural France and rural England and shall probably get to know rural Germany as well. I was four months in England; now almost four months in France and say four months in Germany — a total of a year's time abroad ought to be educational enough for anyone. But it shall be a year that we can look back on and say, "We did all right, and we love each other the more for it". I do miss you so.

Your Jimmy

27 Oct., 1944

My Dearest One,

We had a couple of damn fierce fights last night, very local and not mattering much in the big picture, but very personal and mattering a hell of a lot to some of my men. I wasn't in either one of them, but was directing the show from battle headquarters. I hate not being right in it when I order other people in, but I can really do more good seeing that everything is coordinated and that the men are getting the fire support and other things they need. But I hate like hell to order people in sometimes, to what seems like certain wounds. We really punished those bastards last night — I can't help but feel good about it. I am not getting cruel or ugly, really I'm not; but when you see your friends die, it is a very personal thing. And when you get the chance, we really dish it out to them. An outfit like this that has been in combat so long doesn't whimper or cry. They get scared, yes; we all do, but they have a real hate and real motivation and the desire to get even and to punish the Jerries for all this evil. When the enemy does foolish things as they did last night, not once, but twice, we really stack 'em up. It did us all good. This is really a horrible letter and I will continue it tomorrow when I am in a better mood. I hate Germany.

P.S. I was mad but feeling good about what we had done when I wrote this. Excuse the profanity, but I felt strongly.

Your husband,
Jimmy

NOTE: This is just a reference to several other patrol actions along the river.

28, Oct., 1944

My Dearest Beloved:

I have just had some fun on my first night out in a long time. I, with two of my staff officers, went to have supper with the Count and Countess de Mitry, who own our chateau. We took elaborate precautions because I don't trust him too much. The FFI classed him as an opportunist. He stays on the winning side and sells the steel from his mills along the river to whoever will buy it. So we had his house surrounded with a few of my men and set up a messenger to bring in a message once in a while, just to check up. The butler wouldn't let my man, Icekant, in with the message the first time as he said we were eating. So Icekant threw his gun on him and marched the butler in. It sort of stopped conversation for awhile. I was well guarded, never fear, and it made them all respect me all the more as I am virtually king of this district and they all know it.

The Count is small and rather shy but nice and shows me all the courtesies — asks my opinion and promptly agrees with me. We have trouble though as his English and my French are awful. The Countess has nine children — I think I said twelve before, but I was wrong. She is also small, well dressed, vivacious and speaks quite good English. They are staying in a tremendous old house (not Chateau Bettange), well back of the lines, much of which is closed off and which apparently belongs to her uncle. We had a delicious soup and white wine, then lamb and potato cakes, then the next course was cauliflower, both of the last with red wine, then fruit and white wine again, then coffee. A very simple meal, but beautifully prepared and served. The linen was exquisite, with the family coat of arms on it. And the china was also beautiful, but the silver was almost kitchen variety. I was dying to ask about it, but didn't dare. We talked about the war and the local people and French politics which is very involved. We stayed about three hours and I enjoyed it very much. I wished for you and know you would have enjoyed looking at the furniture and so on. The fruit was served on a great platter, all lined with big golden oak leaves and most artistic.

They put up a good front, but they really don't have a great variety of food. They miss cocoa more than anything apparently. So as we have plenty and you know how I hate it, I will send them a big can tomorrow. They always have it for breakfast and said they hadn't had any for over a year. I guess it's just like me doing without coffee for breakfast, so I sympathize.

Paris has now been placed on limits for troops but it is just about as remote as the Moon to the front line soldiers. We haven't even a chance of getting out of the line, much less of getting to Paris. I really despair of sending off any kind of a Christmas box for you.

Your devoted husband,
Jimmy

2 Nov., 1944

Dearest One,

We had to search some towns for civilian weapons of any kind the other day and got quite a collection of guns from one. So now I have a very fine 12 gauge shotgun "over and under" and plenty of shells. Other staff officers are similarly equipped, so we plan to commandeer a bird dog and go on a bird shoot. We already have some quail spotted, but I really fear for any chickens we encounter as the days are a bit lean at present. Unfortunately, a booby trap killed a pig the day before yesterday, so today we had some fresh pork chops that were wonderful. Sometimes I think I command the greatest collection of thieves that were ever gathered together. I'm afraid to ask where any unusual food came from for fear I'll be a witness at the court martial.

There is so much going on that I wanted to tell you about but am not allowed to do so. The really sad part is that everyone will label me as a colossal liar when all of this is over and I try and make people believe the size, composition and mission of my Task Force. Anyway, we are doing a big job and a hard job and are doing it well. My higher headquarters thinks well of us; in other words, our reputation is good, which is really the big thing. It might sound as if I am getting a swelled head, which is not the case. The truth of the matter is that I have a grand bunch of men working for me. We understand one another and we like one another and we are getting the job done. I'm just about as proud as a man can be about his outfit; the new "Brave Rifles" really are good. And a lot of people besides myself think so.

I really hope I am able to bring this outfit home or that you and the children can come over here and live with us if we stay awhile, for I do so want you to be the first lady of the "Brave Rifles". I want you to be the first lady in actuality right on the spot. I want to show you off to my command so they will know you as I do, and it would be fun to have Jody and Jamie be spoiled by all the soldiers and fed delicacies by the mess Sergeants and become the pets of the regiment. Really, the Army of occupation might be all right when the families come over. We could have a lovely house and the children would benefit immensely from it. They would learn a foreign language and know Europeans probably far better than we would. And we would live with a great deal of prestige and style and maybe I'll be governor of Munich or some such thing. Wouldn't that be the life? Just dreaming.

Your James

NOTE: At this point, the Corps was making preparations for an assault crossing of the Moselle River in strength and cutting off Metz from both the north and south. Therefore, there was a great deal of shifting around of troop units and repositioning artillery units and very active patrolling on the river so that the Germans would get no ideas of what was about to happen.

4 Nov., 1944

My Dearest Joey:

Today has been a real stinker. I was up most of last night, out in the rain most of the day, and now I am waiting for some future developments and then I must go out again. Tomorrow looks like a rough day also. More of this business ordering good men out to die and how I hate it. But they are magnificent about it, truly magnificent. And it makes you proud and humble all in one. I often wonder what makes them go forward. Pray for me that I ask them to do the right thing and give them the right orders and the total support they deserve.

I was driving down the road yesterday and recognized Ham Howze in a passing jeep. Stopped and had only the briefest of chats with him as I had a hell of a lot to do. His unit is in Italy. And he came here as an observer instead of taking home leave — can you imagine that?

We bid adieu to our chateau today. Everyone hated to leave as we have been most comfortable there and the servants have been grand. I really got waited on when I came in muddy and tired. We gave them a lot of cocoa and they wept on our departure.

Your devoted,
Jimmy

NOTE: *The following is quoted from the XX Corps After Action Report relating to the assault crossing of the Moselle River.*
"During the movement of the 90th Infantry Division to the Cattenom area, all vehicle markings and shoulder patches were changed to correspond with those of the 3rd Cavalry Group which had been operating for some weeks in that area. As an additional deceptive measure, the 23rd Special Troops were assigned the job of maintaining the pre-existing old artillery picture. Under cover of darkness, they moved with their dummy rubber guns to the abandoned positions of earlier artillery. Gun positions, camouflage, motor traffic and radio communications of the old setup were maintained by this group. Flashes of chemical powders were set up simultaneously to simulate the firing of XX Corps artillery.
"The 3rd Cavalry Group, reinforced by a Battalion of Tank Destroyers was spread over a front of 20 miles along the Moselle River. It screened the troop movements to its rear from Thionville to the northern boundaries of the XX Corps zone to conceal our attack positions."

NOTE: We were busy making preparations to attack and capture the town of Berg situated on a hill on a re-entrant of the Moselle River, a very strong position and the only position on our side of the River that the Germans still held. We lost a few men on the approach that day, but the big attack was slated for the next day, Nov. 5th.

10 Nov., 1944

Dearest One,

I haven't written you for some days. I know I didn't write you on our wedding anniversary as it was impossible. But I thought of you the whole day long. The past few days have been very rugged, but all is well now. I am very proud of my unit as we did awfully well. Everyone has been most complimentary and the Corps Commander pinned the Bronze Star on me in his office — not for my own deeds, please don't misunderstand me, I wasn't particularly brave or heroic, — but rather for a smart and well-led fight. I am very proud of it and some men died to get that Bronze Star for me.

We are still in the line but have been moved to a quiet sector further north — at least it's supposed to be quiet and has been so far the past several days. There was a period of eight hours when we were actually out of the line and I had no front line responsibilities. However, that's all over now and we are back at playing cat and mouse.

I am dog tired. I have gotten hold of a pint of gin so I am going to take a big slug and fall into bed. The big drive is on, so pray for good weather and we can end it. I'll write more tomorrow. You are ever present in my thoughts.

Your Jimmy

NOTE: We captured Berg on the 5th of Nov. after a very hard fight, much of it hand to hand in the town. Our casualties amounted to two officers wounded, four men killed and 34 enlisted men wounded. We also lost two tanks. The enemy lost about 60 killed and wounded and we took 45 prisoners. In interrogating these prisoners, we learned that Lt. Col. Cross and Captain Nelson had been captured and were not hurt.

11 Nov., 1944 (Luxembourg)

Dearest One,

I hope my letter of yesterday didn't upset you as we have done damn well, but it has been a strain. If you can look back in the papers of about Nov. 5th or maybe Nov. 6th in your papers, about the only action in this whole Army was my own unit's action. It got a play on the Berlin broadcast the next day as a vicious fight on a small scale, which it was.

I feel very proud of my Bronze Star because my men fought so hard to get it for me. I guess the higher ranking you get, the more decorations you receive for what your unit has done and not for what you yourself have done. It is certainly true in this case.

False rumors often get started and it concerns me. I have had many people ask me about Harry Wilson's death, which of course, is untrue, yet many people over here believed it. The same is true of Peewee Collier and both rumors are wrong. Peewee is very healthy. If you should happen to get such a rumor or letter from a friend about me, don't you believe it. The War Department is very fast on notification and will beat any rumors or letters from friends. As a matter of fact, we are strictly forbidden to name any casualties at all, even a long time after, except official letters of condolence which are then cleared through the war department.

I had an officer captured the other day, we know he was captured and quite well, yet he is reported as missing in action and we cannot tell his wife until the Germans tell the Swiss who tell the U.S. Government. It seems hard, but it's really better that way as so many rumors start that are not true. Do not believe rumors, but rather subscribe to the Army/Navy Journal. They have the correct dope.

Luxembourg is a lovely little country, much like Virginia or Pennsylvania, except for the little clusters of stone villages. I am in one such now. We have a small house for a headquarters, low ceilings, inadequate toilet facilities, manure piles and cows in the streets and in all the houses except ours. The chickens have a little door into the houses with a sort of leaning step ladder to get up to it. It's really comical to see them go up the ladder and then into the house.

My headquarters troop had a movie in the village (I didn't have time to go) for the first time in a long while last night. The movie was, "Until We Meet Again" which couldn't have been worse. All about war, sad and dramatic, but it didn't look authentic to the men so there was much hooting and yelling and laughing. One part they all objected to, as they told me, was that when a German officer was shot, no one of the French made a rush to get his gun and shoes. You can never see a dead German with shoes on. The French seem to grab them the minute the shot gets them. All of us have German guns. I have a machine pistol that's a honey. I hope I can bring it home, but I doubt it very much. The only trouble is that it is so characteristic in sound and unmistakably German that I am afraid to shoot it for fear someone will mistake me for a Jerry. More tomorrow. Just got some orders and have to get to work. I will write you more with a little leisure time soon.

Your own,
Jimmy

NOTE: The bridgehead across the Moselle had been well established by now by the 90th Division and the 10th Armored Division and we (Task Force Polk), that is, the 3rd Cavalry Group with a number of attachments, were ordered to cross behind the 10th Armored Division and move up to the left between the Saar and the Moselle Rivers.

13 Nov., 1944

My Dearest One,

Just finished a letter to your mother amid much interruptions as we are in the process of drafting a new operations order. I have a really wonderful staff that takes a great load off my shoulders. Three men in particular whom I lean on very heavily are worth describing in detail.

1) Phil Davidson, my Executive Officer, West Point, Class of '39. My height but heavier, ruddy complexion, prominent nose, nearly bald with fuzzy hair, smart and active and fit and perfectly capable of commanding a Group. He is most polite and deferential to me, but when he gets excited, he raises his voice and beats one fist into the other palm, accents his words as you used to do, "oh man, what a scare, that damn shell went right by me, I dove in the ditch" etc. I trust his decisions completely and would be lost without him.

2) Aaron Cohn, a Major, Operations and Planning Officer. A stocky man with red hair, a graduate lawyer from Georgia, 1939. He has a most unmilitary bearing, but smart as a whip, beautifully educated and a likable personality. We constantly kid him about the day the S.S. nearly caught him and it really would have been hard for him. He really hates the Germans. He killed one with a rifle at 600 yards and rubbed his hands together in joy. He writes all my orders, does all the detail planning after I give him the broad outline, and generally runs the office while Phil Davidson and I fight the troops. Thanks to him we put out the best orders in this Corps.

3) Tom Greenfield, graduated from Arizona about 1939, majored in physical education and played great football. He took basic English, as he tells us, about seven times and still murders the King's English. He played three years professional football with the Green Bay Packers at center. He is about 6'5" tall, weighs about 240 lb., can hit the ditch faster than any man in the Group. He is as brave as a lion -absolutely fearless and is deceptive as he has a great deal of native intelligence. He does exactly what I tell him to do and God help the man, friend or enemy, who gets in his way. He's like a big smart bear and we all love him. When I want something done whole hog, I always send old Tom. I fear for his safety though, as he takes awful chances and is such a big target.

The other members of the staff don't count much. I give them hell and they do what they are told to do, to the best of their abilities. They all try hard for me and I am developing a rather fatherly affection for them all. I'm glad that we are a harmonious headquarters, but as you see, I lean on three men who can be characterized as follows.

1) Smart Regular Army — my Executive Officer
2) Brains — my Planning Officer
3) Brawn — my Operations Officer

Each night about ten we decide what must be done the next day, the four of us in conference. And they are not "yes" men but put forth their ideas. Then we parcel out the jobs and decide who must stay at headquarters to make what decisions, who must make staff inspections of troops, who will visit adjacent or supporting units, who will see the hot action, how we will coordinate the fire support or the mine clearing or the demolitions or what have you. And we go to bed with it all wrapped up — not for certain for nothing in War is certain; but with the feeling that we all know the broad outline of what is needed, with the knowledge that the man on the spot must make the decision and that the rest of us will back him up all the way.

Can you see us at work, my love? Can you see the bond of mutual respect and dangers shared and of the brotherhood that bind us together? Can you see us pooling our ideas until I finally say that it will be done this way? Sometimes we disagree, but when I make the final decision, hateful or dangerous as it sometimes is, we are one and we all know it will be done that very way. These are three fine men that I know and respect and almost love. They would die for me and probably I would die for them. Who knows?

We were pulled out of the line yesterday and went into reserve, the first time out of the line for three months for this gang. So I am all relaxed and have no responsibility for a few days. However, it won't last long, maybe two days more. But I got a good bath and am sitting here with a bit of Scotch I have been saving. However, even in reserve, I have responsibilities and I have to plan on the next job. It looks like it will be a rough one, so I really can't relax. God, if you were only here to unwind me, to relieve this tight feeling of strain and to revel in your lovely personality and your support.

God bless you, my love.

Your Jimmy

NOTE: We were getting ready to cross the Moselle River, relieve several battalions of the 90th Infantry Division and strike to the north/northeast between the Saar and the Moselle River toward Saarburg and the Siegfried Line.

Lt. Col. James H. Polk. Regimental Executive Officer, 106th Cavalry Group. Front row, center. In training for D-Day; near Nantwich, Cheshire, England. Spring, 1944.

General George S. Patton and Col. J. H. Polk, 20 Sept. 1944 outside Bettembourg, Luxembourg. On this date the 3rd Cavalry Group was designated Task Force Polk, with other units attached in anticipation of defending and crossing the Moselle River.

3rd Cavalry Group Officers, left to right: Lt. Col. Philip Davidson, Regimental Exec. Officer; Lt. Col. Marshall Wallach, 3rd Squadron Commander; and Major Harry Sewell, 43rd Squadron Exec. Officer. Fall, 1944 preparing to fly as observers on a bombing run over the Ruhr Valley in a Martin B-26 Marauder, courtesy U. S. Army Air Corps.

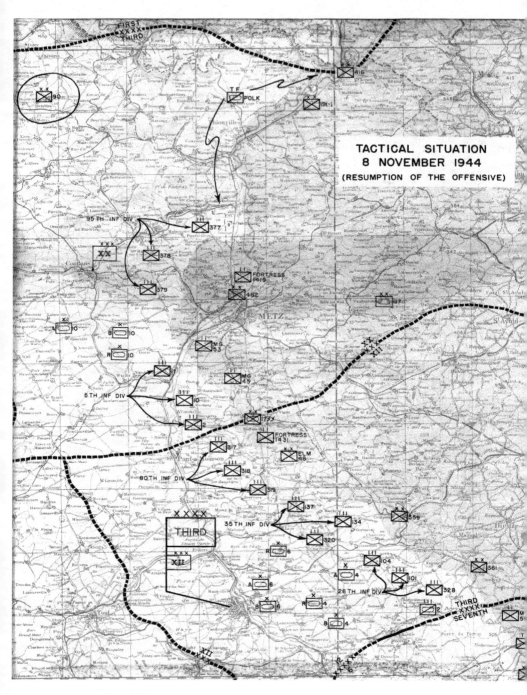

Tactical Situation Map, 8 November 1944, showing Task Force Polk arrayed along a 20-mile front on the west side of the Moselle River near Thionville, France, prior to an assault crossing by elements of XX Corps.

France, 19 January 1945. 1LT James D. Jackson (R) receives the Distinguished Service Cross from Colonel James H. Polk, C. O. of the 3rd Cavalry Group (Mecz.), for leading his troop 75 miles behind enemy lines to Thionville, France to secure the bridge over the Moselle River there. Jackson and his platoon, from Troop B, 3rd Recon Squadron, inflicted heavy casualties on the enemy and Jackson personally prevented the demolition of the bridge.

Col. Polk displaying his new Colonel's Eagles.
Photo taken somewhere in the Moselle-Saar Triangle,
December 1944.

3rd Cav. Grp. Headquarters Staff. Winter, 1945 in Germany. Front Row,
L to R: Maj. John Logan, Lt. Col. Philip Davidson (Exec. Off.), Col. J.H.
Polk (C.O.), Maj. Aaron Cohn (S-3), Maj. Burt Genung (S-2). Second Row,
L to R: Capt. John Hunt, Capt. Don Voorhees, Capt. George Hoogkamp,
Capt. Elmer Rychert, Capt. Tom Greenfield. Back Row: Lt. McCreay .

Col. James H. Polk, C.O., 3rd Cavalry Group with Jeep near Gelnhausen, Germany Spring, 1945. Named after his wife "Joey" for good luck.

R E S T R I C T E D

HQ XX CORPS
APO 340

GENERAL ORDER)   4 November 1944

NUMBER   46)

I   AWARD OF BRONZE STAR MEDAL: Under the provisions of AR 600-45, 22 September 1943, as amended, the Bronze Star Medal is awarded to:

JAMES H. POLK, 019028, Lieutenant Colonel, CAV, Headquarters 3d Cavalry Group (Mechanized), for meritorious achievement in connection with military operations against the enemy in France on 5 November 1944. Lieutenant Colonel POLK displayed unusually sound judgment, and keen tactical foresight in planning and coordinating the attack of elements of the ***Cavalry Reconnaissance Squadron (Mechanized) and attached units against the extremely important town of ****, France, on 5 November 1944. These plans were so efficiently and meticulously prepared and their execution so carefully timed that the town, strongly held by German forces, was captured in less than three hours. His enthusiastic leadership set an example to the officers and men serving under him inspiring them with the courage and determination necessary to rout the enemy from their firmly-held positions. Lieutenant Colonel POLK's actions reflect great credit upon himself and are in keeping with the highest traditions of the Military Service. Entered United States Military Academy from the United States at Large.

By command of Major General WALKER:

                                                         W. A. COLLIER,
                                                         Colonel, GSC
                                                         Chief of Staff.

OFFICIAL:

        s/ Robert E. Cullen
        t/ ROBERT E. CULLEN
           Colonel, A. G. D.,
           Adjutant General.

DISTRIBUTION:
    "A & F"

A CERTIFIED TRUE COPY:

        JOHN A. LOGAN
        Major, Cavalry
        Adjutant

                    R E S T R I C T E D

BRONZE STAR

HEADQUARTERS XX CORPS
APO 340 - U.S. ARMY.
- - - - - - - - - -

2nd. December, 1944

FROM: Captain Guy de la VASSELAIS - Chief of the French
Tactical Liaison - H.Q. XX Corps - APO 340 - U.S. Army.

TO : Colonel POLK - 3rd. Cavalry Group Commanding.

My dear Colonel,

Allow me, as officer of motorized cavalry, to address you
my most sincere personnal congratulations for the Croix de Guerre
with palm I gave you this morning. This decoration was presented
on behalf of the French Army, in grateful acknowledgement of your
war deeds during the battles for the liberation of France.

There is no need to prove anew the real friendship which
exits between our two countries but I believe that the homage
paid to the Army of the United States through the award of the
French war decorations will go straight to the heart of these
who fought so that France could regain her liberty.

I feel that I must point out to you that you have been the
first American officer to have been decorated by a French officer
on German soil. It has been a great honour for me to be chosen
for this mission.

Respectfully,

Captain Guy de la VASSELAIS,
Chief of the French Tactical Liaison.

(Copy from original)

Portrait of Joey Polk with one right earring, carried by Col. Polk throughout the war.

PART III

The Invasion of Germany and the Surrender
18 November, 1944 -23 May, 1945

18 Nov., 1944

My Dearest One,

Just a note to let you know that I am well and unharmed. Our little period of being in reserve lasted only 36 hours. We went back into the thick of it. We have a good cavalry job, an independent mission, and have done damn well these last three days. Yesterday, one of my units was the first into Germany in the whole of 3rd Army and I am about in it tonight. Tomorrow we will be well into Germany if all goes well. Life is busy and exciting.

I have just finished my commander's meeting and have drawn up plans for tomorrow. This finds me exhausted but proud and confident. We didn't actually have them on the run, but at least tired and discoordinated: we mean to keep it that way. We pray that this is the big push that will end it. Everyone is giving it all that he has got and we don't intend to stop short of Berlin.

Today was beautiful, about 32^{oF} but clear and crisp. I was out all day and so was our Air Force. We had a P-51 Squadron working for us and they really softened old Jerry up with first the 500 lb. bombs and then the 50 caliber machine guns — pray for good weather for that's what we really need. Sunshine and airplanes make for a real nice war.

I'll write you more detail when things slow down. Right now the pace is swift. I'll be seeing you soon.

Your Jimmy

NOTE: *At this point we were pushing north and northeast in what was known as the Saar/Moselle triangle. The Saar and the Moselle come together at Saarburg. The resistance was scattered but bitter so that we had small fights in many of the little villages and were capturing a number of prisoners and paying a small price for it. However, our casualties were not excessive and we felt good about driving the Germans back toward Germany.*
At this point we did fear for a counter attack by the 11th Panzer Division which had been active in the area, so that we had the 705 Tank Destroyer Battalion with us and we were very happy that they were along as they were a self-propelled battalion with high-velocity 76mm guns. They were the only thing with the outfit that could handle the bigger German tanks.

22 Nov., 1944

My Dear Mrs. Col. Polk,

I am happy to announce that your old man is now a full-fledged chicken Colonel in the Army of the United States at the age of 32. The word came yesterday afternoon by a courier from higher headquarters with the official order in his right hand, effective the 16th of Nov. by command of General Eisenhower. It is very nice and I am very proud. But the sad part is that I have no Eagles to put on as we are still on the front line and any store carrying such articles doesn't seem to be around. However, all my men are out scouting and I ought to have some soon.

It will be a great help as I get nervous every time a full fledged Cavalry Colonel comes around as I feel sure he is looking for my job. Also I have a lot of conferring to do with various Generals on my right and left, so that having a bit more rank will help in getting into their command posts.

We had a little celebration last night in my honor that I will always remember. We were in some SS headquarters in Germany that some of my tankers had captured the day before. The refreshments were kindly donated by the German Army, consisting of a standard bar complete with cocktail glasses and one bottle each of rum, cognac, vermouth and blackberry brandy, all thrown together in an earthen cookpot in a rather horrible mixture. And we had some fried chicken which was kindly donated by the local German inhabitants. There was a sign on the door renaming the place the M5A1 Club (that's the model of our Tank Company's tanks). And the only female was a store front dummy like Heil Brown had in her house, with her dress slipping off her shoulders and displaying a rather large pair of pink-nippled bosoms. All this was in the midst of a perfect shambles of broken furniture, glass, shell holes and dirt. All the officers were alive and gay as we had just pulled off a brilliant attack that had knocked off some 60 Jerries and we didn't lose a man. Then the counter-artillery fire came socking back into the town but no one gave a damn. It had been such a good day for us all.

This outfit is really getting hot. They all fight a smart fight now and I am so proud of them that I could bust. They all toasted me their new Colonel. I can't tell you or describe the feelings of mutual admiration and respect and comradeship we all feel for each other. We are all so exhilarated that the punch was only a symbol of our mutual esteem. The Stars and Stripes described our action as "slashing" and I think that really fits it. Also, I hope that the papers carried the fact back home that my own 3rd Cavalry was the leading element of 3rd Army in Germany. We captured a town called Perl, inside Germany proper.

Things are looking up now. Metz has finally fallen. We are on our way to another river on the Siegfried Line. But no one is afraid of it. We all think we can punch through and go on through to Berlin itself and there is a great surge of feeling that we are on our way at last. Plenty of food, men, gasoline and equipment are now at hand to see the job through. The weather is foul as usual — cold and rain and near-freezing, but no one complains. It would indeed make you proud to be an American.

The quality of the German soldiers we have been meeting is truly pitiful. They are all either very old or very young, and they know they are beaten. However, they do fight hard until you get the drop on them. But they don't fight smart and are usually quite hungry. I pray this is really it.

Your devoted husband
Jimmy

PS: I need you this night to share my pride and my happiness. I love you.

Your Jimmy

23 Nov., 1944

My Darling One,

Today is Thanksgiving and I can see you all at home gathered around the festive board with all the kids, the great turkey, the cranberry sauce and pumpkin pie. It makes me homesick, but at least I can see it all in my mind's eye. I know just how the dining room looked and who was there and what was said and how the food was and everything. And I know you have wished for me to be there too.

We have had our own feast today since the Army is at such pains to provide on occasions like this. It was really good too, and we enjoyed the turkey and dressing and we particularly enjoyed all the spices. Our food is normally so flat. Also, we had real raisin bread and some captured wine. All my staff sat at a long table and we tried to be happy, but I'm afraid that most of our hearts were far away with our loved ones. The troops as a whole did awfully well. Most of them had their dinners in the local church or schoolhouse in the village on the front line they occupy. But of course, the meal had to be staggered as it is dangerous to collect very many men because of the intermittent artillery fire that might fall on such a gathering.

I visited as many as I could and never saw such high spirits and such pride of unit as these men display. One unit in immediate reserve even got hold of a few kegs of beer and decorated their schoolhouse with autumn leaves and pumpkins. It was exactly like a troop party in the United States. Everyone really does amazingly well when all things are considered. If we only had a ten-day spell of sunshine then we could win this thing hands down.

I can now tell you that my chateau belonged to Count de Mitry and was located on a hill behind Thionville. I was responsible for holding about twenty miles of the Moselle River above and below that place. It was an interesting game as we were stretched thin to allow the power of the Corps to concentrate and strike elsewhere.

It is late and I am sleepy so will bid you good night. God bless you and keep you, my precious one.

Your Jimmy

NOTE: *While the above letter sounds pretty calm, we had by this time run into what was known as the "Switchline" of the Siegfried Line. This is the string of fortifications that ran from the Siegfried Line on the Saar River over to the extension of the Siegfried Line up the Moselle River and lies across the base of the Saar-Moselle triangle. We had bumped into it without any warning, no intelligence people had told us that there was such a line at this point and so we lost some casualties because it was such a surprise to us. We took some casualties in Borg from very heavy mortar fire; so it took us two or three days to shake down and properly know how to handle this fortified line. It was a series of large concrete pill-boxes containing cannon, surrounded by wire and mines and protected by dragon's teeth so that our tanks couldn't advance against it. It was very formidable fortification and very hard to defeat.*

26 Nov., 1944 (France)

My Dearest One,

We are now all out of the line, busy getting everyone his first bath in weeks, change of clothes, Red Cross donut truck and tonight there is a movie. I am the only one left in the Command Post as all the rest are at the show. But I would far rather write to you. Our Command Post is in an old hotel, Germanized, but just over the border in France called a "Rat House". So far, we haven't seen any rats, but it was apparently a Jerry C.P. also and I guess the company was too much for the rats. The boys are getting a well earned rest but with the big push now going on, I don't expect to stay out much more than a couple of days.

I haven't had a chance to relax as there is a tremendous amount to be done when we come out, seeing that everyone is taken care of and rehabilitated and now I'm back on the planning stage of going back in, figuring out our new dispositions, making terrain and road studies, poring over aerial photographs of our new sector, planning and making reconnaissance of our routes so we can get up and into the line in the dark without any troubles. I guess I take my job pretty hard. But I have a horror of being slipshod when men's lives are at stake. It is so easy to put off until tomorrow that I must drive, drive all the time. There is no doubt that all this responsibility is making me older. But at the same time, it is making me wiser and more tolerant of other people. It is making me gentler on the outside, but sometimes hard as iron on the inside when big things are at stake. I think I am well liked by my subordinates. I think I have gained their respect. And I certainly command their unquestioned and immediate obedience when I desire it. I know that I have a harmonious and a smart staff and I know that I command a great fighting outfit.

It's just this business of never being able to relax, of always being the Commanding Officer. I really never have any hour of the day off duty, for something can happen anytime. I never have any real contemporary who fully understands my problems.

You should understand that men don't die in the glory of battle in some gallant charge amidst the music of bugles and the roll of drums. They die often in abject fear in dirt, in mud, in filth and exhaustion, and in the taking of some miserable little hill or some dirty little town. There are some glorious moments that transcend all the badness of it, but they are few and far between.

Damn, here I am, writing all this to you when I would never say it to anyone. I would never admit it to my men, but I have to unburden myself to you. You will understand for you know me so well.

Your devoted husband,
Jimmy

NOTE: —*We went back into the line on the 28th. of Nov. with pretty much the same Task Force, Artillery, Tank Destroyers and Engineers attached. Our job was to relieve the 10th Armored Division and to occupy the line from the Moselle River on our left and 83rd Division across the River, down to the Saar River and the 10th Armored Division on our right. We were bucked up against the switchline and our orders were to keep everything clear on our side of the switchline and to scout out likely places where we might break through the line — with some help, of course.*

30 Nov., 1944 (Germany)

Dearest My Love,

Today has been a hard day. It always seems that I write you at night when my nerves are frayed and I'm worn out, not with anything dangerous or exciting, but just that things haven't gone to suit me, sloppy performances, needless casualties, upsetting things that cause me to raise Cain with someone and get that feeling that I must keep driving to do the right and the smart thing.

We are bang up against the Siegfried Line now and to add to my troubles, today I got a colored outfit as part of my force (this was the 614th Tank Destroyer Battalion). They really have done quite well, but they do impose a lot of minor trouble. Of course, we are all in this thing together and no feeling of race can be tolerated. They are full of pride and undoubtedly will make the papers at home. You might remember the outfit as they lived near my outfit while you were staying with Heil Brown (this is telling her it is a Tank Destroyer Battalion). It is always difficult to break in new troops as we all go through an initial period of great fear. But they did well under their first shell-fire. This really puts the lid on it though; at one time or another, I have had every-thing in God's world working for me except the CB's, and I will probably get them tomorrow.

Col. Gordon and your other Army friends will be interested to know that John McDonald has a command now, similar to mine (he has taken over the 5th Cav.) and that Joe Tully was stepped up from it and made a General. I like Col. Tully so much. You might remember his son who was a Cadet in my Company. My happiness would be complete if they would just make Vennard Wilson a General. I never see any of the old 106th gang as they are some distance from me.

One of your Christmas boxes arrived today and I had a lot of fun opening it. You are so cute and adorable and the Santa Claus was so appropriate and attractive. All my staff remarked on your good taste and what a charming idea it was. I shall save the cranberry sauce for our Christmas turkey and smoke the cigars and eat the olives immediately. I shall also wear the socks as I have some loose shoes and they look so nice and warm. Thank you, my dear. I couldn't help but open the box. Everyone opens theirs at once, and as the whole office force gets about one package a day, our ration of candy is spread out nicely over the whole of December.

It made me very homesick though. It will be a hard Christmas to spend so far away from my loved ones. When this reaches you, I can imagine the frenzy of shopping that will be going on, the hiding of packages from the children, the trip to see Santa at the Popular and all that. Christmas is the time to be with the children and here I am so far away. The Moon carried my message of love to you last night. I talked to you and I pray that you heard me. Bless you, my love.

Jimmy

NOTE: Major George Swanson, the Executive Officer of the 43rd Squadron was killed about this time. He was standing near some Engineers who were repairing a bridge and one shell came in and got him. Nobody else in the group was even scratched. He was a great loss and a wonderful man.

The Siegfried Line along this front consisted of a row of dragon's teeth, as we call them; that is, a series of concrete posts set strongly into the ground and perfectly capable of stopping any tank we have. These are surrounded by mines and wire. Very often, behind the row of dragon's teeth, is an anti-tank ditch. One was described as being 20' wide and 12' deep with about 2' of water in the bottom. These are backed up by concrete pill-boxes, some of them quite large, large enough to contain maybe a small cannon and four or five machine guns pointed in all directions. The pill-boxes support each other; that is, if you attack one, you could be fired on from the side and back from another. They were really very formidable obstacles and very difficult to penetrate.

3 Dec. 1944

Dearest One,

A perfect flood of mail arrived today, some of it as old as seven weeks, and I read them slowly so that I could spread out my pleasures. I hate to get so much mail all at once, but I guess this attack has disrupted the mail service — it always does.

Your life sounds very crowded with all the rummage sales, parties and so forth. I was glad to hear you had slowed down. I do wish I could go to some of those parties you mentioned. It sounds like such fun.

Howie Snyder, whom I see quite a lot as he is the G-3 of my Corps, has recovered from his wound and is back on duty although still pale and puny, but doing a grand job — he's a very fine man.

Yesterday, I was decorated with the French Croix de Guerre by the French government. Our liaison officer at Corps from the government, Capt. Guy de la Vasselas, did the Honors and kissed me on both cheeks. Things have really been happening to me of late. I am sending the citation given to me in a separate envelope. It should not be published as some of the information is restricted. Restricted means that it should not appear in the newspapers. However, they took my picture and will probably send it to the El Paso newspaper. I must impress upon you to let the Army Publicity Service take care of all that.

We are still bang up against the Siegfried Line, but things are going well in other parts of my particular Corps so we may soon get shaken loose again and get out into the open. The weather isn't too bad, no snow to amount to anything, some rain and lots of fog or mist. My C.P. is in a good strong house and I have a good bed and we have one good bathroom which is a great luxury. It works.

The vitamin pills arrived yesterday also, and I shall start on them at once. I have a touch of the flu so went to bed yesterday at suppertime and took some aspirin. Today I am slightly subnormal and will continue to stay in bed all day as there is not much happening on the line. I get every attention, a doctor hovering over me and special soup, apples, fruit juice and so forth. It really is a rest for me to relax all day in the bunk with all this attention. I have a good book, all your letters and every attention, so shall go downstairs with renewed vigor tomorrow. I shall keep you informed. But by the time you get this, it will be all over, so don't do any long distance worrying about something that happened three weeks ago.

Your loving husband,
Jimmy

NOTE: I was given the Croix de Guerre because the 3rd Cavalry was the first unit of 3rd Army to enter Germany, when we captured the town of Borg, and probably the first of our American forces to enter Germany in the whole of Central Europe, as far as I know. We got cables of congratulations from both Gen. Patton and Gen. Walker.

4 Dec., 1944

Dearest Josephine,

Just a note to let you know that I am back on my feet again. I have stayed indoors all day and still feel a bit puny but have suffered no ill effects and will probably make some short front line visits tomorrow —just to let everyone know that the old man is well again and keeping his beady eye on them.

Your Christmas box with the fruit cake from Mabie arrived and all the other useful and nice things. I gave the bar of soap to my laundress and you would think I had given her a great present. She will do my laundry for two weeks and still make a handsome profit of some soap. Our laundry is still being done at the old chateau some miles to our rear. We can't seem to shake away from the place. It's on the 3rd Cav. supply lines so all our supply people go by it daily and look after it.

Your devoted husband,
Jimmy

7 Dec. 1944 (Germany)

My Dearest One,

Today finds me feeling fine. I spent rather an active day yesterday and came home in good humor as everything I saw suited me well. The troops do amazingly well for the adverse weather they face and most of them manage to keep exceptionally clean with all things considered. Our food is still B ration instead of that awful K ration, which means as much fresh things as possible (potatoes, carrots and sometimes meat). The cigarette shortage has never bothered front-line troops; we always have more than we can smoke. It's only the service troops on the rear who have been without them.

The ammunition shortage was terribly critical a month ago and held up our attack for a long time, but is licked now. However, there is no doubt that it cost some lives. The trouble is that we had gone so far ahead of schedule that the ammunition just couldn't keep up — nor could the gasoline. I really think the supply people have done a wonderful job when you consider that practically everything came over the beach and then by truck all the way across France.

The Red Ball Highway was really something to see in its big day. All these black truck drivers with huge trucks from $2^1/_2$ tons up to huge trailers with a big red ball on the front of the truck. They were really kings of the highway with top priority over anything on the road. And they never went under 40 mph. You have to see some of these French roads and villages to appreciate it. If there was an accident, the trucks were just thrown off the road to be repaired later. Nothing could be allowed to stop traffic. They really handled an amazing amount of freight and the drivers really loved it.

We are allowed to send a driblet of men to Paris every so often, so we use it as a reward for the outstanding soldiers and officers. The first contingent got back yesterday and were full of enthusiasm. It is very well done as they were housed and fed GI meals by the Red Cross. They said they spent their first half day standing on street corners watchirg all the women who bicycle pass. All beautifully dressed and with the craziest hats ever seen by this world. The place is terribly expensive. They report a steak cost $25.00 and everything else in proportion. Don't worry about my getting such a holiday and going on a tear in the big cities. It's as remote as the moon at this time.

I saw Joe Tully yesterday. He has been promoted and is in the same outfit with Johnny Thimer (that's the 90th Division). We had a nice chat with much reminiscing about the Fort Riley days.

Today we have rain as usual, but yesterday was a beautiful day, one of the few. This is really beautiful country we are in, between the Saar and the Moselle, and reminds me of Pennsylvania, the same rolling hills, cultivated fields and frequent forests. Some of our observation posts command a really breathtaking view of the countryside. However, I know you can understand how difficult it is to fight over this terrain as it gives the defenders so many opportunities for ambush and he situates himself on top of the hills and looks down our throats. It seems we are always struggling uphill against the Jerries. That's enough for tonight, my dear. I love you.

Your husband,
Jimmy

NOTE: *The 90th Division had been consolidated and made an assault crossing of the Saar River. We, in turn, had been extended so that our front ran from the Moselle, across the switchline and down the Saar to contact with the 90th Division, all in all about 20 miles. We were fortunate, however, to have four battalions of field artillery supporting us, so that any sort of an emergency could put at least 18 guns in a fire support situation.*
South of us, the 90th and 95th Divisions were really in brutal combat trying to fight their way through the Siegfried Line and having some bloody success. However, the Germans had concentrated against them and that left our sector fairly quiet...thank Heavens.

10 Dec., 1944

My Dearest One,

Today has been dull and quiet. The weather keeps both us and the enemy quiet in this particular sector. No one is getting hurt very much and we are living tolerably well. My headquarters is in a nasty little town (the town is Remeling) that smells to high Heaven of manure of which each house has a pile out in front of it. Most of the roofs are leaking and most of the buildings have gaping holes in them. But they do offer some shelter and my command post has a nice big stove. I have a bed of sorts that I throw my sleeping bag on.

I've just finished reading a most unsatisfactory book. My first in ages, called *The Razor's Edge* by Somerset Maugham. All full of improbable people and faked philosophy. I think I shall stick to detective stories and other light reading as I am in no mood to read about other people's emotional crises.

I sent to Abercrombie and Fitch for some fleece-lined gauntlets for myself. They are wonderful and I hope they get here soon, as the fur-lined gloves that you gave me last Christmas are just about finished. I told them to send the bill to you so please pay for it. I have no doubt that they will be quite expensive, but from a pair I saw, they are well worth the money and the comfort they provide.

I broke my shaving mirror, so will you please send me another, either steel or glass in a case about 3" x 6", also a toothbrush as the issue ones are horrible. Other items that are not vital but gladly received are exotic foods like sardines, good jam or jelly, but for God's sake, no marmalade. We have plenty of that; Kraft cheese, Worcestershire sauce, chili sauce, anything good for night snacks. We have plenty of crackers. You can slack off on the candy and soap and razor blades as we can get them now from our local PX. Cigars are impossible to get and I am greatly enjoying the box that Charles sent me. Keep them coming. Our meals are good and wholesome but rather monotonous, which is why I asked for the sauces. If you haven't sent me the long cotton underwear, don't bother, as I am now in regular long army woolen ones. I can wear the long cotton drawers in the spring.

This letter sounds all full of asking, but most of it is just trifles that I really don't need. We are well taken care of. My usual costume is as follows: one white T undershirt, one long wool undershirt, one long wool drawers, one pair of wool socks, one wool shirt and trousers, brown sweater, combat jacket, combat trousers, galoshes over paratroop boots, knit cap, steel helmet, silk scarf, belt with pistol, knife, first aid packet and compass. I forgot the fur-lined gloves. I put my trench coat on over it all and pull a hood over my head. I must weigh 180 lbs. when I get it all together. But a jeep with the top down is cold to ride in any time now. If you can take in that picture, add field glasses and a carbine when I'm up front and throw mud over all of it and you have a perfect picture of me. I look like "Man Mountain Dean" when I get it all on and possibly stagger when I walk, but come what may, I am warm.

Life seems awfully dull and rather an endless prospect before us — I can't see the end before spring or summer. It all lacks so much point on nights like this. I think I have been a bachelor long enough now — better than a year, really — and I'm getting damn well sick of it. I think this bad weather depresses everyone. It is almost dark by 5:00 and the nights seem endless and long. The days have a certain excitement or at least I am busy. Will this damn thing ever end? It must end sometime and until then I am just existing.

Your own,
Jimmy

NOTE: We had a large wood in our sector called the Campholtz Woods, and instead of manning trenches or strong points inside the woods, we laid off so we were not right up against the Siegfried Line in that particular part of our sector. However, we patrolled into the woods with great regularity up to the Siegfried Line and I allowed the men to hunt the small German deer on their way back out. We used to meet the patrols whenever we could and it always made us very nervous when you saw them carrying something (two men, with a long pole between them) as to was it a man or a deer. Fortunately, most of the time, it was a deer, but it gave us an awful fright sometimes.

12 Dec., 1944

My Darling One,

I often wonder what you think of my letters. I must tell you under what difficult conditions I write you. The only lights are Coleman lanterns in our Command Post so I have to write from there. About 6-8 men in an ordinary size room with phones, maps, messengers popping in and out and some form of orders or discussions or just plain "bull" going on all the time. It is awfully hard to concentrate as I am interrupted, always.

I do have a private room next to the stable, but no lights, just a sleeping bag. The room has the most ungodly smell as the roof leaks in spots and runs down the wall so it smells of wet wallpaper paste and cow manure. The stable is part of the house as that's the way they do it over here.

Johnny Thimer has a new job and quite a lot of artillery under his command. His job is to support me and the 3rd Cavalry so we see quite a lot of each other and often talk of El Paso. However, he's a rather difficult person to know and rather opinionated and given to making flat statements. He isn't what I could call a real close friend, but at least a contemporary and a link with home. Do you ever see his wife and compare notes?

Tomorrow is my birthday and I shall miss you and the happy times we always have on those days and particularly miss you at the breakfast when the presents are passed around. But we can do that next year.

Your devoted husband,
Jim

NOTE: *Johnny Thimer was in command of the 5th Field Artillery Group and commanded the four Field Artillery Battalions that were supporting us. Despite the comments in the letter, he became a very close friend and was a superb artilleryman. I really enjoyed matters when the 5th Artillery Group was supporting us.*

About this time, when we were doing a lot of patrolling across the Saar River and into the switchline of the Siegfried Line, or at least up to it, I was down at a little river town where a two-man patrol was going across in hopes of catching a prisoner. We had a lot of artillery and mortars with a box barrage planned plus several tanks so that if the patrol got in any trouble, we could bring down a hail of fire and box Lt. Cartwright and the Sgt. with him in it, so that they would be able to return safely. As the patrol was launched and things weren't going very well, Aaron Cohn (G-3) radioed me from Group Headquarters that Gen. Van Fleet, the very new Commanding General of the 90th Division, was in the Headquarters and was coming down to see the patrol. This horrified me because we never had a General in the front line at night in the first place, and in the second place, things weren't going very well and it was one of these scroungy dirty towns, with dirty soldiers and tin cans all around and really kind of a horrible picture. I told Aaron to keep him there and I would come back. My G-3 said he couldn't keep him and he was coming down to see us. So we just prayed for the best. As luck would have it, and it really was luck, just before Gen. Van Fleet came into the Troop Headquarters down on the river in this little stinky town, Lt. Cartwright radioed back and said that he and the Sgt. had a prisoner (they had pulled one out of a foxhole) and he said, "Turn it all loose". So we turned the box barrage loose and we even had multi 50-caliber guns firing overhead tracers so he could tell what direction to come — it was a real fireworks display. General Van Fleet walked in about the same time that Cartwright walked in with his prisoner. The prisoner was pretty dumb, he didn't know anything really. Gen. Van Fleet and I interrogated him and the upshot was that he had a commanders meeting the next morning with his three Infantry Regimental Commanders, two of them very close friends of mine (Ray Bell and Chris Clark) and he laced them up and down because they hadn't gotten any prisoners and on the other hand, Task Force Polk had really shown how it was done. This had a lasting effect on my career because Gen. Van Fleet thought that the 3rd Cavalry, from then on, were the greatest bunch that ever were associated with him. The funny part of it was that Chris Clark accused me of "maybe this German prisoner was an American and it was all an act" or "maybe we had just had him stock-piled and got him the night before and put on this show for Gen. Van Fleet". Ray Bell and Chris Clark still believe I snookered them on this patrol when actually, it was perfectly honest. (Much later, General Van Fleet made me his G2 of Eighth Army in the Korean War.)

14 Dec. 1944 (Germany)

My Dearest Wife,

I have laughed over your latest Christmas package until my sides ache. Say it isn't so — are you trying to tell me we are going to have an addition to the family? With all this baby food and baby powder, because if we are, you sure better hurry up and have it or I might suspect you. And please tell me, does the Mexican heat powder cool one off or heat one up? I hope it is heating as I can put it to good use. It was a wonderful package, my dear, and I am so grateful.

And please don't be mad at me for opening them now. We move so often that there simply isn't any place to carry packages. I shall try and save one or two items for Christmas day if possible, but I simply could not resist opening the packages that have come so far. It is sort of like a birthday box coming the day after Dec. 13th.

Today I had a note from Betty Drury saying that Fred was all right and a prisoner of war in Germany. You know that he was my predecessor before his capture when he was ambushed outside Metz. So please write her a note as I gather that she is quite depressed.

I flew over my sector in a plane today and truly the country is beautiful. It was a bright sunny day for a change, although awfully cold. I got a good look at the Siegfried Line, dragon's teeth, trenches, pill-boxes, anti-tank ditches, etc. and it certainly looks imposing. Especially when you consider that there is a river in front of it in some parts, and part of it is situated on a steep hill. When we get through that, we are really in pay-dirt. The 90th Division is knocking off one or two of those giant concrete forts a day in very vicious fighting.

Good night, my love.
Jimmy

NOTE: *We were just on the eve of the great German counter-offensive of the Battle of the Bulge and we had no inkling whatsoever, at least as far as I was informed, that it was coming.*

16 Dec., 1944

My Dearest One,

The weather has been clear and cold and I have been out a great deal, stirring around, looking over my forward positions. I have also been up in a plane a few times, casing the joint as it were. We have been making a study of enemy fortifications and have a good part of them spotted. The Germans are great diggers and they put all the population to digging. There are more trenches than any army could possibly occupy and some of them are dug in the craziest of places.

I had a visitor at the C.P., Mac McClellan. He is here visiting me for a couple of days as an observer. His unit has not been in action as yet, so he is finding out how to fight the war. I've had a lot of fun showing my old troop commander how it is done, and he really laps it up. It is almost funny how people who have never been in action want to get shot at, and also what outrageous lies they will believe. It really is a shame, but they are so eager for deeds of valor that it is hard to disappoint them.

I am mighty glad I am not back under his thumb as he hasn't changed a bit and I feel for his outfit. It has been good to see him though and we have been talking horses and the old days at Myer. He went up to Luxembourg and promised to bring us back a barrel of beer. That town is quite an amazing place as they also have apple pies and ice cream, or so we hear.

We are a bit on edge now as the Jerries seem to be putting on a big counter-offensive, a last desperate effort, apparently. It hasn't hit as yet in our sector, but we are ready. I think everyone welcomes it as perhaps the showdown battle of the war. In other words, if we can really bust this one wide open, it might mean the end sooner than anyone would dare hope for. We know we are going to win, it is just a question of time. So if the Jerries are willing to gamble it all on one throw of the dice, I think we are too. It is all very exciting and I am and shall be very busy so my letters may thin out until things quiet down a bit.

This letter is very disconnected as I have had many interruptions and tomorrow promises to be a busy day.

Your loving husband,
Jimmy

NOTE: When the Battle of the Bulge started, we had on our left and across the Moselle, the 4th Infantry Division. Then we stretched from the Moselle over to the Saar just inside the border of Germany and then on our right and to the south was the 90th Division, fighting its way into the Siegfried Line around Saarlouis. We were about 30 miles from the heavy fighting at Echternach north of us, which was the nearest point of the big German attack. We could hear the cannonading quite clearly that morning and at our regular liaison meeting at about 7:30, the liaison officer from the 4th Division came in and said that they had quite a little fight going on at Echternach, but that Gen. Barton could handle it. Consequently, at that point, we weren't too concerned. At the 5:00 pm liaison meeting, the same liaison officer came back in and said, "Suffering God, we're throwing in the bakers and the cooks and we're fighting for our lives, and our infantry battalion in Echternach is cut off". That changed our whole view of the battle immediately. At that point, I called Jimmy Curtis, the G-2 at XX Corps and asked him what he knew about the battle. Since the 4th Division was not in our Corps but in the Corps north of us, he didn't apparently know anything. And nobody had alerted him yet that this great battle was on. I told him he better find out pretty quick because there was really hell to pay up north of us. Then about 11:00 that same night (the 16th), Curtis called me and said that he had word that the 11th Panzer Division was going to hit us right on the nose the first thing in the morning. I then asked him what help he was going to send up for us and he said they didn't have any and he wasn't going to send any help. My comment was that he better get that Corps Headquarters mobile because we couldn't hold the 11th Panzer Division at all. As a matter of fact, I didn't relay this to my squadron commanders as I knew it would scare them to death. Fortunately, the report was totally false and we were not attacked.

20 Dec., 1944

My Dearest One,

These last few days have been rather trying for us all. I know the papers are full of the big German attack and by the time this reaches you, it will be over or hopefully so...a rather comforting thought. We all hope we can really smash this one and it will certainly hurry things up if we can. It does illustrate what a fool's paradise everyone lived in for a while. However, the combat troops realized there was plenty of fighting ahead as early as the middle of September. But I read an issue of Time dated 20 Oct. just yesterday and it predicted the end of the war by Thanksgiving. What a laugh. What we need is sunshine. Pray that we get clear air for three days in a row and that will be all we really need. The weather has been beastly, just about freezing with low clouds all day long and impossible for our Air Force to work.

We are not in any heavy fighting as yet. It didn't hit here. But of course, we are all standing by ready for anything, so my next letter may be from another place. There are lots of troop movements all the time.

I sent a small package yesterday with a present for you given to me by Count de Mitry for you. The Countess got it in Paris. I shall be glad when all this meanness is over and we are together once again. Sometimes the prospect seems endless.

Your Jimmy

NOTE: I learned some months later that Gen. von Rundstedt had actually ordered the 11th Panzer Division to attack down through the Saar/Moselle triangle and that our intelligence service had picked up these orders by radio intercept. However, we learned that Hitler had counter- manded the order and didn't want the shoulders of the Bulge enlarged as did von Rundstedt. I have always been very grateful to Hitler for that magnificent command decision.

22 Dec., 1944 (Friday)

My Dearest One,

I am enclosing George Patton's prayer as I think it is a real classic. We roared with laughter as it reminds me of the way the father in "Life with Father" prayed for what he wanted. George wants the Lord to restrain these immoderate rains, like we all do, but I can see him shaking his fist at the Heavens and roaring it out.

It will be hard to find the children so changed as you write. It is impossible for them not to be, Jody so much bigger and smarter, with pigtails and book-learning and Jamie wasn't even walking when I left, just crawling about and laughing. I gather that he is still a happy child and not serious as Jody was as a tyke. I hope to be home to play with them very soon.

My sector has been very quiet these last few days. But the fighting has been terrific nearby as I know you have read in the papers. Tonight is clear and cold. It's almost never clear in the daytime and we can hear the sounds of many guns in the distance and see the flashes on the horizon. We are indeed lucky to be where we are, at least so far. The reports have been very alarming and everyone has been terribly on edge, ready for it and expecting it to spread down this way. But today marks the turning point, I believe, and the news should start getting good soon. I think it marks the climax of the war and I have complete faith in a great victory. It will be bitter indeed if this is not so. And I refuse to think of it. I can see all of you hanging on the radio and pray that you are not worrying about me too much. It's needless to be worrying anytime because you really can't know when I am in danger.

Not much of a Christmas to look forward to, but again, much to be thankful for to the Good Lord in all His kindness.

Jimmy

NOTE: *The 10th Armored Division had departed from our rear area (they were our backup reserve) and moved up to the Battle of the Bulge. We were reinforced with engineers and artillery and did some shifting around so that the main roads south from Saarburg were heavily protected. We also shifted artillery and were assigned additional tank destroyers. While I say in my letter that it was very quiet in my sector, we were shelled very heavily during this period and there were indications, as I mentioned earlier, of an attack down through our sector which happily never materialized.*

23 Dec., 1944

Dearest One,

Today we moved the C.P. to a more comfortable location (the town is Sierck) and it is a great relief to get out of that manure-ville and the cow that slept in the room next to me. She would start to moo about 6:30 as I guess her udders hurt and she wanted to be milked. We are now in sort of a big, beat-up apartment house that had been shelled quite a bit earlier in the game. But by shopping around, everyone is settled in an intact room. I have a nice bed and cold running water that works, really quite a luxury in these parts. Also, there are a couple of intact johnnies, unheard of luxuries. It's just too good to last. Another luxury that you all don't appreciate is electric lights. We never have them and continually work in the dark or by candle, flashlight or Coleman lantern. I've forgotten what it is like to see streetlights when driving a car at night with the lights on.

Another point that has become a matter of keen interest to us all is food. You don't know how I moan when you included a menu of the party you were giving awhile back. Your mention of such things as pie and hot biscuits, positively made me drool. We did have a great treat the other day. We actually had some ice cream. We furnished the ingredients and a firm in Luxembourg made it for us. We also have lengthy discussions on the merits of various American beers — all absolutely unobtainable. But once in awhile, we get some of the local beer, but it is poor stuff.

We will have a white Christmas as it snowed last night and today the weather is freezing and crystal clear. It really was a relief and none of us minded the cold as it was so bracing and beautiful. Also, I guess the Lord is answering George Patton's prayer as our airplanes were out in force and things look much better for a change. All I now hope is that we get to stay on our present job in this location and keep out of that nearby melee.

Your devoted husband,
Jimmy

NOTE: —We had assembled a lot of men, although we were in the line, from the 3rd and 43rd Squadrons and the engineers, to hear a talk by Gen. Walker who was going to come up and speak to us. Before he arrived, we got strafed by 6 or 8 P-47s bearing American markings. The attack lasted fifteen minutes and we lost 26 men, 3 seriously wounded. Also, we had some trucks burn up and other vehicles damaged. At first, we thought the attack was made by Germans flying Allied planes. But higher headquarters reported that inexperienced American pilots were responsible and had mistaken the river lines. When Gen. Walker arrived a little bit after this attack, he was visibly shaken when shown where he was going to stand to talk to the troops. In fact, if he had been there, it probably would have killed him. He decided not to talk and that assembling these men was dangerous. We agreed, so he got in his jeep and left.

26 Dec. 1944

My Adorable Wife,

I haven't written for three days. My life has been helter-skelter busy doing things. But all day Christmas and the day before, I followed you through your day, at the candlelight church service, trimming the tree, filling the stockings, perhaps attending the Caballeros party, the kids' excitement, Christmas gifts, squeals over gifts and colored paper all over the room, the excited breakfast and making the rounds all day. Damn, but I wanted to be there. This miserable war!

I got another package from you the day before Christmas and also one from Mother. I saved them and opened them on Christmas day. Thanks, my dear, for the cigars, coffee, socks, hankies and soap. It was really the wrappings that I loved — the little personal touches of just your own.

I spent most of Christmas day inspecting the front-line troops and they did amazingly well. The adaptability of the American soldier is a never-ending source of amazement to me.

There are many Christmas trees in the river-town billets and even in the gun positions, all decorated in great style. The German ornaments are the same as ours and we looted a lot of them. Sentries and patrols and gun crews were rotated so that everyone got turkey and some even had baked pies and cakes in their little rear area. At one place, they had an orchestra with instruments, picked up around the town. At every position I had to sample the menus, so that when it came time for our turkey at my own headquarters, I had little or no room. We had the cranberry sauce Mabie sent with our turkey.

The day was crystal clear, snow on everything, and it is still cold. It really is a beautiful sight as this country can be on such days. My headquarters had service beside one of those wayside crosses out in the open. It really seemed truly devout and with meaning, and my prayers were for you and the little ones. We sang a few Christmas carols and wished that we were home. Then we all came inside and had several drinks and tried to be happy, but it was mighty hard going.

I am well and in no particular danger, as this unit has had an easy job at present as compared to what a lot of other troops are going through north of us. We are doing okay and the big picture is beginning to look good. We are really fighting the elements here more than the enemy. Christmas is a hard time to be away from you.

Your adoring husband,
Jimmy

NOTE: Almost by mutual-agreement, there was practically no firing on our front all day Christmas and Christmas night, although there certainly was no fraternization either.

29 Dec., 1944

Dearest One,

I had a wonderful bath in a tub full of luscious hot water. You can't appreciate the luxury of it until you have been without one for three weeks. It was a very strange bath, though, and I will always remember it as it was in an absolute front-line town. It is one of the oddities of war, as part of the wall of the house was blown out and patched up with canvas. A chilling breeze raced through the bathroom but the tub and old-fashioned water heater had been untouched by the shell-fire. I bathed and soaked, courtesy of Lt. Cartwright, almost submerged to keep out of the chill, then leapt out and raced into my long underwear while the shells, mostly friendly, were zipping overhead. It was really unbelievable to think of the whole crazy performance, but I do feel good from it.

The enemy air has stepped up a lot in the past few days, as I suppose has been noted by the papers. We have had two very exciting attacks with bombs dropping and guns popping all over the place. I say exciting, but it really scared the hell out of me. I have decided that there are all sorts of men braver than I am or at least more foolhardy. One attack turned out to be by a couple of American glamor boys, as happened last week, who had gotten slightly lost and we shot one down. He was actually a Major and it was fortunate he had hurt no one, nor was he hurt. The funny part of it was that he thought he was quite a hero and that he had dealt the Germans all sorts of damage. When they shoot at us, we shoot at them and no one pays any attention to the markings on the planes, nor apparently do they note the markings on our vehicles. This war has suddenly gone crazy and Jerries are seen under every bush as there are many rumors of spies, Germans in uniforms and flying planes with our markings. It is literally worth your life to wear anything non-GI or not to know the password.

I've had no mail from you in ten days, only a pitiful letter from Frank Oliver's widow, written way back in August and on the way ever since. I do regret his death.

I love you completely, my dear.

Your Jimmy

NOTE: On this date, I had one of the most frightening experiences I had in the whole war. I was inspecting our front line positions and they are frequently a mile or two miles apart, generally in little villages or clumps of woods, and there was a main road that ran along our positions. I decided when I reached the far flank of the 3rd Squadron, foolishly as it later seems, to go and visit the adjoining strongpoint held by the 90th. Division.

I wasn't worried because we had run up and down this road when the 3rd Squadron had held that strong-point for some weeks. As we neared the 90th Division position, they called a general alert, swung all their guns on us, brought us to a screeching halt and made us stick our hands up. A Sgt. who was half out of his mind, almost frothing at the mouth, dirty, unkempt and obviously frightened, thought that we were some of the Skorzany German troops in American uniforms. He just couldn't believe that a full Col. would be running around the front lines like this and he was certain that I was a German spy. While the other people held their guns on Sabu and Icekant, this guy put his rifle about 6' from my breast-bone, took off the safety and was absolutely ready to shoot me right on the spot. I really thought he was going to shoot me dead, right then. I begged him not to shoot me. I begged him — almost got down on my knees; and I had my hands over my head and I said, "For God's sake, take me to one of your officers." He finally consented. He got the three of us out of the jeep, marched us with our hands up about a quarter of a mile down into the village where the Command Post of the Company was located. The Captain checked me out and realized that I was Col. Polk of the 3rd Cavalry; but it took some talking even with him. In the meantime, the Sgt. was standing around there, still just dying to shoot me. He thought he had really captured a German spy. From beginning to end, it taught me a lesson. I didn't go driving into any other strange outfit that didn't know me from then on throughout the rest of the war. It was as near to death as I ever came.

The last day of December, we had four splendid Platoon Sgts. promoted to 2nd Lt. I had reached the point that we simply would not accept replacement Lts. as they were not well trained and they were not competent to lead in combat. These marvelous Platoon Sgts. were as good as any officers we had. During the month of December, we had one officer and nine enlisted men killed. We had two officers and about thirty enlisted men badly wounded. We figured that we killed about 150 enemy, wounded about 68 and captured 42 German prisoners.

31 Dec., 1944
HAPPY BIRTHDAY

My Adorable Old Lady,

Today you passed another milestone and are one year older. Could it be 32? Good Heavens! It doesn't seem possible. But I do wish I had been there to see you open your presents and to get out on the big New Year's party with you and all the friends. I wonder where you are tonight, who you are out celebrating with, or if you are, and just what kind of New Year's celebration the old place is having.

My Task Force, my Army as it were, fluctuates with the job I have to do. If it is very tough, I get other troops to help me. Right now, Johnny Thimer is supporting me with his artillery. But it varies from week to week almost. If I have a big front or there are a lot of German tanks or some bridges get blown up, then my Corps gives me the type of troop to help me out. I do hope you understand that it is very difficult to write about with all the censorship regulations in mind.

Things are going all right. At present, we have a sharp short fight once in a while when the Jerries venture out from behind his pillboxes or when we send in a patrol to catch him. I have my C.P. still in an old apartment house, sort of on the edge of a small German town. The operations room itself has a stove, and we have blacked out the windows and rigged some lights so we are quite comfortable. However, going to bed and getting up is really a problem. The room is freezing cold. I cast off my clothes and leap into my sleeping bag. In the morning, it takes me ten minutes to get up my courage to jump out into that blast.

Darling, I certainly am living a bachelor and Spartan existence without any hint of feminine touch about it. I really won't know how to act in a home. My language and table manners will be terrible, I will never take a bath, never turn on the light, run out into the yard when I have to answer nature's call, make unkind remarks about the food and all the other terrible habits that I have fallen into. But I expect you will soon train me again. Bless you.

Your Jimmy

3 Jan., 1945

My Dearest One,

I haven't written for about three days as I have been very busy in the daytime and worn out at night. Today was sort of a tough day, but I think things have simmered down for a few days and I certainly hope so. It is always so hard to order people into something tough and then wait for the returns to come in. It is most unnerving as generally, you sit and take a lot of artillery fire and the first people you see are the wounded coming back. They tell horrible tales. You sort of sweat it out and wonder if the plans are correct. Sometimes they are and sometimes they aren't. But they never quite work out the way you expect. We weren't too successful today, but very few soldiers got hurt so I guess all in all, it could be considered a success.

We are all very much excited about the new leave policy, 7 days leave for all combat officers, not counting travel time. You are allowed to go anywhere in France except Paris, which is special, or to England to get rested up. It is still in the rumor stages, but the rumor is most persistent. Where do you think I should go? Certainly not to England as I have seen enough of that place. I believe the south of France sounds best, somewhere on the Riviera where I can lie on the sand in the sunshine and just relax. It certainly would be nice to be away from all responsibility for a while, as I guess it wears on me — and, to see a little sunshine. There is also leave for four men a month out of the whole outfit to spend a month in the good old U.S.A., to be given to the most deserving who have been wounded and decorated. At that rate, such a leave would get everyone home in thirty years, so I have no hope on that score. I guess we'll just have to win this damn war to get home. This is a short note, but I am weary.

Your devoted husband,
Jimmy

NOTE: *We were under orders to get prisoners and it was very difficult. We lost people trying to get in to the Siegfried Line since the Germans had pretty much stopped patrolling into our area. Therefore, we thought up a new scheme and decided that we would pull a deception in the hopes of luring a German patrol out of their pill-boxes to come investigate. What we did was move a fair number of vehicles in this little town with a number of smoke pots and a lot of hay and then early one morning (2 Jan.) we set the town on fire. All the vehicles went storming out of there making a lot of noise. The trap was to have the Germans come and see what the hell was going on and then we could ambush them. That night, sure enough, about 10:00 p.m., a patrol of about 20 German soldiers came out of a pill-box and felt their way through their own wire and mines and came down toward the village. The leading members of the patrol actually entered the village when our troops cut down on them. The fight was led by Captain Tom Downing, later a Congressman from Norfolk and a marvellous officer, but the outcome was horrible. Our soldiers killed 19 Germans and one got away so we didn't have one single live prisoner. I was furious that after all the exercise and planning, we had failed to get one single live prisoner, but rather killed them all. I gave Tom Downing one of the worst dressings down that anybody ever had in the Army.*

7 Jan., 1945

My Dearest One,

My life has been a mad world of activity these last few days. I have been out late and on the road two nights in succession, but at last I am back in my C.P. again. However, it is a beehive of activity with people popping in and out, orders going out and all kinds of turmoil. I haven't written in some four days, I think, so am seizing this moment to dash this off.

I made a trip up to Luxembourg city yesterday on business and got a couple of hours off. I had supper with Paul Harkins. He has gotten fat from his desk job and looks much older, but the same old Paul, cigarette holder and all.

Luxembourg has suffered very little from the war. I bought a pie and had some real ice cream. The people are quite well dressed and the city most attractive. How I loved the drive up in the brilliant sunshine across the lovely country, all covered with about 6" of snow. It was a treat. I did so wish you were there to enjoy it with me. Whenever I see the luxury hotels and nice beds and food on china plates, it has the effect of making me terribly homesick. My life is generally so masculine and rough that it is not a constant reminder of home.

Isn't it tragic about little Simmy's death. Mother wrote me. A real tragedy with Sim over here. I haven't seen him. All my love, my precious. I am well and warm.

Your own,
Jimmy

NOTE: —*All the activity was occasioned by the fact that we just had the 3rd Squadron relieved by the 94th Division and there was a lot of shifting around to do. It put us down on the Saar River completely up against the Siegfried Line from the switch-line where we had been. The 94th Division was brand new in the theatre, very naive and very nervous, and kind of hard to get along with. I was called up to Luxembourg city by Gen. Patton as the 3rd Army Headquarters had moved up there during the Battle of the Bulge. I didn't know what he wanted me for and, of course, was quite nervous about it and thought that maybe we were going to get in some tough action. I was ushered into his office immediately by Paul Harkins — and when I got there Gen. Patton first greeted me warmly and then showed me a picture of a horse that his wife, Beatrice, had just bought. I admired the horse, but I knew that he hadn't called me up there for that. Finally, he handed me a blue-covered typewritten manuscript of a court martial, a Lt. Col. Matlack of the 6th Cavalry had been court-martialled by Joe Ficket for carrying around a French or German nurse in one of his ambulances and living with her. Gen. Patton said to me, "Read it and then I'll talk to you." It was quite voluminous and I read the whole thing while he was running the war. It was very interesting to sit in his office and hear him cracking out orders and all that kind of thing. The sentence was that Col. Matlack be dismissed from the Army. Finally, I finished and put it down and after awhile Gen. Patton said to me, "I can do three things. I can approve it; I can mitigate the sentence to some extent, or I can give him a letter of reprimand and another combat job. Is he a good fighting man?" I said. "Yes sir, he is, I know him well." Gen. Patton asked, "Could he command an infantry battalion?". I answered, "Yes sir, he could". He said, "What do you recommend?". I said, "I recommend you give him a reprimand and give him an infantry battalion." He called in Paul Harkins and said, "Who is short of infantry battalion commanders?" Col. Harkins said, "The 80th Division." Gen. Patton said, "All right, write me out a reprimand to Col. Matlack and give him a battalion in the 80th Division." He said, "Thank you very much, Jimmy, I do appreciate your advice. That's all." How wonderful that he would take time out for this personal affair in the midst of a great battle.*

9 Jan., 1945

My Adorable One,

Today, we are set up in a new "manure-ville" and are busy getting comfortable. We always seem to have the C.P. in the best house of the village, which always seems to be the bar room of the local inn, and we always have the message center behind the bar. We have yet to find one with any beer on tap or any wine in the cellars, as the C.P. is always a couple of miles behind the combat troops. And between the retreating Germans and the advancing Americans, one side or the other always does a very thorough job on the tap room.

Today, another package arrived with that grand all-wool sweater. Tell Mabie I love it. It is so light and warm. Also the things you sent me, the vitamin pills and all. I am fixed up with the necessities of life and am particularly glad to get the toothbrush as good ones are hard to come by. We promptly ate the Nabiscos and will save the candy and chocolate wafers for tomorrow. And you are so good the way you put in the list of contents, and obey all the regulations to the letter... a very good Army wife, I should say.

Our front has been very quiet the last few days; still in the same general location watching that same old river and the Siegfried Line. The big attack up north seems to be contained, and from all accounts they are knocking over a lot of Huns. It really looked bad for a while but I know we gave them better than we got. The weather has been bitterly cold and there is about 8" of snow on the ground, all very pretty but not so nice to move in. My unit certainly is lucky on that one, not to get involved in that knock-down, drag-out affair up North.

There really isn't any point in your worrying about what you read in the papers because you really can't tell if I'm in it or not. But my Cavalry Group isn't usually required to attack as Infantry. So when you read about some terrific attack, I have usually finished my part of the show and am off protecting a flank or something like that.

Your devoted husband,
Jimmy

NOTE: My new C.P. location at this time was in a town called Wald-wisse.

12 Jan. 1945

Joey My Love,

Life has been a bit monotonous these last few days. Not much other than a few front-line inspections, and as the unit is getting along well and is doing as it is told, I don't have much to buck them up about. The weather continues to be bitter cold and I'm out most of the day, visiting about and bundled up to the ears, as an open jeep is an awfully cold ride.

We have a civilian barber in our present location which is a great luxury. He gave me a fine haircut and shampoo the other day, my first in many days. He is also an expert shaver. As he speaks not only French, but German also, I don't enjoy it when he wields that big razor. However, it is a joy to get a real civilian shave, as well.

The people around here are funny. A man yesterday said he was an American because he was French when the French Army was here, German when the German Army was here and now the American Army is here. That just about sums up their attitude. They don't really care who wins or what country they are in, just so they are left alone. They are a dirty and uncouth race around here, not to be compared to the real French peasants of western and central France.

This winter does seem eternal. I miss you.

Your loving husband,
Jimmy

NOTE: We are in the part of France called Lorraine. It has been successively German and French. It was French until the war of 1871, then German until World War I, then French, and captured by the Germans in World War II and occupied for some 4-5 years. Now that we have overrun it, it's back to being French again. The people almost always speak both French and German and as mentioned in the letter are willing to change sides and help whichever country seems to be winning. They have no patriotism, as far as we can tell, for either France or Germany.

13 Jan. 1945

Dearest Punkin,

Today has been quiet and the weather a good deal better, the sun out for a while and not the bitter cold we have been having lately. I visited around a bit and while at my Corps Headquarters, ran into Jimmy Curtis, who will take over a staff job as G-2 there. It was good to see him and nice to know that he will be working there as he's a smart officer. Can you imagine, he is still a Lt. Col., but will have a Colonel's job so that he can now start sweating out his three months in the job before his promotion. And he has been overseas for thirty months, imagine that. He and I had a real old bull session about El Paso and it did my heart good.

George Ruhlen, I discovered from the Stars and Stripes, is somewhere near me, so I shall try to get over and see him and show him that picture of our two good wives on a toot in Juarez. Maybe we can put on a toot ourselves, as our liquor ration has at last been straightened out. Each officer is allowed a quart of scotch and a pint of gin a month, both good English brands for the cost of about $2.50 for the works — quite a bargain and strictly medicine in this cold weather. I usually drink a toast to you at bedtime and dive into the old sleeping bag about 10:30 each night.

Some of this may seem screwy, but I cannot change my $300.00/ month allotment without an awful lot of trouble. Therefore, I've left the allotment alone ($300.00 goes to Junction City Bank in our joint account) and also have the government send a check for $75.00 to you direct each month. Then the money orders I send are just what I save from my left-over pay, about $90.00/month is what I keep and I can hardly spend a cent of it, so I have fun sending it with money orders to either you or Mother.

The clothing stores, GI, now have those Eisenhower jackets in stock, so I plan to get one and get it all fixed up fancy with the eagles you are sending and so forth. The trouble is I have no place I can wear it, but I want to have it handy for V-Day; but it really looks like there is no great hurry to get it.

Darling, I know you are saving some money, but please do whatever you want to with the stuff I send home. Please plan a trip in the spring or something. I'm going to send Mother some money to take her spring trip so ask her to visit you. I want her to see the kids. All my love and God bless you.

Your old man,
Col. J. H. Polk -not too old!

16 Jan., 1945

My Darling Wife,

Life continues rather dull and monotonous. We are playing a sort
of waiting game on this front while the Huns are getting a good chewing with the pocket being reduced. However, it seems that whenever
things are calm, then something happens.

We are really marvelously provided for by the American Army,
particularly now that the supply situation is all cleared up. Front line
troops are furnished everything that troops in the rear have to buy
from the Post Exchanges. And the last week or so, we have been getting good candy, chewing gum, all the cigarettes we can smoke, all
clothing necessary except a few items that you have supplied to me. I
mentioned earlier our liquor ration, and lately the troops have been
seeing new movies while back in local reserve positions just about a
mile or so behind the lines. Our really big trouble is carrying all the
stuff we have now, not so much in my type of unit as in the infantry.
Also, everyone has latched on to some type of stove to carry along,
about the most important part of the baggage, really. But we are now
halfway through the winter and by the time this gets to you, it ought
to be almost done and we can really get going and end this thing. The
recent news of the Russian winter offensive sounds awful good, so I
guess everyone will soon resume the attack and get on with it.

We were strafed by some German planes yesterday. They made
one very fast pass at us and then they were gone with some American
fighters chasing them, and nobody got hurt very much. To get a report
ready, I called a conference there on the spot. It is amazing all the
conflicting stories one gets after the excitement is over. The number
of planes reported was all the way from one to six, the markings were
reported as German, U.S., British and one man even said it looked
like Japanese to him. The final payoff was when one man said he knew
it was a four-engine bomber. What a rat race. The trouble is that the
gunners are too busy shooting and everyone else is too busy diving
into a cellar or ditch to get a decent look. What mad confusion the
Germans must have when our planes work them over in swarms. I'm
glad we have air superiority or our lives would indeed be miserable.

Your devoted husband,
Jimmy

18 Jan., 1945

Dearest One,

There has been a bit of excitement today, but now things are cooling down and I can take a deep breath and relax. The whole command is outraged at the mail situation. None of us has received a letter in ages. It seems to pertain throughout the whole Corps. My last letter from you was written the 21st of December, almost a month ago. And it was a short letter. I understand even the generals are cussing out the mailman.

I'm getting pretty optimistic over the overall picture. There are bad situations here and there in the line, but all indications are that the enemy is getting pretty desperate. Also the Russian attack seems to be going great guns. Therefore, I wouldn't be surprised to see this thing crack wide open all of a sudden. Maybe as soon as three weeks or as long as three months, but when it finally goes, it will go fast.

I doubt that there will be a general armistice; that is, on a certain day, Germany will surrender. I think instead, that enemy battalions or regiments will surrender piecemeal and that we will make a mad dash to the Rhine and beyond.

Right now, we are in the process of making up a pool on the date of the Allied entry into Berlin. The conditions are: 1) entry fee, $10, 2) winner take all the proceeds or sent to the next of kin, 3) name hour, day and year to avoid ties, 4) jackpot will not be carried forward to the Group Command Post to avoid capture, 5) in the event the C.P. is attacked, the Adjutant must secure the funds. All of this was interrupted by a terrific argument on the above, everyone expressing his ideas. We then argued about the Pacific and whether or not we would ship over there by the way of the United States or go the short way. Terrific moans at this point so the argument was abandoned. However, the consensus of opinion is that we are better troops for the Army of Occupation than for the jungle warfare they have in the Pacific. Everyone figures out something, but it seems impossible to tell. However, when I think of Jimmy Curtis being over here 2 years and something already, it makes me shiver. As you once said, I'm missing the best years of my wife!

Your loving husband,
Jimmy

20 Jan., 1945

Dearest One,

I'm afraid we shall have to move our command post to another town shortly. The artillery has just placed a battery of huge guns about two blocks behind us. They don't shoot very often, but when they do, it sounds like the crack of doom. The battery moved in yesterday and fired its first shot about midnight, and it woke us all up in shock as a complete surprise to everyone.

My first reaction when I hear a shell is to duck. After the second shot or so, I know it will be far or near, friendly or enemy, and I can act calmly and go on about my business. However, these awful things behind us go off at irregular intervals, shake the windows, rattle the slate off the roof and we collectively jump out of our skins from surprise. I guess we shall have to move nearer to the front line for the sake of our nerves. But I am in a house with nice thick walls and a good roof, so will try a day or so more to get used to it. Tell Helen Thimer that I am pretty sore at Johnny about this business and it may mean the end of our friendship, particularly if it pulls in some counter-battery fire on top of us.

I'm only joking, of course, and he is one of my few friends. Tell his wife that I think him a fine soldier, full of helpful suggestions and always ready to do all he can for me and mine. He runs a damn fine outfit and that, from me, is real credit. I wish we could stay together all the rest of the war.

Your devoted husband,
Jimmy

22 Jan., 1945

Dearest One,

Today I had a visitor in the person of George Ruhlen. He came bearing gifts in the nature of a quart of champagne and also a picture of you and Mim standing beside a large bottle of whiskey in Juarez. We had quite a time talking over old times. Tom Burshell's Bar, Juarez, Fort Bliss and the rest. He stayed about an hour and ate lunch with us. His unit is in reserve near our old chateau resting up after Bastogne. However, his artillery battalion had practically no losses in that ruckus which is really remarkable. He is very lucky.

I spent most of the afternoon out in an artillery observation post, looking at the Siegfried Line from a good safe dugout and directing fire. I went through a pine forest on the way up there that was beautiful — all the trees laid out in a regular pattern, all the underbrush cleared away and a carpet of snow underneath. It was quite dark and majestic under those huge trees and a bit spooky too. Most of the forests over here are very carefully tended but have been allowed to go to pot a bit in the last few years — just enough to make it in between a forest and a beautiful garden.

The war picture looks pretty good now. Germans kicked out of the Bulge, Russians beating the hell out of them, and I presume we will soon again attack. Who knows? Maybe my luck will hold and someone will want me on his staff in Washington. You never know. Maybe someday I will suddenly call you up and say, "Meet me at the airport tomorrow morning." What would you do? Well there is no such luck, I fear. I love you always.

Your devoted,
Jimmy

25 Jan., 1945

Dearest One,

Today has been bitter cold, around zero most of the day and it is now about 3°F. We also had more snow yesterday so the real winter is upon us. However, I think it is better than that cold rain we had in the late fall.

I have been out at night quite a bit lately. Last night we had a half moon and with the snow it was almost as light as day. One could see more than a mile. I was down in some of these deserted river towns from which all the German citizens have been evacuated and there are just a few soldiers on alert with strong battle positions here and there ready for action. It was beautiful but ghostly and weird, particularly when a goat stepped out of a barn and scared the wits out of us. The snow covers up a lot of the ruin and desolation of this part of the country. And it has really been wrecked, believe me.

My guess on the end of the war, or rather the allies' entry into Berlin, was 4 May. But if the Russians keep on going like they have, I will lose my money. However, that is one ten-dollar bet that I won't mind losing in the slightest. Someone else can have the proceeds gladly if they beat that date.

We had an officer leave for the States yesterday. He was over-aged and grey, being a captain at 41 years old, and he was losing his nerve and not very much good to us. So I gave him ten dollars to call you up from Chicago when he gets there. He will probably be greeted as a hero. He can tell you all about me. I hope the call doesn't scare the wits out of you as I didn't think of that angle of it when I gave it to him.

Oh damn this war. I am so full of longing for you with memories of our life together and companionship and love and happiness. I am tired of this life of drabness, unending responsibility, of few friendships and few moments of real, happiness. I wish it were over, over right now, done with and finished so that we could both make plans for our future life. But at least the end is in sight. God grant us a speedy victory and a speedy return to those we love.

Your Jimmy

27 Jan., 1945

My Adorable Wife,

I got two letters last night which made me very happy. Poor little Jody and her teeth. It must be an absolute horror to her to have to go to the dentist all the time. Tell her I think she is a fine, brave girl to have all that work done and that she will have pretty teeth just like her ma when she grows up.

My front has been quite quiet. No one is getting hurt very much, lots of additional troops in my command to strengthen us up and the weather is almost too bitter for active operations. We have some snow almost daily, the sky is generally overcast during the day and clear at night — I don't understand why. The temperature stays below freezing all the time. I believe we're at the height of the winter weather and it should take a turn for the better soon.

I was out last night again, in the moonlight, for some hours and it was beautiful. Almost a full moon with brilliant deep snow and the sky clear. There are times like this when it would be such fun to have you here with me to go tramping through the snow in the moonlight. I hate not being able to share some of these experiences with you and also hate not being able to share some of yours. I definitely want to bring you over here later and show you this part of Lorraine that I have come to know so well. We could stay at the Hotel Metropol in Thionville. And I will show you the very windows we used to shoot from and go visit Count de Mitry and the chateau where we stayed so long. Also, I would like to bring you to this little town where we are now. It would be fun to buy a drink at the bar in this guest house that is now our operations desk. You can show me Paris and I will show you rural France as I know it and we'll have a lot of fun. I do adore you.

Your Jimmy

NOTE: *On one of these moonlight expeditions around my command, I almost got killed. I was going to visit the 3rd Squadron Headquarters and had radioed ahead for them to expect me in their particular little village. When I drove into the command C.P., I started raising hell with Col. Marshall*

Wallach because no one had challenged me. What kind of security was it when I could drive into the town and no one would even challenge me? It turned out later that they had a new replacement 2nd Lt. in an armored car watching the particular road that I came in on and he was frozen with terror. He had pointed his cannon at me coming down the road in my jeep and had his foot on the foot trigger (it is a very common trigger and goes off very easily), but fortunately, didn't fire. This is just the kind of luck you need but I became pretty careful about going into people's outposts after this.

30 Jan., 1945

Dearest Punkin,

I have just finished laboring with a batch of efficiency reports and it is an awful chore. Today has been quiet and I have been out most of the day inspecting some of my units in reserve and also looking over the German civilians entrusted to my tender care. Some of the families turned out to be lousy, so we had a great dusting today and I have itched ever since. I know I have those damn cooties just from being around those people; but still have hopes it is just my imagination. The Germans are very well behaved, though. They do exactly as we tell them; far better than when we were in France.

Tomorrow we have a big lottery to see who gets to go to Paris. The allotment is one officer and four enlisted men from my Group Headquarters and Headquarters troop. I really can't decide who will have the pleasure as all of these lads have done their very best for me. So a lottery is the answer.

It is all over now, thank Heaven, but it was really spooky during the early days of the Battle of the Bulge. One night a Corps Headquarters Intelligence man called me up and said, "Now I don't want to worry or upset you, I just want you to be prepared because the 11th Panzer Division is going to attack you at dawn. Well, goodnight, old boy." Man, what a night we put in waiting, getting ready for that one. Thank Heavens that that dumb joker was wrong. But the big point is that if you read that the 3rd Army is putting on an attack, don't fret. We are not generally the type of troops that attack and you should know it by this time. We are usually on the flanks.

Good night my sweet.

Your own man,
Jimmy

NOTE: *During the entire month of stabilized warfare in January, the Unit operated from forward positions within close proximity to the enemy fortified line. In the earlier part of the month, the fortified positions confronting the troops were the switch-line from Nehnig to the Saar River while later on the 3rd Squadron was relieved from that area and our troops were faced by the Siegfried Line on the east bank of the Saar River. Due to severe weather, attempts were always made to prepare strong-points in the various villages while covering the intervening ground with strong combat patrol and dug-in emplacements. Units in these emplacements were frequently rotated to prevent so-called weather casualties. The Saar Valley position was particularly suited to this type of defense as there were numerous stone villages along the western bank of the River, all affording considerable protection from enemy fire and offering excellent concealed observation posts. We took very few casualties during this period. Summarizing the mission of the Group throughout the month, we had a defensive mission of containing the enemy, generally known as an economy-in-force role.*

Feb. 1, 1945

My Dearest One,

Today we are having a big thaw. It is like spring outside; our first mild weather since before Christmas. The roads are simply a sea of mud. Snow still covers the hills and all of the buildings in our town are leaking like sieves from the holes in the roof. It is only temporary though, but at least we are over the hump of the winter.

We had the lottery to see who wins the leave to Paris and guess what — the Chaplain won. We were all glad as he is a very fine and Godly man and has done a great deal of good for all of us. But it was very comical, first because he hated to take it and also because of all the remarks passed about virtue being its own reward, and about the Good Lord being on his side. Also, my driver Icekant gets to go and he is so excited that his usefulness has simply ceased. But he can tell me about it on his return, and I know it will be a spicy tale as he is a wild kid, full of energy and courage and the type that will enjoy the place.

Our sector continues to be quiet. I take occasional visitors up to the front lines and they are always amazed that it is so quiet. It is a deadly sort of quiet, occasionally broken by a burst of machine gun fire or some shells going overhead. But not nearly the action you are led to expect from the movies. The visitors seem to expect a roar of shooting that goes on continually, houses burning, the earth shaking and so forth which, of course, is true in some of the big attacks, but not true at all in our present sector. We have occasional raids and patrols and so does the enemy. But generally, it is just a few snipers in some outposts or artillery observers that are on alert that do any shooting. Things are much more tense at night than in daylight.

As a matter of fact, we are all getting kind of stale with this type of life. It has settled into a routine. The days seem to drag past. There is such a burning spirit of "let's get this thing over with" that we envy the Russians being on the move again and wish that we were also. If we could just shake out of this area into the open, past all these dreadful pill-boxes, and get going again, I think we all would be happy. But now it looks like a slow process of grinding away until the sudden crack-up comes and we are rolling again. We have a big map of Germany and follow the Russian moves with avid interest.

Goodnight, my dear, I love you.

Your devoted,
Jimmy

4 Feb. 1945 (9:00pm)

My Adorable One,

As I keep telling you, it isn't too bad now in our front line. No one could stand getting shot at all day long for more than a day and I haven't been shot at in weeks. I've heard a lot of shooting, of course, but most of it is ours; practically all, in fact, and I think the enemy is running low on ammunition. I get about one man hit every day now, and only about one in ten fatal.

You would be truly amazed if I could take you with me on an inspection trip of the front tomorrow. We would ride up about all the way in a jeep, get out and walk about 500 yards through a wood; probably be stopped by a sentry who would tell me where the platoon commander was. We would walk up to his observation post, perhaps crawl the last fifty feet into a comfortable dugout where we would be invited to have some coffee. There would be three or four men around, some sleeping, a telephone, some grenades and rifles and one man watching through a small hole with field glasses. I would probably talk to him awhile and he would probably tell me that he hadn't seen a German in two hours. We could look then, through his glasses down a steep slope to a smallish river. On the other side, if you look carefully, you could see trenches and perhaps ten pill-boxes, but not a sign of life, not a sound. It is the quiet of it that will always amaze you. If there is some movement on the other side, a man will pick up the phone and call for artillery fire. Soon you hear the guns banging behind you, then the shells moan overhead and then you see them strike. The enemy troop all dive into their holes and the quiet settles down again. Together, we will talk about mail, food, health, patrols and enemy activity. Everyone looks surprisingly well and clear-eyed. They will talk with great pride of their accomplishments. They all want to know the big picture, how we are doing. There are, of course, moments of great excitement and tension, but they have been very few of late, and we are thankful for that.

Your devoted husband,
Jimmy

5 Feb. 1945

My Dearest One,

Just a note as I am dead tired tonight — not much doing, but I have been out tramping around the hills in the rain and am ready for bed. Yes, I did get the sheep-skin vest and wrote Charles thanking him for it. It is truly great. Also got the fur-lined gloves that you sent. They are beautiful and useful, but my mittens arrived also today so I will save yours for best and muck around in the others. Yours are much too handsome for such rough work.

Life is dull although the war news is good. The Philippine campaign is thrilling and to think that Jack, Tom and Harry are all there. At last my birthplace, Batangas, Philippine Islands. is back in American hands. I do worry about them all and I'm glad I'm in this theatre, cold weather and all because at least our end is in sight; but I can't say that for theirs, as yet.

I had a soldier make a Valentine for Jody and will mail it V-Mail the same time as this one, so tell me which one gets there first.

Your devoted husband,
Jimmy

NOTE: The references were to my brother Jack Polk who was commanding a battalion in the 1st Cavalry Division, my brother Tommy Polk who was on the Battleship Colorado and my brother-in-law Harry Wilson who was in the 11th Airborne Division commanding a battalion.

7 Feb., 1945

My Dearest Beloved,

Today finally brought your two letters written Christmas Eve and Christmas day and it took some six weeks on the road. It really makes me sort of mad that so many of your friends and my friends are still in El Paso going about their daily lives the same as usual. Why haven't they been drafted? How will this work-or-fight law affect them? Will they be drafted now, because we are getting replacements that are older and not nearly as physically fit as they used to be? Oh, it's just that I envy them and the existence they lead.

It's now 2:00 a.m. and I have been out on the river as we had a little exciting activity. I am waiting for the final reports to come in so my ear is sort of cocked to the telephone to know how bad it was. Those damn mines. It makes me so bitter to see good, fine, brave men mangled. It makes me bitter as hell and mad as hell at this fiendish enemy we fight. I want to smash them all, wipe them off the face of the earth and show them no mercy.

We can see the end of it far better than you can probably, at home, but we can't tell when it will be. We really have their backs to the wall now. But the weather, terrain and fortifications are on their side. It takes blood to root them out. God knows how long it will take.

Your devoted husband
Jimmy

NOTE: Letters of 10 and 13 Feb. are omitted as being of little substance and full of complaints about the weather and food.

17 Feb., 1945

My Dearest One,

I missed a few days in writing to you, not on account of any great activity on our front, but more because for the last three nights, I have been out inspecting some places that cannot be visited in the daytime. The weather has been lovely for three days, sunshine, spring temperatures, so I took advantage of it to stir around and see a lot of things I hadn't been able to see before. All the snow is gone and the grass is actually turning green and buds are on some of the trees. I know it is premature, but it makes us feel good anyway.

I leave tomorrow for my 72 hours in London, drive back part of the way and fly back the rest so it's quite a short trip. Both Johnny Thimer and Howie Snyder had planned to go but had to drop out today. I am sweating out a phone call saying that mine is cancelled also. But so far, it's on. I will try to phone you from London if it is at all possible. But I doubt if they will let me do it. However, it's worth trying just to hear your voice again.

I have no nice clothes, so will go out looking very combatish. They tell me you get better service anyway, and I will purchase a battle jacket over there. I shall have breakfast in bed for three days, take six baths and generally relax.

I know that your immediate thought is that I will be naughty or something. But you need have no fears about that. I'm your husband to have and to hold from this day forth till death do us part. I swore that vow 8+ years ago and I still mean it now as much as I ever did then. So I hope to see a few shows, sight-see some, shop some and just plain feel free of this responsibility that is always hanging around my neck.

Your devoted husband,
Jimmy

NOTE: Orders are finally out for XX Corps to go on the attack. The plan is that the 94th Infantry Division will smash through the switch-line of the Siegfried Line followed by the 10th Armored, followed by the 3rd Cav. We are to reduce the Saar-Moselle triangle. The reason I was still permitted to go was, I believe, that they thought at Corps that it would take 4-5 days for the 94th Division to breach the switch-line and therefore, it was okay for me to go to London. But since Snyder was the G-3, he was responsible for planning and that is why he was cancelled. Thimer, I would guess, was in the same thing. Also, I think Gen. Walker, after a couple of visits, was beginning to think that I was getting a case of battle fatigue and needed a rest badly. He was probably right.

25 Feb., 1945

My Dearest One,

Got back late last night to my old C.P. and found the situation generally unchanged and everyone doing fine. As a matter of fact, they are doing so well, I rather had my feelings hurt. But it all boils down to the fact that I have a fine staff and a static situation; it has gotten to be almost routine or so I tell myself.

It really was a good trip and did me a world of good. The travelling was a bit annoying as I had to sit around airports a lot. I had to leave my hotel this morning at 5:30 and the plane didn't get off until 9:00. No breakfast, and coffee for lunch; so when I finally got back to Corps Headquarters about 7:30 last night, I stopped and ate a tremendous meal of beans and Vienna sausage and even that tasted good with the appetite I had worked up by that time. Arrived back at my C.P. about 11:00 pm after a long blackout drive and was really ready for the bunk. We travelled in C-47 planes which are also used to haul paratroopers, supplies and casualties. So it isn't luxurious. You sit in an aluminum bucket seat with no back to it. It took three different rides to get back. We flew right over Paris again and the weather was lovely; so all in all the expedition was quite successful. I feel refreshed and raring to go, and it looks like things ought to start moving mighty quick.

This thing must be over soon, it simply must be. It can't go on forever. And I have had enough to satisfy my professional pride and far more than enough for having been away from you. And all this loose talk of troops shipping direct to CBI Theatre chills my blood. And it chills me even more to see some people who have been overseas for three years. It almost makes you want to get wounded, just to get a trip back to the States. The trouble is, the wound has to be dreadful or they just patch you up and send you back into the line. It isn't much of a solution!

Your adoring husband,
Jimmy

NOTE: *While I was away, the 94th Division broke through the switch-line at Butzdorf and raced north to capture Saarburg. The 10th Armored Division followed them through so that the entire Saar-Moselle triangle was captured in fairly short order. The 3rd Cavalry was ordered through the break following the 10th Armored Division and we established the line* on the Saar River from the bend of the river where we were earlier, but this time through the fortifications and north to Saarburg. That included the towns of Serrig and Hamm on the east side of the river and again, we were facing a new branch of the Siegfried Line. On the 27th of February, the C.P. was moved to Saarburg and it looked like the war was beginning to break open.

28 Feb., 1945 (Germany)

Dearest One,

I saw Hank Cherry today for the first time in a good while. He was in a rush as they were moving up to get going (he's a Battalion Commander in the 10th Armored Division), but he did have time to show me a pin-up that his wife Suzanne had sent him. It was a scream, really. He said he was afraid to show it to anybody but her old friends. It was a portrait of her from about the waist up, some sort of a drape over her and very, very decolletage. Of course, she doesn't suffer in that line.

We are on the move again and it doesn't look too hard as the bastards are definitely disorganized. I do hope and pray that we can get them on the run and rush them all the way to the Rhine. The unit next to mine has broken the Siegfried Line but the country is very rugged and difficult for my type of outfit to work in. If we can just keep them on the move enough to prevent them from mining the hell out of every road and path and house, it will be a nice war. Artillery fire and small arms fire we expect, and even if hit, one has a chance to recover. But if these mines don't kill you, they invariably take off a foot or something and very often they take off your private something. I shudder to think of such a catastrophe ever happening to me.

While I was away in London, my driver Icekant had the bantam all fixed up, overhauled and painted and greased. And painted in flowing script right on the middle of the armor plate windshield is "Joey" in big white letters. You don't know what a thrill it gave me and what a big kick my driver got out of my pleasure. I shall get a picture of it and send it to you. I guess every man in the regiment will know your first name rather shortly.

If anything should happen to me, don't expect letters from anyone in the outfit for quite a long time, as they are not allowed to write until you have been officially notified. When you are notified, then you write Phil Davidson and he can then answer you. Not that I expect anything, but a shell isn't too choosy about who it hits. However, soon we can stop sweating it out. It really looks like the beginning of the end this time. I know the above will scare the daylights out of you, but don't let it because I know I will come home and get out of it okay.

Your loving husband,
Jimmy

NOTE: With the capture of the Saar-Moselle triangle, we had really punished the German army on our front. We took all kinds of prisoners, inflicted lots of casualties on them and the roads were littered with burned-out tanks, trucks and things that men throw away in a precipitous retreat. It was a splendid campaign. We were on the flanks of it and fortunately not in the hard fighting.

1 Mar., 1945

My Adorable One,

Just a note to let you know that all is quiet at present. I might have alarmed you with my letter of yesterday needlessly. We are, of course, busy making plans but it looks as if 3rd Army is to play a rather secondary role for a while and let us sit. Of course, one never knows; the big plans never get down as far as little old me.

The weather has been grand these last few days, spring-like and we are all full of zip and most everyone has a slight case of sniffles. I landed in England one year ago today which now entitles me to wear two gold bars on my left sleeve, one for each six months in the theatre. I would just as soon not get any more. Two is enough to classify me as a veteran and I am now ready to return to the bosom of my family. I am tired tonight so would bid you good night.

Bless you, my love.

Your Jimmy

NOTE: The 10th Armored had captured Trier and breached the Siegfried Line totally, so we were well into Germany proper and past their fortifications. We were ordered to take up a position on the north flank of XX Corps with the Moselle River on our left and extending down a long ridge with the Ruwer River on our front, just west of Trier. XII Corps was on our north just across the river and the 94th Division was on our south on the same high ridge that we occupied.

4 Mar., 1945

Dearest One,

We are on the move again. Been here a day and expect to jump off again tomorrow. We have been doing good work and it hasn't cost us much, in a large part due to the boldness and courage of my two Squadron Commanders. They are really good. I had my first experience with rockets today, called "screaming memies" by the troops and they are well named. You can hear them coming a long way off which is fine as you have plenty of time to duck into a ditch. I am getting to be one of the fastest men into a ditch that you have ever seen. I came up covered with mud. What a sight. I shall never get clean.

We are well into Germany proper now and the civilians are plenty hostile; not like those along the border where we were so long. They have really suffered though, here, and will continue to suffer. Their big towns are simply flattened. Such devastation is really indescribable and has to be seen to be believed. And Hitler's Siegfried Line is kaput, gone. We are through it and it really wasn't too hard — not nearly as hard as everyone had imagined it would be. It would have been terrible, but most of them have lost the will to fight and "don't want to die for a lost cause" as they put it. I wish they all felt that way. But of course, there are enough of those fanatics to still make it mighty tough.

We move slowly, then faster and faster and faster. We ought to be all up to the Rhine all the way along the river in a couple of weeks. Then a short rest and bingo, in we go to end it. Don't worry about me. The whole Group looks after my safety like I was a helpless child. They will get me back to you.

Much, much love.

Your adoring,
Jimmy

NOTE: *The scheme of defense along the Ruwer was simple and effective; taking maximum advantage of the draw through which the river ran in front of us, the squadrons had placed their troops in strong points and in towns on all the high terrain west of the river and on the commanding ground overlooking it. Observation was excellent and all enemy movements during the day could be easily ascertained. At night, strong-points of armored cars and automatic weapons employing a perimeter defense were utilized, coordinated with well-placed listening posts, much like the old Indian-fighting army. The tank companies were in mobile positions back near the two Squadron Command Posts on a good road net, alert to launch a mounted attack on 30 minutes notice to repel any enemy penetrations of our thinly-held positions, on approximately an 8 mile front.*

There were some 2,500 civilians in our front line towns which caused a great problem. We had to go through them and determine from pay-books and identification who were German soldiers on leave and who were in the Volksturm and remove them to P.W. cages. It was the cause of considerable concern to us and was deeply resented by the German people.

10 Mar., 1945

Dearest One,

It's late and I'm dog tired. We have moved again and will be moving again soon. I have a magnificent outfit which has done wonders and the best is yet to come from the way this thing is cracking wide open. We ought to make the papers as the 3rd Cavalry soon. (We had been forbidden any publicity as the Germans thought we were a Division.)

I am well and dirty and seldom in any danger as I have such a big command that I just don't have any time to get really well forward. So all I can do is to direct the show from the C.P. and hope to fight a smart war.

And we are fighting a smart war and I pray to continue that way. My letters will be sporadic and few. But don't worry. Just read the newspapers and picture me directing my show.

There is one river that will live in my memory forever. We can't ever seem to get away from the damn thing; that twisting, turning, steep-sided, stinking Moselle that continues to haunt me.

I need your prayers and guidance in the next few days to be worthy of my great command.

Your adoring husband,
Jimmy

NOTE: On the 6th of March, early in the morning, a troop of the 3rd Squadron with some troops on each side, was hit by a very heavy attack from an Infantry Battalion of the 256th Infantry Division. They came in hard and we counter-attacked hard with our two tank companies. To quote from the After Action Report, the following is verbatim: "The Group Headquarters located on the high ground in Kernscheid overlooking the town of Irsch maintained a perfect observation post for the spot recording of the progress of battle. From this position, the Group staff could determine the location of any machine guns, could watch Col. Marshall Wallach as he led his tanks through Irsch to attack the enemy's rear, while a troop in Gutweiler lay down heavy machine gun fire. The arrival of tanks just about broke up the party. By 8:30, the attack had ceased and almost all the enemy were either killed or captured. 100 P.W. were taken as a result of this operation while we suffered only minor casualties. Unfortunately, 25 of the P.W.'s were killed in Korlingen by their own artillery fire while they were grouped *together awaiting interrogation. We also had two guards wounded. South of us, the second S.S. Mountain Division was attacking the 94th Division, primarily the nearest Battalion on our flank."*

At the end of this attack, we captured the attack order of the Division and had a great compliment paid to us. The G-2 (Intelligence Officer) of the Division said, "The 3rd Cavalry will counter-attack with one Company of tanks in 30 minutes or less and a second Company, ten minutes later. In addition, the counter-attack to support the 94th Division's Battalion to the south of us will not occur until late afternoon." Actually, the 94th Division did not counter-attack until the next morning, some 25 hours after they were hit, while we counter-attacked in 25 minutes.

15 Mar., 1945

Dearest One,

I've lost all sense of time and don't know when I wrote you last. We are in the midst of a difficult operation, but the heat is really on the Jerries now. However, my command has had, it seems, the whole damn German army, almost, compressed into our front. And our moving is really rough. Hard work all the way. I have a huge force at present and I am given a lot of help.

Saw Paul Harkins yesterday, and he said we soon would be taken out of the line for a good rest. I don't know how soon this "soon" means, but we are ready.

A German officer was interrogated in a 3rd Army prisoner's cage and said, "3rd Army is the only Army feared by the Germans. But when the 90th Division, the 4th Armored Division or the 3rd Cavalry is on our front, we really catch hell. Those three outfits of the 3rd Army never let us have any rest. When they appear on the front, we know we are going to get it." Wasn't that a nice compliment from those bastards?

I've lost some weight but feel well, particularly as I know we can rest soon. The Rhine River will sure look good to these brown eyes because I am sure tired of that Moselle.

I can now tell you that all during January and early February we held a stretch along the Saar River from Orscholtz to Dillingen and I have looked at Murzig many times. We really blasted the hell out of it. My C.P. was at Waldwisse just inside France by half a mile, but as all my troops were in Germany, so I used to date my letters from Germany. After all, I was in Germany at least twelve hours a day.

I will send you the addresses of my staff wives soon. Phil Davidson got the Purple Heart yesterday from a nick in the face from a rocket that hit near him. He was lucky, thank God.

I have work to do so must end this. When it reaches you, I hope I will be in reserve.

Love you,
Jimmy

NOTE: On the 9th of March, we had the 16th Cavalry Group attached to us. They were new to the theater and the idea was that under my command, we could break them to combat conditions easily. They were commanded by a Col. Buzbee who was a bird. I told him that he had to establish a certain reputation for bravery in order to direct his command. The first attack they mounted was with their tank company leading and he rode on the deck of the leading tank, firing a 50-caliber machine gun. I told him later I thought he was somewhat overdoing it.

As kind of a joke, we put out an operations order, labeling ourselves as the 316th Provisional Cavalry Brigade, Armored. The funny thing was that both Corps and Army picked it up without us ever having any sort of order that we were such a Brigade. Without any sort of authorization, it started appearing on operations maps all around the theatre. We thought we might get in trouble for being so presumptuous, but everyone bought it.

19 Mar., 1945

My Dearest One,

We are on the move again. The Hun has collapsed on our front and we have had fun and the Air Corps has had a picnic shooting them up. We ought to buck up to the Rhine in a few days and get our promised rest then.

The Krauts will not forget this war for a long time to come. I have seen Murzig, Saarburg and Trier and the destruction is devastating. The whole Saar Valley is a complete deserted ruin. Trier is about as big as El Paso and is deserted and the whole center of town is flattened; stores, churches, hotels, railroad yards, all a heap of rubble. It will really take years to restore and the German people really know what war is now. How they must hate us. Yet strangely enough, they don't show much hate. They are simply glad that it is over for them when we capture a town. They even warn us of where mines and booby-traps are; an incomprehensible people. They fight like hell and yet when captured they will tell you anything, even when it means death to some of their comrades. I loathe them all.

This old war is really cracking up. We will be on the run for a few days and then I hope I can write you that I have spit in the Rhine River. Tonight I am bone tired and must be up and about early so I will hasten to bed with thoughts of you and to a speedy end to the war. I hope this hectic life doesn't make an old man of me.

Your Jimmy

NOTE: On the 10th, 11th and 12th of March we had some very severe fighting and on the 12th, we had four men killed, 23 wounded and 3 missing in action and lost 4 M-18 Tank Destroyer guns, knocked out by direct fire from an 88mm battery. The 88mm were anti-aircraft, high-velocity guns, but they could fire level fire and were the best anti-tank weapons the Germans had.

We did have one very strange event. We had one light tank on an operation that was separated from the rest of the platoon, and lost its orientation and drove straight in to the German lines. We called it a one tank jamboree because they by-passed an enemy mine-field and got in the rear area behind the 88 mm battery and well behind the German front lines. Everybody took a shot at them. The tank eventually returned after about an hour of wandering around, finally got themselves straightened out and came back *to our lines. They had at least 200 bullet splashes on the tank, the storage sponson boxes and the fenders were all cut to pieces, the antenna was shot off and they were out of ammunition and just about out of fuel but curiously enough not one of the crew was hurt. It was really a miracle. And we were sure that this tank, roaming around behind the German lines like a bull in a China shop, must have caused real consternation in their ranks.*

On the 14th, in addition to advancing and quite heavy fighting, we lost one whole tank platoon which blundered into another battery of 88mm high velocity guns and all 20 of the crew were either killed or wounded. However, we flanked this battery and either captured or killed all the members of it so we think we got even.

One soldier, Private Wysocki of the 3ʳᵈ Squadron, a member of the crew of one of the knocked-out tanks, was captured, treated by a German medic and was a prisoner for about three days. He spoke fluent Polish and started arguing with some of the soldiers of Polish descent, telling them that they ought to surrender. After three days, he talked them into it and marched back into our lines with 16 German prisoners that he had captured without a weapon.

23 Mar., 1945

My Precious One,

Today, we pulled back into reserve for a short rest after the great drive of the 3rd Army through what is known as the Palatinate. We are clean up to the Rhine now and it is a great feeling. I haven't seen the river yet because when we were near it, there was such a great crush of American Troops converging from every direction that we had to pull back and get off the roads.

It has been an amazing week. The second time I have seen the German army in utter rout, crushed, destroyed or captured. The sights, sound and smell of it I want so terribly to tell you about in great detail; of the bitter, bitter fighting we were in around Trier, the mass of artillery and rockets that were thrown at us, the mines, the pill-boxes and stench of death. Then the first signs of their alarm because other troops had maneuvered to their rear, and the week of beautiful weather, how our air caught them in movement on the roads, how the breakthrough started, how we poured through until there were no more mines or artillery, only broken remnants that we caught and slashed and ripped.

We are really deep in Germany now and into their very heart. This town is full of German civilians. The big towns are terribly smashed and even the small towns have been hit. Germany is paying for this war and we are glad. We, the Headquarters Troop and my staff, are installed in a nice row of six houses, all modern. We just marched up and gave the people fifteen minutes to leave. We didn't give a damn where they went, just get out. So I have a nice bed and tomorrow I shall have a hot bath, my first since London. It's just as if we drove up and ordered a block of your home on Federal Street evacuated in fifteen minutes. Does it seem cruel? Damn them all, they have it coming.

If you could see the released slave labor we have freed, Russians, Poles, Czechs, Italians, French, all completely starved and tattered. All taking to the highways to get home after five bitter years. They are pitiful and terrible creatures, men, women and children as released slaves. And the Germans fear them and well they might, for they will steal and kill to eat, rape to satisfy their lust. We are collecting them to feed them and get them to the Red Cross, but as yet they are like wild things, like animals released from pens who will not be penned again. They beg any kind of food and wolf it down; and while the German people are fat, the God damned swines, they will really pay for this one. And the funny part is that when we first capture a town, they put out white flags and then wave and line the streets like it was a parade. It is a beautiful country, but filled with wreckage and human sorrow. The crime of this slave labor stinks up the whole world, this crime that the Germans can never pay enough for. You cannot conceive of how they have made beasts of people.

The Saar Valley is a deserted ruins where the Siegfried Line was, and it is wonderful to get away from the stink of it into fresh air and the absence of mines. We are now through the great mine belt. I give this war a couple of more months and then finis. It cannot last as they are fighting with remnants only, but still fighting, the fools. With every day they fight, more of this Germany is going to be smashed flat by our artillery and air. I am bitter, bitter, bitter, tonight.

Love, Jimmy

NOTE: We pulled off the road in a little town called Isenberg, about halfway between Kaiserslautern and Mainz, and remained there for two days as the traffic was so heavy with the 3rd and 7th Army all converging in the center of the Palatinate.

24 Mar., 1945

Dearest One,

I was really worked up last night when I wrote to you. I hope it didn't upset you. I probably tell you things that frighten and upset you, and make you think what a great change has come over me. Such is really not the case, but you are really my only confidante. So sometimes, I have to let off steam to you. This slave labor thing really has me going.

Today has been simply beautiful, a clear spring day with lots of sunshine and we have all loafed and soaked it up. I had a haircut, a wonderful bath, cut my nails and did all the things I have been needing to do like sorting my clothes, cleaning my gun and airing my bedding. Now I am all rejuvenated and full of hell.

All the townsfolk had to turn in their guns and knives so I am sending four of the Hitler Jugend knives home; one for Tom, Chuck, Bubba and Jamie. When he grows up to it, he will like it. We also liberated a very expensive air gun, sort of a glorified BB gun that shoots little lead pellets. So we have been sniping out the window, shooting unsuspecting brother officers in the tail as they pass our window. Everyone is like a kid on a holiday today. The Group Headquarters has been challenged to a baseball game tomorrow by the officers of one of the Squadrons. It is grand for everyone to get a release from nervous tension after the exciting two weeks we have just been through and to get all cleaned and our equipment in readiness again. I think we have a chance at a real rest this time. I certainly hope so. But even this short spell has worked wonders with everyone.

Does this letter sound happy, because I am happy today, bubbling with life and supremely confident of the war's end in a few months. The situation is really good on all fronts.

Your devoted husband,
Jimmy

27 Mar., 1945

My Darling One,

We have moved up twice since I wrote you last. Very hectic moves over crowded roads, passing all sorts of destroyed German equipment all along the way and truckloads of Jerries going to the rear as prisoners. We are waiting for room on the bridges to get over the Rhine and get going. It isn't like those lean days of last summer and fall, when there were few troops and short rations and damn little ammunition. Now there is everything; all sorts of troops crowding each other to get over the bridges, all sorts of everything crowding up. The spirit of everyone is a joy to behold. We know we are in the greatest Army in the world, the "Mighty 3rd", that nothing can stop us. My group is really a cocky bunch now, raring to get at them, and George Patton has really fought a masterful campaign these last two weeks.

We are in a nice clean German village, not beaten up at all and with plenty of chickens so that we have eggs for breakfast. Two women cried violently when we threw them out of this house. They couldn't understand why we did it when, as they said, "The Germans never harmed anyone". Then they claimed they were Polish. Well, we have a Polish 1st Sgt., and when they couldn't speak a word of Polish, out they went. Boy, I hate them all.

We will soon be back in active operations.

All my love,
Jimmy

28 Mar., 1945

Dearest One,

Last night when I was writing you, the phone rang and I was ordered to report to Corps immediately for orders. It meant a long blackout drive there and back, frantic planning, alerting troops and issuing orders. Then the changes started coming in. We have had three changes in orders so far and are still sitting in the same place awaiting something else. It is rather nerve-racking to be kept like a monkey on a hot stove, but this old war is busting so wide open that plans and orders can't keep up with the troops. We are ready to go in any direction and do anything, but I am afraid even to go out for a walk for fear we will get some sudden orders again. It has been fine for the troops though. We have been really more or less out of enemy contact for almost a week. I have lost all track of time and only know the day and date when I write you.

The weather continues to be fine. It is really a great break as it has appeared before the spring rains and before the Rhine swells from the melting snows of the Alps. The country is very pretty and very peaceful where we are. There is a ball game going on outside and all is serene.

I got your letter written at Gallup last night; had no idea that Charles' interests in business had grown to such proportions. I shall watch my ammunitions boxes to see if he has made any of them. Ask him how they are marked. Is it the Leavell Box Company?

All my love.
Your devoted husband,
Jimmy

3 April, 1945

Dearest One,

I can't tell you yet of our more recent operations, sufficient to say that we have come a long way from where we crossed the Rhine. We all thought the war was over when bang, we ran into it again. We are out in the open once more. However, there are just enough fanatics and just enough tanks and 88's left that every so often, the Jerries are able to lay a trap or make a stand and some more Americans get hurt. We have been pretty lucky so far, however. We shall have to fight to the bitter end and occupy the whole of Germany and kill every fanatic in the country before it will be over. It is true that they can't last much longer, but elements of them are going to go down fighting to the bitter end, the miserable fools.

The terrible thing to us is, how rich a country Germany is with her marvelous factories, beautiful fields and woods, her natural resources. And they really have everything when compared to France — yet they covet the world. All of the villages are well kept, no slums, no shanty towns, reasonably good plumbing, good climate — yet they can't be satisfied. Her towns are far better than those in England. It makes me want to burn every town to the ground. I really want to shell every place before it is occupied just to bring home to the women and children what a hell Germany has inflicted upon the world, so that the children will grow up with a horror of war.

The weather has been fine, occasional rain but no one minds it, and the average temperature is around 50°. We are on C- and K-rations again because we are moving so fast. I just detest the stuff. It is all I can do to eat it. However, we have been getting fresh eggs for breakfast, or at least the mess sergeant has them for me.

Please send me mayonnaise, chili sauce, hot sauce, Worcestershire sauce, celery salt, chili powder and such, also sardines and shrimp. Very expensive list, but it does buck up the unvarying menu. Boy, what I wouldn't give for a dinner of steak, green salad and ice cream. Love you always.

Your man,
Jimmy

(No one knows what day of the week it is!)

My Dearly Beloved,

Today finds us assembled in reserve behind the lines after some very eventful days. There is a big change in our direction of attack. We had to turn and are now ready to start off in another direction tomorrow. But at least tonight we have friendly troops all around us. Orders are issued for our initial march tomorrow, our passage through the Infantry and then our break-out into the open. So I am tense and nervous, hoping my orders have been wise, well understood and that all will be well.

We are settled in a little German village and as usual, have moved out the occupants. We are completely out of touch with the outside world, no Stars And Stripes, no mail, no messages, no nothing. I don't have time to listen to the radio. We have been on a diet of C-rations for days. But it is surprising how happy and full of vim everyone is — for we know that time is short and it will all be over. No one has been hurt in the outfit for several days and we have done the Germans a lot of damage. Also, we captured a complete warehouse full of Rhine wine and we had to go tearing on so we didn't get any of it. I did get a beautiful Luger pistol off a German Colonel and shall hang onto it, but I'm not allowed to send it home as yet.

I feel sure you can almost tell our route by the progress of 3rd Army. Boy, it really is a wild life. We have covered so many miles, I am dizzy and tomorrow will mean at least 50 more. You would be amazed at how brown and healthy I am with it all. But it is a tight drawn, nervous life. I sometimes feel I am burning myself up. But it can't keep on forever.

I hope you get this. I found out today that a lot of our mail isn't getting back as the APO is 200 miles behind us. Oh my darling, my thoughts are all mixed up tonight, so I shall end this wild thing and get some sleep.

Bless you, my one and only.
Your Jimmy

NOTE: On the seven days between this and the previous letter, we were really on the go. The night of the 28th, we crossed the Rhine River in the vicinity of Mainz and Hochheim and assembled in the bridgehead of the 5th Infantry

*Division which had made an assault crossing several days before. At 10:00
a.m. we moved out through their bridgehead and into virgin territory. We
were all very nervous because we really didn't know what to expect, and the
thought of being on the east bank of the Rhine and going towards Frankfurt,
we had visions of much fighting in the streets and so forth. We were pleas-
antly surprised as there was no resistance whatsoever. No uniformed enemy
to fight, but many surrendering. All the villages had sheets hanging out the
windows, but the very few people just stuck in their houses. By nightfall,
we occupied the valley between Frankfurt and the Taunus Mountains and
my Command Post was at Bonames which I later got to know when I was
ADC of the 3rd Armored Division. At the close of the day, we met the 6th
Armored Division which had swept east of Frankfurt, thus isolating the city
which we by-passed. Following troops were to capture it.*

*On the 29th, more of the same. We moved about 50 miles to the northeast
and the center island of the autobahn was filled with prisoners marching to
our rear. There were so many we really couldn't count them. Also, hordes of
men in their striped clothing from their concentration and work camps acting like a bunch of crazies and we couldn't blame them. Without resistance,
we got up as far as Alsfeld and were overrunning all sorts of equipment and
manufacturing firms making aircraft engines, film and ammunition. We
also captured a Colonel who was Chief of Ordinance for Frankfurt who
stated that there was no real German Army left and that the war would end
shortly. He said that the Army was in a great state of confusion and most
organizations were composed of stragglers. He was evacuated to Corps and
then direct to 3rd Army, and it was believed that his statements were given
wide publicity by the allied press.*

*On the 31st, still moving up both sides of the autobahn toward Kassel, we
began to run into resistance. Lost several armored cars to anti-tank guns
and ran into numerous roadblocks set up and partially defended. So, we
were back in the fight again. We were bucking up towards the Fulda River
and were notified that the 4th Armored Division was fighting in Hershfeld
as were we in our advance. Our objective at this point was toward Bebra.
The Fulda River with its blown bridges, road-blocks defended by anti-tank
fire, tanks, SP guns and anti-tank barriers, formed a new and formidable
enemy main line of resistance. It was effective enough to halt the advance of
both the 4th Armored Division on our right and the 6th Armored Division
on our left as we were halted at Bebra.*

*During the last three days of March, the Group advanced approximately 150
miles while capturing and destroying numerous enemy items of equipment*

and capturing uncounted prisoners. The close of the month found us disposed west of the Fulda River, prepared to advance to the east and northeast, still deeper into the Third Reich.

The reference to our changing direction simply meant that when we got close to Kassel, we turned due east with XX Corps, four Divisions and the 3rd Cavalry Group advancing straight east toward Chemnitz. The Corps was in a box formation, the Armored Divisions leading, the Cavalry Squadrons on the flanks and the two Infantry Divisions cleaning up the rear.

8 April, 1945

My Dearest One,

Tonight I am seated at an immense and beautiful desk in a former German staff college building. In fact, it is the General's desk and I am having a glass of his excellent white Rhine wine and shall shortly sleep in his bed. His bedroom furniture is really beautiful. I wish you could see it — Napoleonic with beautiful red polished wood and golden fittings all over it. What a wonderful bunk to have and no one to share it with.

We are really going on a tour of rural Germany and everyone exclaims over and over about what a beautiful country it is. These people really had everything and it makes us furious. Also, today I got a beautiful pair of 8-power German officer's binoculars, very light, small and easy to carry and a beautiful instrument. I shall probably wind up giving it away as I do most anything else that comes my way.

A little officer named Dale Bowman, a supply officer in one of the squadrons, says he went to high school with you. Also, Pres Utterback, one of my Squadron Commanders, is from Brackettville and served a year at Bliss. Finally, Shirley Cook is a former enlisted man at Bliss — now a Major and a good one. Anyway, the four of us got to talking about getting together with our wives and giving Juarez the old whirl when we got back. It will really be a party with four veterans of the 3rd Cavalry reunited in Juarez. A woman would really learn more about the war on a night like that than in talking alone to her husband in ten years. Wouldn't that be fun.

We've had it pretty easy today and it doesn't look bad tomorrow. But you never can tell. These Krauts surrender in car-load lots and it is a picnic for a couple of days and then we run into a bunch of fanatics and all of a sudden, it's just a hell of a fight. Some of these crazy fools don't know the war is over and are still willing to give their all for the dear old fatherland. We have 120 more miles to go and will be into Czechoslovakia. Then where do we go? That is the question.

It's hateful not to share beautiful days like these today...hateful not be able to at least talk it over at the end of the day and drift off to sleep with you.

Your own,
Jimmy

NOTE: On the 10th of April, Bob Allen was reported missing and was alleged to have gone through my front lines. He was the Allen of the famous Pierson and Allen column of the Washington Post, widely syndicated and very highly respected and, at this time, the Assistant Chief of Staff G-2 of 3rd Army. Upon investigation, we found out that Lt. Col. Allen and a jeep with some others and a second jeepload of MP's following behind had indeed driven through my area without checking with anyone, and when last seen, had driven through an outpost. We asked the Sgt. if he had stopped them to warn them and he said, "No, should I have? Here's a Lt. Col. going through my position and we weren't contacted so I just assumed he knew what he was doing." This had happened before, people driving through our lines who weren't aware of the situation and weren't aware of how thin we were at times. Since there was no shooting going on, these inexperienced people didn't think they were in danger. Bob Allen was badly wounded, had half his arm amputated when he was recovered several weeks later, and I was mildly chastized.

11 April, 1945 (?)
(I really don't know)

My Beloved Woman,

Several days ago, we sent off our mail clerk with his bed roll and rations and told him not to come back until he found our APO (Army Post Office). The poor man came in triumphant this morning and how he found us I can never guess; but he had four letters from you and one from mother, the last written March 2 when we were crossing the Rhine. Seems a long time ago as we have come a long distance since then. We have been constantly on the move, really fighting U.S. traffic jams more than Germans. Everything is on the road moving up to a front that keeps moving also. Some days we are in front, some days we are all protecting a flank, and then we spend another day fighting traffic to get back up to the front again.

No one in my command has gotten hurt in about a week except for a few casualties from Nazi air. We are so close to their airfields and so far from our own that their air has become quite active. Recently, we get a couple of attacks a day.

It really is funny when it happens because first of all, everyone shoots like mad; also orders are that the columns keep moving, but about half jump off in a convenient ditch and half keep going, all shooting. So it is a perfect bedlam of noise and confusion. It is over in a flash and the people in the ditch look embarrassed and the people that kept going look superior, and amid much cursing and orders, calm is restored and we move on once again. What a rat race. The war really is over. But it's just that no one can agree to stop shooting.

General Marshall really chilled our blood about "high priority" troops rushing straight to the Pacific from this theatre. Now we are all busy wondering who has this "high priority". I do think a lot of service troops such as engineers and ordnances will have to go first, which will allow the combat troops to stop over in the U.S. Also, it does seem the Cavalry is well suited to the Army of Occupation here in Germany and for such things as riot duty. So we really don't know where we stand and have had not an inkling of official thought on the matter. Everyone is busy spreading stinko rumors and trying to convince the other fellow that he is the "high priority" they talk about. I know there will damn near be a riot if they put us on a boat for the Pacific. I have done enough gypsying around and sight-seeing to last me a good long while. I pray that it is over soon.

Your devoted husband,
Jimmy

NOTE: We had an unusual incident on April 15th. One of our platoons was in a small German village and had posted a guard for the night. Lt. Parker, who has been mentioned before, heard some noise outside, looked out the window and saw five Germans surrounding our armored car on sentry duty with the driver standing in the turret, his hands in the air. Lt. Parker calmly took up his rifle, shot four of them and the fifth one threw down his weapon and got away. The poor sentry had to be sent back to rest up as he was a nervous wreck after that experience.

13 April, 1945

Dearest One,

We are in a terrific rat race. It is really moving very fast now and I figure we'll be in another country in about two days. Yesterday, we captured over 800 prisoners and no one was hurt in our outfit to the best of my knowledge. One enemy battalion surrendered as a unit with their Colonel leading the parade. It really was a sight. And they even had their wagon trains with a few women perched on them, one, the wife of the Colonel who wanted to go along, like you do, my love. There was much weeping when we told her she couldn't go to the PW cage with her husband.

We just heard the news about Roosevelt's death and were stunned by it. I guess everyone has gotten away from the idea that he might die in office. Now we are all speculating about the new President. He has some awfully big shoes to fill.

I know I have lost weight, but then we all have, as our lives are so hectic and our rations are all canned stews. But it must end soon and then we can relax for a bit.

Much, much love,
Jimmy

NOTE: *The outfit that surrendered was the 5th Battalion, 88th Hungarian Training Regiment. And they were really glad that the war was over. They marched by in very military fashion and when they came by the Group Headquarters, saluted as would any good military organization.*

About this time, Col. Mehan, the G-1 of XX Corps, showed me a letter wherein Gen. Walker recommended that I be promoted to Brigadier General. I don't have the letter and always regretted that I never secured a copy because it was full of praise and flattering remarks. It was approved in a very nice endorsement by Gen. Patton and sent up to Gen. Bradley's Headquarters, who disapproved it by saying that I was too young. I never have been too fond of Gen. Bradley ever since then, as I would have been the youngest Brigadier in the American Army.

14 April, 1945 (Germany)

My Beloved One,

The last two days has seen us constantly on the move. We are now very close to Czechoslovakia and still no one gets hurt and we go ripping along. Most amazing things happen in these crazy pursuits. Some true happenings of the last two days are as follows:

1) We captured a Major General, complete with monacle who came out of his cellar and accosted one of our cooks and demanded to see an officer so he could properly surrender. He looked just like a comic-opera general and was disgusted with his command as they had all surrendered (this was B Troop of the 43rd in the town of Gera).

2) We were tearing down the autobahn which looks like the Pennsylvania Highway, and here was a bunch of Krauts trying to surrender. No one picked them up and everyone just motioned them to keep on walking to the rear. They looked very pitiful waving their white flags and all our outfit just ignoring them and ripping on past.

3) The German children line the roads and wave white hankerchiefs and cheer us on forward.

4) A Russian fighter plane circled over our bivouac. The pilot opened his canopy and leaned out and gave us a clenched fist salute.

5) The telephones even work in this town so someone tried to call Hitler and someone else called and asked for "Herr Commandant". We put on an interpreter and this guy said something must be done as the Italian prisoners of war from the concentration camp were looting the box-cars in the railroad yards to which the interpreter replied, "You lousy son of a bitch, you bother them, we'll kill you."

6) A most comical sight. A whole bunch of German civilians looting one of their own trucks that had broken down and the whole cargo consisted of green fireman's pants.

7) One of our outposts called on the radio and said that two Volkswagens doing 60 miles an hour and loaded with Germans had come by so fast that they didn't fire. So we rolled two tanks into the road and burned them up as they rounded a curve.

8) One of the 4th Armored tank columns was tearing down the road, met a German tank column going equally as fast in the other direction, and no one fired until about six tanks passed each other. Then all hell broke loose.

Really this war takes on the craziest proportions when everyone goes so fast. It's amazing so few get hurt. But the Jerries are so confused that we continue to surprise them in all sorts of funny situations. The S.S. are really the only ones who want to fight and all the others are dying to surrender and do so whenever they get the slightest chance.

We moved into a very nice house this evening with good beds, the electricity, water, telephone all work, and we got a few eggs from the back yard so I won't have to eat a can of corned beef hash for breakfast. I know you are excited by the news of how it is all going and I expect to be able to describe the Russian Army to you in anything from a day to a week depending on our orders and not on what the Hun can do to stop us. Must go to bed now as it has been a hard and exciting day. But in closing, I think I should say that I think your worries for my safety are about over and it should be finished when this reaches you. Now we can start sweating out getting my orders for home. I do adore you.

Your own,
Jimmy

NOTE: On this date, we captured the town of Gera and picked up a Lt. General with all his staff who was the commander in this section. Also, we overran a hospital with some 4,000 German wounded which we were required to protect. Lt. Gen. Niedhaldt said that his captors had treated him with the greatest respect and he had a very high regard for the 3rd Cavalry.

18 April, 1945 (Germany)

My Darling One,

In a letter from you yesterday, you sounded quite upset about the war. I do hope that you are not still feeling that way. Of course, the war is not over yet and will probably continue for several weeks or even a month. But it is not the war as we knew it. We have had practically no casualties lately, no artillery or rocket fire and very little of what could be called fighting. It is now a question of sweeping up all the remnants of the German Army that are scattered all about the countryside. They make stands at the important towns and the rest of it is usually blown bridges and clearing road-blocks and flushing them out of the woods. And they are more than glad to surrender. I am not in one tenth of the danger that I was last fall and last winter — really, that's the truth.

I have been asleep most of the day as we had a very long night march that wore everyone out. However, I just had a hot bath in a fine bathroom and feel all fresh and healthy now. The trouble is that our baggage hasn't caught up with us so I had to put my dirty clothes back on, but I still feel fine anyway.

Boy, have we ever covered the miles in the last thirty days. I can now tell you a little more of our progress earlier in the drive. After we crossed the Rhine, we jumped out in front of the Corps and drove north-east, just above Frankfurt, then turned almost north and moved about 70 more miles in two days until we hit the Fulda River at Bebra and Rotenburg. There, we got in quite a scrap but finally captured both towns. Then we circled around Kassel from south to west to north while the Infantry took the town from the south. We really had one good day there and played hell with them when they were trying to get out of the town. It was fun. And no one ever got scratched, just one of those things that you read about.

I would say that Kassel is a town about the size of Fort Worth and it is really flattened. The whole center of town is simply one big brick pile of rubble, far worse than Trier and I thought that was bad. I am allowed to tell you things that are more than two weeks old so you can sort of trace my course on a map and should know where I have been, even if it is about a month late.

I had a very interesting talk with a war correspondent yesterday. He said 3rd Army is the only interesting Army and that one can tell the difference even in the rear areas. He said in other armies, all the ration and ammunition trucks obey the speed limit, while in 3rd Army, the ammo trucks go 60 miles an hour. He says everyone in 3rd Army is usually vague about the situation and who is on his right or left, but that everyone is loaded down with ammunition and in a hell of a hurry. When he sees a column coming down the road at 50 miles per hour, doughboys sticking out all over the truck, sitting on the barrels of their artillery, riding in captured German trucks, whooping and generally lost but in a hell of a hurry to get forward, then he knows he is back in good old 3rd Army. We also have a custom, which I have already written you about, of throwing the civilians out of their houses on George's orders, that the other armies don't practice. It is a very proud Army and it would break our hearts to ever get shifted over to some other one.

I am out of cigars. Also, please don't forget to send me some of those sauces. These C-rations are really getting hard to bear.

Your adoring husband,
Jimmy

21 April, 1945

Dearest One,

Tonight is one of those tense nights again when I have issued all my orders and conferred with all the commanders and done all I can at present to insure that the jump-off is well prepared. Now it is in the prayer stage where I pray that I have been a smart Commander and done the right thing. My main concern is that the forward units fight a smart and clever war and avail themselves of all the support and help that I can get to them.

Funny thing about Easter. We were in such a horrible rat race on the road all day that I didn't realize what day it was until that very night. I pray I can start enjoying such holidays sometime in the not too distant future. Sometimes it seems endless the way these fanatical crazies keep on going. Will they ever quit or will we have to kill or capture every one of them. Well, tomorrow the outfit will have another try at it.

Bless you, my dear.
Your Jimmy

NOTE: *About this time as the enemy retreated to the east, it appeared that he was planning to concentrate his fanatical S.S. troops in what was called the National Redoubt and make his final stand around the Hitler mountainous stronghold in the Bavarian Alps. 3rd Army was ordered to shift south to approach this National Redoubt from the northwest and attack these final positions. XX Corps was to assemble just northeast of Nurnburg and attack toward Regensburg and this is the jump-off that I had mentioned. The general plan was that we were to attack southeast in zone and contact the Soviet forces advancing west from Vienna. Our particular plan was to pass through the 65th and 7lst Infantry Divisions at 6:00 a.m. on the 22nd of April and lead the Corps.*

The 5th Ranger Battalion was again attached to us and we made up quite a formidable strike force. The six Recon. Troops of the Group were reinforced with one platoon of tanks, one platoon of M-18 self-propelled tank destroyers and one company of Rangers, all riding on our armored vehicles. Thus, we had six armored infantry strike forces heading for Vienna.

27 April, 1945

My Dearest One,

Yesterday we took over 1,000 prisoners and had one man wounded. Isn't that something? And today, the Russians and Americans joined forces on the Elbe. Boy, this war is really rushing to a climax. We move every day. Today, we are again in a little manure-ville and tomorrow we cross the Blue Danube and keep going towards Vienna. Only the river looks green to me.

I saw Bill Damon yesterday. The 14th Cavalry really had it in the Battle of the Bulge and both the executive officer and the colonel commanding were relieved. It was just like Gen. Patton said, "You get overrun, you get relieved."

A box came from you today with the cigars, face soap and insignia. Thank you so much. I was all out of cigars and have been smoking captured German ones — real trash, believe me. The crossed sabers with the "3" on them are real fine and I shall put them on my battle jacket. It is now stored at the Chateau Bettange in Thionville and I shall have to wait on that event. I am busy and working hard.

Your devoted husband,
Jimmy

NOTE: We cleared the area in front of the Corps from around Nurnburg down to Regensburg and moved up all along the north shore of the Danube River, clearing everything out on our side. We ran into a lot of little mean fights in this advance, generally centered around a village with probably a couple of S. S. and some Volks Grenadiers that were made to put up a fight. Our method of dealing with this was to hit the town hard with some artillery, then rush in with tanks and tank destroyers with Rangers riding on top, shooting in all directions — a fiercesome display of fire-power that overcame resistance almost immediately. Our casualties were almost zero, we took lots of prisoners and were, as I frequently said, "fighting a smart war", not getting hurt and hurting lots of Germans.

24 April, 1945

My Dearest One,

I haven't written in some days, perhaps about three or four, as we have been out of contact with the outside world except by radio for about that period of time. We all feel quite proud because we got top billing on the news radio. Our drive was announced as an armored sprint of 3rd Army, and only the Russians got on the radio ahead of us.

It really was amazingly good. We were, at times, 30 miles out in front of anyone and all by ourselves. In three days, we captured 1400 prisoners, untold warehouses, railroad trains and everything you can think of. And with it all, we had about nine casualties — I mean men who were hurt, not killed. I really am proud of this outfit. The Corps and Army Commanders both sent a "well done" by radio on this mission and I am in hopes that our outfit will be mentioned by name, now that the mission is completed (I refer here to our drive from Nurnburg down to the Danube River at Regensburg).

The country we are now in reminds me of a famous waltz (I am telling her we are in Austria). Also, the beer is excellent. Our present CP actually has it on ice; the first ice I can remember since the good old U.S.A. We are, as usual, set up in a wayside inn. I have a nice room with attractive rustic scenes on the wall. Also I am dying to buy or steal some of the beer mugs that line the beer hall. Each steady customer apparently had his private stein with his name engraved on it — very ornate with beautiful scenes painted on them. I know you would really like them, to have as a set of vases or something.

We really were glad to see the infantry come up and catch us today. Although we were sitting along a pretty blue river (I am referring to the Danube), we were just about out of gas and out of food also. This war does seem terribly endless at times though. We study the map and figure where the Russians are and where the end of Germany is and how much farther we have to go. It is coming to a rapid climax, however. We see more evidence of it everyday.

I had an amazing experience today. I was going down the road between a bunch of British prisoners (we released 2200 of them and the prison later became the headquarters for the U. S. Army training area called Hohenfels). One of the Brits handed me a newspaper printed yesterday in Paris. I was completely floored but came to find out that the Air Corps had dropped them the previous night to the prison camp. And there it was, the latest world news in print. And we thought we were completely cut off from the outside world.

I am tired tonight, a reaction from three days of great excitement, hit-or-miss meals and little sleep.

Bless you. Goodnight.
Jimmy

NOTE: While I didn't mention it in my letter, I had a frightening experience in Hohenfels. I went into the Headquarters of the PW camp and normally, if I go into an uncleared building, either my driver or my radio operator would come along as a bodyguard. I didn't think it necessary, however, in this headquarters with all the British PWs around. In any event, I was walking through a room when a door to a closet opened and out stepped a German soldier, completely armed with a Schmeisser sub- machine gun. I made a grab for my carbine, pulled it down off my shoulder and instead of hitting the safety, I hit the clip release and the bullets all fell on the floor; so there I stood with an empty gun. Fortunately, the German wanted to surrender, so he threw his gun down and I marched him out the front door with an empty gun and turned him over to my driver. I later wrote the Chief of Ordinance and said it was ridiculous to put both the safety and the clip release buttons in front of the trigger guard, both on the right hand side. I just hit the wrong button. I suggested he should have the safety on one side of the gun and the clip release on the other. I got a very nice reply from him saying he had other similar complaints.

29 April, 1945

My Dearest Beloved,

It is about noon of a bright and sunshiny day and I am sitting in a little house in a little country town. Nothing much to do, as we are stopped along a little river waiting for the infantry to get a bridgehead over it and then we will move on. I feel well content as I just saw a division commander who is an old friend of the family (this was Major Gen. Bill Wyman, Commanding the 71st Division). He complimented me on my fine outfit and said it had an enviable record and a superior reputation. I just hope we can finish it up that way and it looks nearly done.

A whole bus-load of Krauts just drove in to one of my outposts and surrendered, driver, bus and all the soldiers. They are the damnedest people. Now I expect to see that big Greyhound bus ripping down the road in my column. We have a terrific assortment of captured vehicles that my soldiers just won't turn in to the proper authorities. We look like Coxey's Army.

I did have a wonderful steak dinner last night at a Division Head-quarters mess. It's funny — our two main topics of conversation are food and home. We don't even discuss the war except for the funny things that constantly happen. That (the war) is such old stuff to us. After 252 days in the front line, it is commonplace. We don't even get excited about Berlin being surrounded or the rumors of Hitler's request for unconditional surrender to only the U. S. and the Brits. It is all such old stuff, these rumors of the end. We are complete cynics now and will believe it when it happens.

We haven't received the slightest hint of what is in store for us when complete victory finally arrives, other than the general vicinity of that part of Germany we will occupy and police. I think the authorities are making a great effort to keep the CBI troop list a secret as there is bound to be a great roar of rage when the news gets out. However, my personal idea is that a lot of these late arrivals who have just had a taste of combat are the candidates for direct shipment via the Suez Canal. After all, we have all been over here more than a year and have been fighting three quarters of that time. There are, on the other hand, quite a few units similar to mine who really have just arrived. They are good candidates in my book. If we have to go to the Pacific, we will surely get a month's leave in the United States on the way through.

Your own,
Jimmy

6 May, 1945 (Austria)

My Adorable Wife,

I know you must be upset in not hearing from me. It is true that I haven't written in about five days. But tonight, even the 3rd Army is finished! *The War Is OVER!* My Command Post is at Steyr on the Enns River in Austria. The Enns River is the halt line where we sit and await the Russians per the Yalta Agreement. How happy we all are. How unbelievable it seems. We just can't realize it. There hasn't been any sort of a celebration of any kind. We are just too worn out and too exhausted and too unbelieving to celebrate. I imagine it is about the same at home.

It just doesn't seem true. The last few days have been too exciting and too hectic and too unreal to leave any emotion in us. I just feel drained of all feeling. We went 80 miles yesterday, 60 the day before and, I don't know, it just sort of all runs together in a mad scramble.

We are deep in Austria and the Austrian Alps are just outside my window in view. We have stopped in a nice house beside a beautiful lake (we had moved back to Seewalchen on the Atter Kammer See at this point), with a simply breath-taking view of the snow-covered peaks across this huge lake and about 20 miles away. Yet I have so many worries, that I have no time for scenery. In my sector of responsibility which we've just finished cleaning up, there is a concentration camp of 17,000 poor starving humans. They are dying at the rate of 300 a day from starvation (this is the Ebensee Concentration Camp). I have seen suffering before, I thought, but I really didn't know the depth of despair and depravity that people can sink to. But enough of this. It should be a day of rejoicing and prayers of thanksgiving. To me it is a day of hard work and bitterness.

Today we captured two major generals and I have enjoyed giving them hell and scaring the daylights out of them, intimating that we will turn them over to the Russians. That really puts the fear of God in them. I really would like to turn the whole German Army over to the Russians.

Darling, it is not a sane day and I am exhausted — so will close by saying that we can both thank God in all sincerity that I have lived through this war without a scratch. And that my men who died, did not do so in vain.

I love you,
Jimmy

NOTE: Our last fight of the war was at Vocklabruck where we ran into about 50 Hungarian S. S. fanatics that wanted to fight. We had to put on a full dress armor-infantry attack but beat them up good, but unfortunately, lost one armored car and the whole crew. "B" Troop of the 3rd Squadron was moving down the road toward Vocklabruck when the two leading platoons took a wrong turn. The captain riding behind the second platoon, diverted the third platoon to the correct road and called the other two back. Unfortunately, the third platton was led by a 2nd Lt. who had just arrived about four days before and he blundered into the ambush. I think, perhaps, had it been one of my experienced platoon leaders, it wouldn't have happened. It really broke our hearts that three days before the war was over, this splendid young man and his crew were all killed.

The drive on this last day up to the Enns River was really weird because we were going up the back of a German Army facing in the other direction to oppose the Russians. They just waved us on. They were fully armed and kept waving us to go on, knowing that the further we went the less the Russians would gain of their country. It was very fortunate that nobody fired because we were completely out-numbered. I was riding with the leading recon troop and we were surrounded by Germans. When we got to Steyr, there was a whole infantry brigade there in position facing east. We had the Col. commanding line them all up in the town square in a formal ceremony as he wanted to surrender properly. I took it and then we had them march down to the Enns River and throw in all their weapons. We had so many weapons by this time that we didn't want any more and we sure didn't want them with any.

7 May, 1945 (Austria)

My Darling,

Today, we got the official "cease fire" order by radio from Corps Headquarters and I am enclosing a copy for the scrap-book as I think it is a rather historic message. There were great whoops and shouts when my message center called out the news. I wrote yesterday that it was over, but this makes it official.

I spent most of the day organizing the concentration camp and help is rolling to them; a mobile Army hospital unit, convoys of food and an administrative headquarters to run it. We scavenged food from all the surrounding towns today and made them a rich soup as normal food would probably kill most of them. Their joy and gratitude of our help makes me feel humble, yet proud that we were the means of their deliverance. Truly, we have been fighting a holy war as our Chaplain has said. Such sights and such tragedy leave little time for rejoicing. I'm simply drained of emotion by it all. The taste of it is still in my mouth.

I might write you where we have been. From Kassel we went east past Gera, Jena and Weimar near Chemnitz. It was nice as we had an armored division on each side of us and we really knocked them over. Then the 3rd Army turned south and we moved from one flank of the Army to the other, made a long march behind the lines and wound up south of Nurnburg. Next, we jumped out in front again and were announced as an Armored Division of 3rd Army, driving on Regensburg. We hit the Danube, stopped while the Infantry came up and forced a crossing over the River, then moved out in front again and fought our way down to Braunau on the Inn River. It was a short rest again while the infantry got across and we were off into Austria. Since then, we have been on a race through Austria. We pulled up day before yesterday and have been sitting since then. My Command Post is on a truly lovely spot in a nice chateau overlooking a beautiful, big lake. It was the summer resort, in the old days of course, of many of the prominent residents of Vienna, and is supposed to be wonderful hunting and fishing country. In fact, the Emperor Franz Joseph had his hunting lodge in this area, some place.

My dear one, my heart is too overflowing with pity and anger to write of anything else. This beautiful country will soon cure me, I hope, and tomorrow, I shall take it easy and go canoeing on the lake and take a bath and get all rested up. I sort of have to unwind myself from the terrible tension of these last days and get back to normal.

Your adoring husband,
Jimmy

NOTE: Actually, on the 7th of May, I became sick. And I was quite sick for three days, running a fever and feeling very ill. After I recovered, I asked the doctor what was wrong with me and he said, "You are 6' tall and down to 135 lbs. You were completely drained emotionally and worn out physically."

9 May, 1945 (Austria)

My Adorable One,

Today has been lovely and I have really enjoyed myself. The weather is heavenly — bright sunshine, this beautiful country and I have a magnificent view of the lake and the mountains beyond. The lake is icy and much too cold to swim in, but all the soldiers have every boat on the lake going full tilt.

This afternoon, I took off to see the Vienna Riding School. It is not in Vienna, of course, but was moved near here because of the war. It is a famous horse training school that specializes in Lippizzaners only. They have about forty horses here, all stallions, and all greys or almost pure white in color. They are bred for generations for just this school. The stallions are as gentle a group of horses as I have ever seen.

They are wonderfully well cared for, beautifully trained and really a joy to behold and see work. The head man, Count Podhorsky, put on a private exhibition for me, showing me all the phases they go through in training, then (and it takes four years) putting on a regular school ride. It was truly fascinating and an unforgettable experience.

Also, I had a countess, if you please, to act as my translator. She was a woman of about 50, rather heavy and squat, but with a mobile face and a very cultured voice. She didn't know technical horse terms so had a difficult time with my questions. There were a number of grooms and servants about who bowed and scraped and flurried around whenever the riding master, who was apparently a very important person, and the countess and I appeared.

The countess had on a hat that you would have loved and I shall try to get you one to wear with your tweeds. It was one of those little Tyrolean jobs with a little feather in the brim, and was covered with all sorts of charms, little skis and silver sleds and other trinkets. I hope I can collect some.

A number of the men here wear the same sort of hat, a pair of leather shorts with dress suspenders and a loud shirt. In fact, the men dress much fancier than the women who as a rule, don't appear in peasant costume, but wear simple factory- made dresses, similar to those in the U.S. They do, as a general rule, wear a rather gaily colored apron over the dress but that is about as far as it goes.

It's a shame we can't stay on here, but we expect to move on to our permanent occupation area in a few days. The hunting, fishing, mountain climbing and later on swimming would be wonderful. But all of this beauty and recreational facilities just make us homesick.

I feel all rested and calm now. We are all getting unwound and are busy making plans for the occupation. Still not the slightest intimation of what is in store for us, nor do I expect it for some time. We are still on the "C" and "K" rations and it is all I can do to eat any of the filthy stuff. Our good rations should catch up with us in the next day or so. There has been a terrific food problem, with so many thousands of prisoners, rescued allied soldiers and these pitiful slave laborers to feed. I really should be grateful that I am eating this well and we are all careful to waste nothing.

Was V-E a great celebration in El Paso, or was it just quiet? There was absolutely no celebration here. We knew it was over several days before as we hit Steyr; and as one soldier said, "Hell, there is nothing to celebrate. We just start sweating out going to the Pacific."

Much, much love.
Jimmy

14 May, 1945

Dearest One,

The world remains heavenly and I was up most of the day looking at our million-dollar scenery. I am getting as brown as a berry, but the lake water is still too cold for me to swim in, even if some of them do. We don't have much in the way of duties right now. Everyone is loafing and gathering up all the stray German soldiers in our area as they are all over the place. We are getting practically all of them in the daily roundup.

We now have a couple of portrait painters in our menagerie. They were inmates of the concentration camp and are most grateful for a chance to work in return for their food, so I intend to sit for my portrait in the next few days (see cover portrait by Mieczylaw Koscielniak). I may as well keep them busy and send you a nice present also. They both have completely unpronounceable Polish names, but have already done a couple of officers and seem quite talented. We also captured a trapeze act and are having them put on a show as soon as we get enough food in them to get their strength back.

In addition, we have been out scouring the country for horses and have managed to acquire quite a stable. At last count, we had about 30 head and they are still coming in. We commandeered five, really beautiful animals from some sort of Kraut staff officers' stable that was for only high-ranking people. Some at least, are beautifully trained and a couple seem to have a lot of jumping ability. We have a bunch of Hungarian PW's for grooms, all ex-cavalrymen and wonderful grooms and glad to work for food. You can actually get almost anything for food over here.

So, you can see that we continue to keep busy with various activities. It really is necessary after those last months of pure excitement. The Army has quite a program in the way of schools, athletics and recreation, but we really can't get started on them until we settle into our final area. However, we are doing some planning now. Also, we are getting back on a balanced food ration again. We actually had pancakes for breakfast today and will have steak tonight. It is great to get back on a decent menu.

Much love,
Jimmy

12 May, 1945

My Dearest One,

I have been out the entire day inspecting troops and looking at scenery. I went out in my private speedboat for an hour's spin and sun-bath — the excuse being to inspect my troops scattered around the lake. Also paid my daily visit to the concentration camp, where things are very much better. They are beginning to look like human beings again. Careful feeding and American medical attention have worked wonders. Only seven died by 3:00 today. Their will to live is amazing.

We are now in the midst of figuring out who will go home and who will stay here. It is quite a simple affair as far as the enlisted men are concerned; points for decorations, points for service, points for good behavior and so forth. But we have no dope on officers in general and of course, my being a regular Army officer makes all the regulations inapplicable. The point system does not apply to the regular Army as I understand it, except that if I have a high number of points, I would get more consideration than someone with a low number. There is a lot of good-natured joking about how having children helps one's score. I figure my score is 120 which is about the highest in the regiment. But it doesn't do me any good! (Considerable comments about finances are omitted).

Your devoted husband,
Jimmy

20 May, 1945 (Austria)

My Darling One,

Today I am allowed to tell you where I am. My CP is located in Seewalchen, Austria on the north end of the Atter Kammer See, which is one of the big lakes in the Austrian Alps. My concentration camp Ebensee is across the next lake to the east and on the other end of it, or rather was, but is no longer in my sector, thank Heavens. We have been here about two weeks now, ever since V-E Day in fact.

About three days before V-E Day, the Infantry made a crossing of the Inn River near Braunau. We crossed behind them that night and the next day jumped off to meet the Russians on the Enns River near Steyr. We got along fine until late that afternoon, captured about a whole Hungarian Division that didn't want to fight, and then ran into the last fight of the war near Vocklabruck; met a bunch of fanatical S.S. troops and had a row for about two hours. I was sort of foolish in the excitement so got decorated with a Silver Star for being a damn fool.

We got into Steyr about noon the next day, ran right up the back of a German S. S. Division which had orders to let us through. They were faced in the other direction toward the Russians and it certainly was a spooky feeling to be moving between Krauts armed to the teeth and no truce or peace or anything, just sort of an unwritten agreement. To tell you the truth, I was scared sick, for if anyone had gotten trigger happy, it would have been too bad.

We sent patrols across the Enns River, but the Russians hadn't gotten close enough. It was quite a disappointment when the infantry came up the next day and relieved us and we were ordered to turn around and come back here. This was a big pocket that had been by-passed in the hurry and was full of German soldiers. However, they all surrendered easily enough. It really was fortunate in the long run as we certainly wound up the war in a lovely spot. I hope this will be our permanent location but can't imagine having such good luck.

We had a terrific shindig yesterday. My head is still whirling from it. It was the 99th anniversary of the organization of the 3rd Cavalry. We planned a ceremony and I hopefully invited General Patton and his staff to attend. We also invited all the former 3rd Cavalrymen in the area. I was amazed when most of them accepted and our guest list read like this:

General George S. Patton, Jr.
Major General William G. Wyman
Brigadier General Holly Maddox
Colonel Paul Harkins
Colonel Bill Leech
Colonel Oscar Koch
Colonel Sammy Walker
Colonel Jimmy Curtis

We had a beautiful ceremony on a hillside with our million-dollar view much in evidence. I made a short speech of welcome and then the three Generals each made the most complimentary speeches possible. General Walker could not be present but sent a letter that was truly extravagant in its praise. I am having copies made and will send you one. It really is a letter to end all letters.

Well, to wind it all up, General Patton got me out in front and gave me the Oakleaf Cluster to the Silver Star for outstanding leadership of an outstanding unit. Obviously, I have never been in such a state. I was very close to tears, I can assure you, and was quite dazed by it all. We then had a lovely luncheon on the balcony above the lake. The setting was perfect and the food delicious, we had scrounged all over the place, and even had some Benedictine and Cognac punch that had everyone on his ear. Afterwards, the whole party went out on the lake for a boat ride, later by the stables to see our horses, and they finally departed by plane about 4:30 p.m. I was in such a state after all the honors and playing host to the Army Commander and all his staff, that I just came back here and went to bed.

With it all, there were photographers all over the place. Consequently, you will probably know about it before this reaches you. They said it was quite a story and should be in plenty of papers in the United States. It really was the signal honor to have them all visit us. Everyone had a wonderful time and they told me that it was the first holiday the 3rd Army staff had taken since Sicily. They left General Hap Gay at the C.P. to run the Army and I was sorry he couldn't make it. Paul Harkins looked grand and I had a lot of fun with him. Of course, the General was magnificent, a typical performance for the troops and they loved it. My real favorite of all the staff is Col. Oscar Koch. You might remember him and General Wyman as they were both instructors when we were at Fort Riley.

General Patton relaxed at the lunch and was most entertaining and attractive. He talked of his family, asked after mother and all the family, and was much amused by mother's remark which I repeated about he and I going hand in hand to rescue Carson Fleming. Jimmy Totten is in the War Department in Washington and Johnny Watters is in some hospital and will recover from his wounds okay it appears. I tried to pump him about our date to leave this theatre, but he said he really didn't know. Also, the Pacific came up for considerable discussion and all he would commit himself on that subject was to the effect that we would get our month at home, which is something, at least.

It really was a great day, both for me and for this great Cavalry Group. I hope it doesn't completely turn my head — but certainly from all the extravagant praise, it is enough to.

Please make a copy of this long letter and send it to mother. I have gone into such detail because I wanted you to know all about it; but am not capable of writing it all over again. And please don't think me a great braggart; it is simply that I am so busting with pride that it just had to spill out.

> Bless you my love.
> Your adoring husband,
> Jimmy

P.S. Did you get the article in the New York Times? It came out in the magazine section on 22 April.
JHP

NOTE: In addition to all the above, at our luncheon, Gen. Patton described how he thought we ought to attack the Russians and drive them back to their pre-war boundaries. He had objectives all figured out for XX Corps and our own 3rd Cavalry. He believed our replacements should come from our own supply troops and that we could get the German Army to operate the rear areas for us. In other words, they could rebuild the bridges and the railroads and the telephone lines and truck up ammunition, fuel and food, and that we could easily whip the Russians; it would be a cinch. Actually with all this, we were simply horrified as we had thought the war was over and we were so naive as to believe the Russians were our gallant allies and not our long-term enemies. In this regard, he certainly had second sight which the rest of us surely lacked.

A portion of General Walker's letter mentioned in the above letter is quoted as following "Today, I call you XX Corps' finest. You were first to reach the Meuse River, first on the Moselle River and the first Americans in Thionville, where you struck terror and dismay into the hearts of the German soldiers. In the reduction of Fortress Metz, your efforts contributed as much as any single unit, be it Armor, Infantry or Artillery, in the elimination of the last great barrier that stood like a shield to our entry into Germany. In fact, yours were the first troops of XX Corps to enter Germany.

"In the envelopment of the Siegfried Line and the pursuit through the Palatinate, the name of Task Force Polk became synonymous with boldness and aggressiveness. Your 150 miles in three days from the Rhine River to the Fulda River, when you permitted an entire Infantry Division to be motorized and moved forward without ever de-trucking, was one of the most important and significant tactical achievements of this war. Of how finally, in the concluding days of this campaign, you acted as a special combat team for the Corps Commander. Your execution of this mission was done with all the dash and daring of Stewart's famous 'Raiders' themselves. Your exploits are far too numerous to mention and I have mentioned only a few to let you know that we are neither unmindful nor unappreciative of your prowess.

"I can think of no more fitting tribute or toast to you than to echo the words of Gen. Winfield Scott which were addressed to the 3rd Cavalry when he saw our national flag erected above Chapultapec by one of your fellow 3rd Cavalryman, and this I quote:

'Brave Rifles, veterans, you have been baptized in fire and blood and have come out steel'."

23 May, 1945

My Precious One,

You say you have been counting up on my point score and I have 44. You do me a real injustice, so I will count up my point score for you. Service in Army since Oct. 1941, 56: Service overseas, 15: Children (2), 24: Three Battle Stars (Normandy, France, Germany), 15: Bronze Star Medal, 5: Croix de Guerre, 5: Silver Star with Oakleaf Cluster, 10. Total, 130.

However, it doesn't count for regular Army Officer — too bad.

We are now at Murau, deep in the Austrian Alps. We are in a long, beautiful, narrow valley with high snow-capped mountains all around us. It has been rather cold and rainy and as most of the men are in tents, it has been rather uncomfortable. I haven't written in about four days but the Tito scare had everyone pretty upset. We got very sudden orders to reactivate the task force and clear a route to Italy. It was quite a rat race as we had gotten lazy in the last few weeks. However, we have become such Gypsies and so used to fighting, so there wasn't too much grumblin' or groaning, just another nasty job to be done, even if V-E Day had come and gone. We rather sweated it out though, as fighting partisans in the Alps would be difficult and very hard to tell friends from foe. However, the scare is all over now and not a shot fired. We are just camped awaiting orders to return to Germany.

You couldn't possibly guess what I have done today. I have gone to a wedding. It was quite a story. When this alert came, I had an Infantry Battalion, among other things, assigned to my task force. The Battalion C.O. came over with a very long face to get his orders and said this sure was playing hell with his wedding plans. It seems he was to marry a Red Cross girl who had come all the way from Orleans for the affair. He had met her when he was wounded and in a hospital back there. They had big plans in his regiment and here he was, off to Trieste on a fighting mission. Well, we got down as far as the Mur Valley and were stopped, so he sent back for her and today was the wedding. It was in a lovely little chapel in a local castle. Everyone present was an officer except for this one poor girl, all of us in combat clothing with steel helmets and weapons. The ceremony was really pitiful but very sweet, and struck me as brave and fine. The bride wore her blue Red Cross outfit and carried a bouquet of lilacs, picked off the local bushes. Afterwards, we had a little supper in a delightful chalet, but it was cold as blazes. The poor girl had the shakes so badly that I thought she would faint during the ceremony. But she carried it off very well. She really is a lovely girl from near Poughkeepsie and educated at Vassar, so now they are honey-mooning up on the mountain, poor kids. What a life those Red Cross girls lead.

Bless you my love.
Your Jimmy

NOTE: Right after our big ceremony on the 19th, the next day we were ordered to reconstitute the task force and open the road across the Alps to Trieste. It seems that Tito and other people were making trouble and it was thought that the XX Corps would have to move across the Alps and reinforce the Allies in northern Italy. I really was afraid that there would be a lot of grumbling or desertions or problems, but everybody was still in fighting trim so we hitched up and took off.

In General Patton's diary, War As I Knew It, the following is quoted from page 330 about this particular incident:

"Little or nothing is known or has ever been said about the 3rd Army's duplication of Hannibal's feat, crossing the Alps.

"At war's end, when the situation in Yugoslavia was not clear, the 3rd Army was ordered to move three divisions into 5th Army and British areas, south of the Alps and north of Trieste. Without so much as a wink of an eyelash, the 3rd United States Cavalry Group moved out in 12 hours and crossed the Alps and was thoroughly mixed up with British troops in northern Italy. Gen. Clark, who had not been informed of such a movement, made haste to congratulate Gen. Patton on the alacrity and boldness of his moves. However, he lost no time in informing Gen. Eisenhower that additional troops were not needed and Gen. Clark requested that these troops be withdrawn. They were, with the same zest and determination as aforementioned."

This was the last operational action of the 3rd Cavalry or Task Force Polk. After we returned to Germany, over the Alps again, the 3rd and 43rd Squadrons were ordered to move out smartly, to return to United States for thirty (30) days leave and onward movement to the Pacific war; fortunately, they didn't have to go as the war with Japan ended before their sailing date.

The Group Hq. and Hq. Company was ordered to take up occupation duties about 30 kilometers south of Munich in the area surrounding the Starnberger See and including the XX Corps Headquarters as well. There were a number of battalions under us, generally corps artillery and engi-

neers. We collected weapons, directed repairs of roads, bridges and telephone lines, screened the population for Nazi party members and carried out the denazification program and generally enforced law and order with patrols and occasional road blocks. We had great difficulty in supervising a Jewish Displaced Persons Camp at Feldafing of about 5,000 souls as they were half starved, very emotional and unwilling to do any work. We, of course, were not able to discipline or confine them, so it was a matter of persuasion which seldom worked.

We kept our horses and Hungarian grooms, had a very active athletic program, operated the Royal Bavarian Yacht Club, had a nice Schloss at Garatshausen with excellent facilities, and generally kept fairly busy. However, everyone longed for home, and the point system sent some back every week until most of the veterans had departed. I finally received my return orders and arrived in El Paso by air on November 7, 1945 on our 9th wedding anniversary, after an absence of twenty months.

Gen. George S. Patton pinning the Silver Star (with Oak Leaf Cluster) on Col. James H. Polk, May 19, 1945, Gmunden, Austria. The occasion was the 99th aniversary of the organization of the 3rd Cavalry Regiment, which Gen. Patton himself commanded from 1938 to 1940.

C I T A T I O N

Oak-Leaf Cluster to Silver Star

Colonel JAMES H. POLK, 019028, Cav., 3d Cavalry Group
(Mechanized). for gallantry in action in Austria on 6 May
1945. Colonel POLK accompanied the forward elements of a
leading Cavalry squadron in a drive to contact Russian
forces on the ENNS RIVER. Near VOCKLABRUCK, the spear-
heading forces suddenly encoutered fifty fanatical SS
Troopers who engaged them in a fierce fire fight. With
gallant disregard for his own safety, Colonel POLK rallied
his men and led them in an overwhelming attack which completely overran the enemy. Contiruing the mission, Colonel
POLK was marching at the head of the column when it came
upon several hundred heavily-armed enemy soldiers. Quickly
perceiving the danger of their position, Colonel POLK
instructed his German-speaking interrogators to command the
hostile force to lay down their arms and surrender because
the war had ended. His daring ruse enabled tha party to
reach their objective without further casualties. Colonel
POLK's outstanding bravery and fearless leadership were
an inspiration to his men and are in keeping with the
highest tradtions of the Army of the United States.
Entered Military Service from Virginia.

Hdq. XX Corps, 3rd Army

A true copy

'OAK LEAF CLUSTER, BRONZE (Army)
Indicates an additional award of the medal
corresponding to the ribbon on which it is worn

Gen. Patton and Col. Polk aboard the German speedboat "Baldar" follow
ing the 3rd Cavalry's 99th aniversary celebration on May 19, 1945. To Patton's le
rear is Maj. John A. Logan, Regimental Staff officer.

Col James H. Polk, May 19, 1945. 3rd Cavalry's
99th anniversary celebration.

Gen. G. S. Patton congratulating Col. Polk for his receipt of the Legion of Merit. Bavaria, Sept. 5, 1945, during ceremonies honoring the fourth anniversary of the organization of General Walton Walker's XX Corps.

September 5, 1945

CITATION FOR LEGION OF MERIT

Colonel James H. Polk (Army Serial No. 019023), Cavalry, United States Army, for exceptionally meritorious conduct in the performance of outstanding services, as Commanding Officer, 3rd Cavalry Group, from 12 September 1944 to 9 May 1945. Through his distinguished qualities of leadership and organizational skill, Colonel Polk led his organization to outstanding military attainment and contributed invaluably to the successes of the XX Corps. During the hard winter months, he brilliantly deployed his troops along a front much larger than that normally assigned a Cavalry Group. In March, he breached the Siegfried defenses, raced to the Rhine, crossed it and hammered his way across Germany to the Danube River. Bridging it, he soon crossed into Austria, capturing hundreds of towns in his onrush. Colonel Polk's tactical brilliance inspired all with whom he served and reflects highest credit upon himself and the armed forces of the United States.

A certified true copy

Surrounded by DP police (with armbands), US military police and other US Army officers, Gen. Dwight D. Eisenhower is taken on a tour of the Feldafing Displaced Persons camp. 17 Sept., 1945.(Photo Credit: USHMM Archives).

Gens. Eisenhower and Patton (behind Eisenhower) tour the DP camp at Feldafing. 17 Sept., 1945. (Photo Credit: USHMM Archives).

Target practice near "Mussolini's Schloss," Austria, 1945. The pistol was a .32 calibre Walther PPK taken from a captured German SS officer and was carried by Col. Polk as a personal sidearm.

Joey Polk sitting on her feet in her mother's garden, as mentioned in Col.
Polk's letter dated 30 Sept., 1945 .

Family portrait of Joey Polk with children, Jody and Jamie, El Paso, Texas,
sent to Col. Polk in fall, 1945.

PART IV

Epilogue: - The Occupation in Bavaria.
12 June - 30 October, 1945

Editor's NOTE: From November, 1987 through April, 1988 General James H. Polk (U.S.Army, Retd.) was interviewed as part of an Oral History program conducted by Jesse Stiller and Rebecca Carver with the University of Texas at El Paso (UTEP), El Paso, Texas. Following is an extract from these interviews pertaining to then Col. Polk's and the 3rd Cavalry's involvement with the Feldafing DP Camp in the fall of 1945.

"....After the war we were given a territory to watch over. Military government teams actually did or tried to do the running of it, but we were the security and made sure everybody behaved and confiscated all weapons. We would pick up people and process prisoners and all that sort of routine.

One of the most onerous jobs was looking after a Jewish DP camp and that is a story in itself.... In the first place the people were starved and kind of crazy. We had about 5 or 6,000 in this former Hitler Jungen camp, very nice camp as a matter of fact...it was a beautiful brick campus. The reason it started there was that near the tail-end of the war a trainload of Jews, enroute to and within 30, 40 miles of Dachau, were strafed mistakenly by an American airplane. It knocked out the train's engine, somebody finally turned them loose, and they were right by this Hitler Jungen camp, so they just started it.

We had about eleven rabbis, and the head rabbi once told me, "There isn't a decent person in this camp. We are all felons or we would not be here. We have all lied, cheated and stolen to survive the Holocaust. I am amongst them. You must forgive some of the things they do here."

It was a very mobile population because there were about four or five such DP camps in Germany, such rendevous, and they were all looking for their children or their relatives. Universally these camps were very, very difficult to manage, and the people had been through such terrible experiences. We never knew on any given day how many people we had. They were free to go anyplace they wanted, and a lot of them walked or they would get a car. The trains slowly started to run again.

Practically none of the Jewish DPs wanted to stay in Germany. There were serious prohibitions against going to Israel at that time, and they were sneaking down there. So Jewish people could not go to Israel legally and if they couldn't go there, they wanted to go to the United States. They were disgruntled about staying there in that camp. And they could not see any immediate end to it, nor could I promise them any immediate end to it. Although Eisenhower inferred that he would get them out of there, I don't think he ever did anything about it. I do not know exactly. But it was a very difficult problem for them. They were a stateless people — they had lost everything in Germany or Russia or Poland or wherever they had been.

I learned another thing that kind of surprised me — that the orthodox Jews did not like the reformed, who did not like the conservatives, etc. And there were some Jews who didn't have any religion and they didn't like each other very much. And then the Polish Jews did not like the German Jews. Well, we had to do everything we could — we set up a slaughterhouse for the orthodox. I learned it is very hard to be an orthodox Jew — their food is so special and their habits are different and everything. I was very sympathetic; we were all very sympathetic, but it was a very difficult situation. We tried to operate through the rabbis, but the rabbis often did not agree with each other. There were different kinds of rabbis, but they didn't get along very well. I thought, "Heck, it'll be just fine. Get the eleven rabbis together and run the camp that way." It did not work.

We were not allowed to impose any discipline on the DPs. For instance, I had my MP platoon...outside the gate and tried to control things in a nice way. But they were undisciplined and food crazy. We were feeding them about 5,000 calories a day, and they would...gain weight very quickly, but were prone to diseases, particularly pneumonia and colds and that kind of thing. A lot of them died. We had a hospital with American personnel, but we had pneumonia and measles and other problems resulting from the DPs deteriorated health and a lack of cleanliness in the camp.

Our guidance was to get them healthy and feed them and house them properly and get them things they needed like sewing machines and carpenter tools and shoes, machines to make shoes with, and so forth. This group, I found out, would not do menial work, would not dig, for instance. They did cabinet work and weaving and shoes and skilled work. I talked to the rabbis about that and they said, "they never had dug and never would."

We had General Patton and General Eisenhower come visit the camp one day (17 September, 1945). That was not a happy occasion because I was not allowed to have any U.S. soldiers inside the camp. So, we had about 50 Jewish MPs trying to keep order among their own people. They had armbands. You drive into the camp and come around a circle and there was the flagpole. And so all the 5,000 Jews gathered, assembled around the flagpole and the Jewish MPs were holding them in a circle. In drives a U.S. MP Jeep and then an open Mercedes with General Patton and General Eisenhower in the back seat. Well, the Jews gave sort of an animal roar, and broke the lines and all, and came in on Eisenhower who didn't realize that this was a friendly welcome. The crowd threw me right up against the car. He turned to me and said, " Can't you control this rabble?". It frightened him badly, and then he realized that I knew he was frightened and then he realized that General Patton was not frightened and that Patton knew Eisenhower was frightened, and then he got mad. And he stayed mad. Oh, I could not do anything right. Boy, I really got it. I thought I was going to be reduced to a Captain — all he had to do was the stroke of a pen, and I was going to be back to my permanent rank. Then they finally left, leaving me with some orders. I got plenty of guidance that day, I'll tell you. When they left, General Patton turned to me aside and said, " This has been one of the most distasteful days of my life."

The sequel was about four or five days later my MPs, outside the gate, caught the head rabbi and the #2 rabbi with a truckload of beef hindquarters going up to Munich to sell them. We had set up a slaughterhouse at the camp for the Kosher people, and apparently they would not eat the beef hindquarters. Well, two of my MPs stopped the truck, saw what it was and started giving the rabbi a hard time and he started sassing them. And so they pulled him out of the truck...and one of them drove the truckload of meat back to the camp, because the Jewish DPs were not all orthodox at all. And the other MP drove the rabbi and put him in our little jail. The word got out awfully fast because there was great sympathy for the Jews and Eisenhower was very sympathetic, quite consious of the political problems involved.

We got orders right away from SHAFE to release him and not to pursue any charges. So, we released him. The next day the Inspector General of SHAFE (Gen. Haines), a Brigadier General, Inspector General of the whole damned American outfit, arrived on one of those little trains they had, in the railroad station at Feldafing and I had lined up my 30 MPs. So they got the rabbi and the Inspector General, and they were going to finger the two MPs that had done this. My MPs looked magnificent — all wounded veterans, big tough guys, and they had white shoe laces and they looked so soldierly with yellow scarves. So the Brigadier General said to me, " Colonel Polk, can you identify the two men who did this?" I said, "No, sir, I haven't tried because there are not going to be any charges filed so I didn't try to find out who did it." "Well," he said, "We will."

So he got the rabbi and he went down the line and he said, "That one?" The rabbi said, "No." "Was it that one?" He said, "No." "Was it that one?" He said, "No." Went all the way down the line. Finally the rabbi realized this was not going to be good news for him, so he said, "Must have been some other MPs." I said, "Yes, it must have been.", although I knew damn well they were my MPs. And so the Brigidier General got on his train to go back to SHAFE and he said, "Well, apparently it wasn't your MPs, but let me tell you something, Colonel Polk, don't you dare let it happen again, you understand?"

I really had a time with that crowd, I'll tell you.

12 June, 1945
Raab, Austria

My adorable one,

It does sound as if your days are full to overflowing. I am glad you have started golf and I accept your challenge — you better practice hard as I am getting to be quite an athlete and will beat the pants off you. Who takes care of the kids when you go whipping off? Do you have a sitter, a nurse, or is poor Mabie pinch hitting. But don't do so much that you get all run down, I want you in the pink when I get back.

I had the most delicious dream of you last night. I was in a C.P. someplace and the Krauts were about, but no one was particularly worried. Then I had a rendezvous with you outside, in the woods. We walked and flirted and had all sorts of fun being romantical. I woke up in such a lovely glow — for it is rare that I dream and all my few dreams until lately have been nightmares of fighting. The dream represents a turning point in my subconscious mind, I think, and now my inner mind has ceased worrying and has turned back to thoughts of love and home — not that those thoughts weren't always completely there, but I did have a constant load of tremendous worry and responsibility that came to the surface when I went to sleep. Phil (Col. Phil Davidson, Regt. Exec.) said that I often moaned and sometimes ground my teeth in my sleep. I guess it is over now.

I just came back from a nice long horseback ride across this lovely countryside. You no doubt remember that it is almost all rolling fields, woods with the underbrush all cleaned out, and meandering country lanes. There are no fences so one can ride any place across country. Today I saw a buck and a doe and also some quail. There is a ridge just out of town — when you ride over it you get the most lovely view of the snow capped Alps in the distance. We have a fine string of well trained and good mannered horses — a couple that are a real joy. But it makes me feel so close to you (the radio is playing now "I got a woman crazy for me, she's funny that way") to go out riding all by myself — I sort of feel that you are right there beside me — I feel so calm and peaceful and rested — so sure of our love and our feelings for each other, of our mutual love of our children and our supreme faith in the future — our future together.

It is strange how much I love you and how close you remain to me — an ever present personality that I love and remember. I have so many, many happy memories of us together — from the first days we met, through our courtship and marriage, and our days of raising a family together. My memories of my pride in you — I am so proud of my beautiful and attractive wife. I brag about you all the time and am forever bringing you into the conversation. I am afraid I have built you up into a great pianist, golfer, and charmer. You really will have a reputation to live up to when we all get together again. Bowman is the only man in the Regt. who knows you and he thinks you are wonderful.

I have wonderful memories of you swimming, driving a car, looking harassed over a stove, or being a gracious hostess at our table or just being a damn fine wife at breakfast. ...... I know you have plenty of guts, plenty of charm, and plenty of sense. Not only that, but..... Oh, darling, you are a lovely, wonderful woman, different and lovable and just you, my Joey woman, my wife and my love! You are the only woman that could possibly interest me, the only woman that I could possibly love, in fact the one and only woman that I want completely for my own, to the exclusion of all others, now and forever. You are the one perfect woman — that was made just for me, just as I am made just for you. We fit — we are a very intricate fit and no one else has the combination. My dear, darling woman, I do love you so — I love you more with each day, if such a thing were possible.

Jimmy

5 September, 1945
Bavaria

My dearest,

I have just come in from a grand ride and am all sweaty and hot and horsy smelling. My mare "Brownwood" is really schooling and jumping nicely now and is a joy to hack around on. I do wish I could bring her back to the states with me when I come as she is a lovely creature. Why do I always love a mare, I guess it is that mannish streak in me but it seems I always have "girl horses." We have two good stallions on the place but I will have none of them.

Today was organization day for XX Corps — their fourth, so I felt quite superior. There was quite a to-do hereabouts for it. They had a parade where I simply sweated buckets but it was worth it as General Patton gave a most characteristic speech, all full of curse words and his own philosophy. He said you can't put out a fire by disbanding the fire department — that we had just put out the greatest fire in history but that the main job of the fire department was to inspect around and prevent fires just like the army's job in the future is to prevent wars. He wound up by saying "Don't ever forget that you belonged to the truly great American Army, go home and be as great citizens as you were soldiers — God Bless you all" and with that he burst out crying.

It really was very effective — he is so sincere and we all worship him but no one could get away with such ham and curse words except the old man. He had on the damnedest get up — green jodhpurs and his fancy helmet and his jacket simply covered with medals. Three squadrons of P-51's roaring overhead and doing all sorts of wild acrobatics — the lake in the background and a beautiful day. I shan't forget it for a long while — for it makes me proud to be an American soldier.

Tonight, as I write, there are all sorts of flares going up across the lake — truly beautiful, red and green and white rockets and parachute flares. But as I look over my shoulder and out the window at all of them I don't quite enjoy them. It all reminds me too vividly of a night along the Saar River last winter, when each flare had a dreadful meaning like "We are being attacked" or "Lift your artillery fire by 100 yards" or such. It reminds me particularly of one night when we put a patrol across the Saar and into the Siegfried line to get prisoners and things went wrong and all kinds of Kraut flares went up and we lost twenty good men. I guess I shall never really enjoy fireworks again.

It really is a heavenly night and the radio beside me is the N.Y. Philharmonic Symphony and they have just played a couple of piano concertos and I am transported out of these surroundings — back to those dear Sunday afternoons we spent together, listening to such heavenly music. Weren't those good days. I never liked Sundays very much until I was married to you, and suddenly they became the most beautiful day of the week. Our lazy, happy, be-together day, taking care of the kids and loafing and listening to the radio, no one to disturb us, just our dear little family sort of on our own and very happy and content about it. It would be good to spend such a day again — as I have told you before, I want to be all alone with you for awhile and then I want to sit around with the kids again and get to know them again — and just have that feeling of being home, with all that really means. I do pray it won't be too long before this dream comes true. Good night my love and God bless you — for I do love and adore you so.

Your husband,
Jimmy

7 September, 1945
Friday — Bavaria

My darling woman,

Well, I am off to the French Riviera and Paris tomorrow. We leave
the Munich airport at 8:30 and if the weather is good will fly over the
Brenner Pass, over Italy, and on in. I had tried to get permission to
drive down that way but was unable to get a clearance so I will just
look at it from the air. I expect to stay there six days, have about two
days in Paris, and then come on back.

I have no particular plans or no friends to meet but everyone says
that you are bound to meet some old friends there. Russ Brosbows
is in Paris, so I shall look him up. I really don't need a rest at all but
it seems a good chance to see the place — just one of the things no
one should miss over here. I also might go by Thionville and spend a
day with Count DeMitry as he wrote me a most cordial letter asking
me to visit him — if I can work out the flying angle I will do it as it
would be interesting to see the old places we fought and also to visit
a Count and Countess — they only have nine children!

I have been trying to remember if you were ever there but I seem
to remember that you went to Italy and skipped it. Anyway I will
look it over and decide if we ought to include it on our itinerary when
we come over together later on. Damn, but I shall miss you on this
trip. I would far rather spend my leave at Cloudcroft (New Mexico)
than at this mecca of all the world but maybe I can do both before
the snow falls.

Now please don't go worrying about me not behaving myself on
this trip. I promise you that you have no worries on that score. You
are always in my thoughts so constantly on a leave that it is just as if
you were there — telling me that I have had enough to drink or that
it is time to go home or something like that.

I doubt if I shall be able to get you much in the way of a present
at the place, as the French have a terrible inflation and our money
isn't worth very much. In Germany there is nothing to buy and in
France it is too expensive! There is a perfume factory and would I be
spoiling my daughter if I sent her a bottle? I'll see.

(Later) The whole army over here is really in a great turmoil,
what with new orders about discharging everyone and sending people
home and everyone going off in all kinds of directions. It looks like
practically the whole troop will be cleaned out, Pres (Third Squadron

C.O.) is going and just about everyone else — Logan (Regt. S-3) is going to Berlin with Col. Drury — and here I sit. I guess that when I come back there will be just me and the Hungarians left to hold down the fort. A damn good army can sure break up fast.

H. Heimer came by to say goodbye. And he is going right to El Paso and will soon see you. I could just die. I sort of wanted to give him all sorts of tender messages but he is not that kind of guy. Anyway he will be seeing you soon and is a sort of personal messenger from me to you — he probably won't tell you that I love you but that's what he is supposed to mean anyway. And how I wish I could hide in his pocket and pop out when he gets home.

19 September, 1945
Bavaria

My darling one,

Have just spent two very trying days working with my D.P.s as the heat is really on the camp now. I have been down to that damn place a dozen times, ordering this and that, making a speech to the block leaders, changing the guard, and practically being a barracks policeman. In addition the 551 AA BN, which has been guarding and running the place, departed for home today and a new FA BN has taken over in its place, so they have to be all re-indoctrinated and started off on the job.

Pres Utterback and two other officers from the headquarters left today for home with the AA BN. It shall be lonesome without him and I shall miss him as he was about the only officer in the headquarters close to my age or that I could ever pal around with. The army is in a complete turmoil over the point system and the hurry up discharges that congress is forcing on us. I have lost absolutely all my key personnel, all my radio operators, and almost all of my officers. I could no more run a Cavalry Group with what I have now than I could fly. And everyone else is the same way. I have been sent infantry men and chemical warfare troops and goodness knows what, just assign them to the Cavalry and someone thinks that they automatically become seasoned cavalrymen. I even have a dentist acting as my assistant operations officer. It really is driving me nuts.

I can't imagine what will happen to the 3rd Cav Group — it would seem best just to break the whole thing up and call it a good job well done and end it on that note. It is very sad to me to see such a good outfit just going to pot before my eyes. It looks like that by October first only me and the Hungarians will be left of the old bunch. Also it makes it terribly hard to accomplish anything with constantly changing personnel, none of whom have any experience. We have overnight become an army of rookies and couldn't fight our way out of a paper bag — the most magnificent army in the world has ever seen four months ago. It seems an awful shame and shows what fools we Americans are in so many ways. We shall have to start training all over again from scratch.

From all your letters El Paso sounds most gay and charming. I am sorry that you missed Gen. Walker but really more sorry that you missed big Tom Greenfield, he is a fine fellow and risked his life for me several times — you can't say much more than that.

To answer some of your questions:

1. For Xmas, just send me trifles — I still think I will be home or rather pray I will be home but don't quite see how. However, the Army is so damn SNAFU that no one over here can possibly tell what will happen from one minute to the next. I don't need a thing.

2. Yes, I got the story of Commodore Hornblower and enjoyed it very much — however, I was horrified at the implied infidelity of my great hero with the Russian babe — did you make out in that cryptic chapter that he wound up in bed with her?

3. Yes, "Captain From Castile" arrived just before I went to the Riviera and I thought I had written and thanked you for it. I haven't had a chance to read it yet but it looks fascinating and I note that it is at the top of the best seller list. Thank you, my love.

4. No, I don't live at Dr. Frick's (Wilhelm Frick, Hitler's Minister of the Interior) house. It is sort of an officers club for us, we frequently eat meals there or give parties there and I usually sleep there Saturday night and sometimes on other nights.

5. No, it would be absolutely impossible to bring home either Baylos or Carrie, our cook, much as I would like to. The army has gotten terribly strict about such things as many troops have tried to smuggle people home, especially these homeless children.

6. I don't know why Gen. Patton turned down the two requests for me except that it is a Third Army and also an ETO policy to keep regular army officers over here for the Army of Occupation. I don't believe he has any special job in mind for me but so many key officers are on their way out with high point scores that there is a need over here for good officers.

7. I am sure that no regular officers wives or any other will be allowed over here before spring and perhaps later than that. By next spring, I suppose the army will settle down and begin to make some sense.

Oh, damn, I just have to get home before we are all old and worn out with life. We are both so full of loving that can only come out for each other — and even I can't help noticing how grey I am getting and how thin my hair is. That grey stripe in the middle of my head is now quite pronounced and my whole head is specked with grey.

Do get another picture of you and the children for me — I hate that one of you that I have on my table, you look so solemn and it just isn't like you. And the children are so much older. And what about those pin-up pictures of you in a bathing suit that you promised to me. I really want one as revealing as possible, so I can see as much of your lovely legs and figure as the censor will allow.

Oh, I do so want to hold you close in my arms again and soon. Have no fear of us learning to love again, my sweet virgin — I and you will relearn it all in a night and more besides — be it in New York or El Paso or a tourist court on the way to someplace. I have so much aching and longing stored up inside of me that I will simply cover you with kisses and caresses and embraces — I will surround you and mash you and squash you and hug you — for I just love you so.

Jimmy

20 September, 1945
10:30 P.M.

My adorable wife,

Another nasty day of fooling around the DP camp, trying to get them to cut wood for their winter needs. They feel that they worked for the Germans for five years, so that now the Krauts should work for them — so they don't want to cut wood. One tried to run away from the work detail and an officer of mine shot into the ground with his pistol to scare him. This fellow fell on the ground and the poor officer was horrified — thought he had hit him, but he didn't have much trouble with his work detail after that.

The days are beginning to get quite brisk now, leaves beginning to come off the trees and a very definite feeling of fall in the air. I really look forward to this winter with a complete sense of dread — I swear, I just can't stand the thought of another winter over here. I guess I must make my mind up to part of it at least. I do know this much — the unit has not been requested to stay over until spring — so it does mean that we will have some time during the winter — our chance in October is almost nil, in November good, and in December excellent. That is absolutely all I could find out today and that is all that Third Army Headquarters knows. It is enough so that you should hold my Xmas packages to almost nothing for I am absolutely determined not to be here for Xmas — I will get home by sheer force of will if nothing else. I have promised you to be home by Xmas and I surely will be if I can.

Why is it that the guys who mess up get home before the ones that do well — it doesn't make sense to me. I really have a terrible sense of frustration tonight, for my work is so piddling and irksome and I want my woman. Oh, God, how I want to be with you tonight — for I am lonely and discouraged and griped and I want to talk it all over with you and decide what is best and have you make me happy. Life is so pointless among these damn Krauts, I hate them all and love you with all my heart and soul.

Your Jimmy

26 September, 1945
10:30 P.M.
Bavaria

My darling woman,

Another dull day and another lonesome night for me — the time really is dragging with not too much work, with dark coming on after supper, and it is too cold to enjoy our water sports. We had fires going today and there was a real chill in the air. All the mountains south of us are now covered with snow on their tops — it is a beautiful sight but makes things a bit chilly thereabouts.

Now Gen Patton has gotten himself in trouble again — this time over "fraternization" and the removal of Nazi's in office. Why can't he keep his mouth shut! The jails are simply full of Nazis awaiting some sort of trial, there are literally thousands in concentration camps, so if the home folks think the Nazis are running Bavaria they are just crazy! Absolutely no one admits to being a Nazi, for as soon as it is known that they were a Nazi before 1939, why then into the jail they go. And all the soldiers and some of the officers (plenty I guess) have been going out with German girls — fraternizing even since V-E day and before. The point is that the fraternization rule is unenforceable, Americans being what they are. He simply realized that such a rule could not be enforced, so he ended it. And it was a wise move, for it has been undermining authority from the very outset. Some Americans would be going out with girls if they were hottentots.

Oh, hell, but he has to get quoted in the home town papers and get nasty editorials by writers who don't understand conditions over here at all. The most important thing is not to get every last Nazi out — they were all more or less Nazis anyway. The important thing is to get these damn people fed and get food in for the winter, get the railroads working, the roads and bridges mended, the telephones and lights going, get in coal and wood for the winter. You can't possibly realize what a huge city like Munich is without those things, what it is to have no mail or telephones or electricity or railroads. This damn country is a wreck and the only people who can run a railroad are Nazis — therefore we keep a few of them to run the damn railroads. The American people make me sick, for our Army is a citizen army, not a professional army, and everyone here is trying to get this country back on its feet — not to be a great power again but just so they will be warm and can eat. Of course we make mistakes — hell, I am governor of a whole country and I make mistakes every day but I would like to see anyone else do any better. You better defend the old man in any arguments, because he is right and the papers are wrong. Seems to me I am always blowing off in letters to you lately, but the state of the Army and the condition of these people is enough to make me heartsick. We won the war and now we are losing the peace.

Enough of that business. Today I heard that Howie Snyder is going home for 30 days leave along with Col Lipke (G-5 of Corps.). Also General Craig just left to go back and command the 7th Service Command in Omaha. Howie has been over a little over two years — (19 months for me plus a bit). He will go to Washington and see Tommy and Sally there. But it represents another one of my friends leaving — just about the last one I have in the near vicinity. I suppose my name will be coming up for it in the next couple of months. But I don't know whether to take it or not, because if one takes it, it sort of means that you are coming back over here at the end of the leave. I haven't reconciled myself to that idea as I still hope to come home with the Group Hq, for good I mean, not just for a leave. It will be a terrible decision to make if I get such a leave offered before we are alerted for shipment home. And I still feel that we will be shipped home by December at the latest.

I think I'll stick it out as commanding officer of this outfit and do my damnedest to bring it home for I know that it is my best chance of coming home and staying there. Oh, darling, I just have to come home, I just simply must be your husband in fact as well as in name. One month would just be heartbreak — I just couldn't bear going off again without you, once I had held you close in my arms. Will our orders ever come? But they simply have to sometime soon — so soon I hope.

I love you,
Jimmy

22 September, 1945
Bavaria

My dearest one,

Just got your nice long letter and I thought I would show you just what my pay card shows as follows:

Base Pay	$400.00
Pay for foreign service	33.00
Pay for rental of your house as no quarters are furnished	120.00
Pay for rations	42.00
Total Per Month	$595.00

Expenses as follows:

Allotment to you	$300.00
Insurance	43.52
War Bond	37.50
Government check to you	100.00
Deducted for my rations	21.00
Paid in cash to me	92.98
	$595.00

As far as going into business over here, it is definitely out as the army is worried about a lot of monkey business that has already been going on. A lot of guys have been getting watches from the states — Mickey Mouse are the best — and selling them to the Russians for sums like $500.00 and the like. Also some of the troops captured a lot of German money and even American money that these Nazis had tucked away or buried in the woods, etc. So now the army has some very strict controls on the amount of money we can send home. So even if you make any money over here you can't send it home. Money really has very little value here as the people want food or goods. At the Riviera a package of cigarettes is worth $1.20 and a pair of army trousers is worth $60.00 — so there has been a lot of shady stuff going on and I wouldn't dare get into the slightest business deal.

It is true that I was recommended to be a general — I never wrote you about it as it sounded awfully egotistical. Also I would appreciate it if you did NOT spread it around as it can never happen now — the army has more generals that they know what to do with. If other people want to spread it around, why that is all right but the proper thing for you to say is that you don't know anything about it. Really, I have no official knowledge of it — only that General Walker told me in an informal conversation that he had so recommended me and Gen Patton confirmed this later in a conversation.

Incidentally, as a matter of interest for yourself ONLY, it was not Gen Patton who first recommended me — it was General Walker. This is a matter of some personal satisfaction to me as it shows that the recommendation was made on my personal ability and not because of a former friendship with Gen Patton or his family. The occasion was when my Task Force jumped off from around Nurnburg ahead of the Corps and headed for Regensburg and the Danube. We amazed everyone with our speed, left an armored division behind, captured a vital bridge intact, and got all sorts of prisoners with almost no casualties.

Anyway, the whole affair is a very fine thing to have on my record and I am satisfied with that. It would be most difficult to be made a General now over so many older men and would cause much resentment on their part. As it is on such an unofficial basis, it is not a subject for either you or I to discuss — please understand and do as I say on this matter.

Bless you, my love, and good night.

I love you,
Jimmy

29 September, 1945
Bavaria
9:30 a.m.

Dearest,

Have read over your letter several times about your friends at Bliss who have been relieved or displaced by Regular Army officers and their feelings about this matter. It really is a very hard matter to discuss as each case seems sort of special and in a class by itself. Everyone sort of takes sides and gets angry, depending on whether the man in question is a friend or not. But I will say that I have never known a man who was relieved of command who was not bitter about it and think he was done an injustice. But also, in my opinion, most of the men who were relieved deserved it.

There have been plenty of good men relieved — I know personally of a great many. But the thing is that even though they were good men, they either made a serious mistake in judgment (and in combat one mistake is enough) or they lost their temper and told a superior officer to go to hell. Well, you can't tell a superior where to go in the army, or any other job for that matter, and get away with it. On the other hand, most officers will hear your side of the case if it is put tactfully and politely. Then if your side is turned down, the only way to do is do it his way but get the orders in writing to protect yourself.

As far as "boot licking" is concerned, there just isn't any for front line troops in combat. The man who can "cut the mustard" is the man who gets along. Everyone stands on his own merit, everyone has his own job to do, and no one gives a damn or even knows if you are a West Pointer or what. When you get back about as high as Corps headquarters I will admit that some of this currying favor goes on, but even there it doesn't get you too far. You can either do the job or you can't.

My guess is that your two friends weren't too close to combat, where a man stands or falls on his own abilities, or else if they were they messed it up. I can list you at least twenty men, all generals or colonels, all West Pointers, and all relieved or reduced because they messed it up — friends, what school they went to, or boot licking didn't have a damn thing to do with it. They simply couldn't get the job done so they got canned.

And finally, I say "Thank God for it." It is a damn difficult thing to relieve a man from command — the thought always is to give him another chance, and another and another. And all the while men are getting killed or the supplies are not getting up or something. Mistakes are made, it is true, but in most cases there is no mistake and it should have been done earlier. Just let me argue with your friends, by God I know they are wrong.

Again, enough of such chatter — I think I should come home, just to protect you and the Regular Army in all these arguments and criticisms that are springing up. Boy, I really have some red hot arguments of my own, straight from the ETO side of it.

The weather continues to be simply foul — we have had continuous rain for a week now, a cold nasty drizzle that gets right into your bones. Almost everyone has a cold but so far I haven't gotten one — expect it most anytime in such weather.

My life is very dull these days, the chief duties being supervising my DP camp, supervising the wood cutting program for winter fuel, and investigating black market or similar matters. I have almost no friends hereabouts and have been reading about a novel a night. We are well supplied with those paper backed books and magazines but most of it is trashy. I am afraid that I am not improving my mind very much. I have my own Group Headquarters and also a Field Artillery Battalion in my command at present.

So I can just manage to keep busy during the day, we eat supper about 5:30, and the evening stretches empty before me, starting about 6:30 P.M. Plenty of time to write letters but not much to write about, plenty of time to think and most of my thoughts are of home. So it all boils down to the fact that I am lonesome and a bit homesick — not to the stage where I mope and feel sorry for myself, just restless and griped and angry at all this time in our lives that we are wasting by being separated. And I am accomplishing so little. I do so need your love and adorable companionship again — for I miss you so.

Jimmy

30 September, 1945
10:00 p.m.

My darling one,

We have spent a very lazy Sunday here, I didn't get up until late as we had a long bull session last night and all reminisced about the war and home and such subjects. We had planned to go to the races in Munich this afternoon but it simply rained buckets so I imagine it was called off. Apparently they were going to have a regular race meet (horse races, I mean) under civilian control or at least so the radio announced. I can't figure out where the race horses will come from but apparently there are some hidden out around here, enough for one day of racing anyway.

This afternoon I just loafed and read and signed a few papers and after supper went up to Tutzing to see a movie, "The Princess and the Bellboy" or something like that. It had a good cast with Heddy Lamar and was an entertaining show but the soldiers moaned and groaned and whistled so much that they almost ruined it. And the theater was not heated so I sat in my trench coat and gloves and was still cold. Gosh, but this is a dull life I lead.

However, tomorrow promises some excitement as Gen. Patton is coming in the afternoon to inspect the DP Camp again. The heat still remains on these camps but we have been working hard on it and conditions are much improved. We still have trouble getting them to do an ounce of work and yesterday and today were holidays so I know the place will look like hell. If we could just get them to use the bathrooms and garbage cans all would be well, but those devices are still a little too civilized for them. There are times when I could just take a club and lash out all around me in that place and other times when I catch myself getting quite fond of these crazy DPs. I know they are the cause of my grey hairs and the baldish spot that is appearing on the back of my head.

I am glad that you wrote me that my grey hairs and my bald spot will not make any difference in our love. However, it makes me seem so damn old but then baldness is supposed to be inherited from your maternal grandfather and as mine was very bald there isn't anything that can be done about it. Or is there? Do you know some good remedy. Even my beard is getting grey and the grey hairs show when I haven't shaved in about 18 hours.

I think I told you about our Mercedes Benz getting confiscated in Munich a couple of weeks ago — well, anyway we have gotten a new one, not quite as snappy at the old one but the motor and tires are better. Also we have finally succeeded in getting this one registered, so it is legal and authorized so we can whip around without fear of confiscation. The only trouble is that it is a touring car and a bit open for this weather but not as open or as windy as a jeep. Also, I see that tires are unrationed now, so maybe you better buy a set as I am sure those recaps are about done for by this time.

I keep sending you pictures and you haven't sent me any in a long while. Did you ever find anyone with a 120 camera — and what about a picture of you in a bathing suit? Really, darling, you don't know how I pine for recent snapshots of you. I think my favorite one of all that I have of you is the one of you in a light colored summer dress, sitting on your feet with hands in your lap, out in your mother's garden. I look at them all so often and always carry my photo case in my pocket and show it to all and sundry on the slightest provocation. But I particularly like that one because it sort of suggests the outline of your breasts and your hands and arms are so attractive but most of all because your expression is so cute and loving and natural. You are just telling me that you love me in it. I want to take your face between my hands and kiss that dear mouth and tell you that I love you with all my heart and soul. And then I want to pick you up and carry you upstairs and really show you just how great and how beautiful this love I hold for you really is. You are such an adorable woman, so lovable, so passionate, and such fun — I do miss you so tonight. Perhaps we shall think of each other tonight — I know I shall, so now I'll hurry to bed.

I love you,
Jimmy

5 October, 1945
Friday
10:00 p.m.

My dearest one,

Have just been listening to the third game of the World Series over here — we are five hours ahead of Detroit — so we are six hours ahead of you now. I didn't really know because our time had changed last month and I supposed that yours had. Anyway it is afternoon back home and maybe you are going to a tea or out with the kids on an errand or just fooling around. What hours does Jody have at school and was her first month's report card good? Do you have to help her with her lessons or has it reached that stage yet?

You don't have to send me any more cigars as I can now get them in our little PX — also there is no need to send any toilet articles such as soap, kleenex, tooth brushes, or any of that stuff as we have plenty of it as well as candy bars and yesterday we even got in some bottled Coca Cola. I had some on the Riviera for the first time and now we have it here.

The weather continues to be simply awful — I didn't know it could keep up a drizzle so long except in the jungle. And in the mountains just south of us there was two inches of snow yesterday. The natives say it is unusual but I am getting used to that remark. However, it works a great hardship on my wood cutting details and other outside workers.

Had a couple of exciting incidents in the DP camp yesterday that I didn't mention in my letter of last night. A truck turned over on the way to Munich and killed nine of them, 23 in the hospital. I passed soon after it happened and never saw such carnage — what a mess. Then my chief of police (DP) caught the meat detail selling the meat on the black market that they were supposed to deliver to the kitchen. And one of the more prominent rabbis was right in the middle of the deal -some of these people will steal from each other just as quickly as from anyone else. If I don't get the scabies or the Chinese Rot or some such from that damn place I will be lucky. And then I was notified by phone today that two more prominent Jews would be here to inspect the camp on Sunday as personal representatives of President Truman. It is getting so we can't get anything done for the inspections we have. And of course the place will look filthy as they will not work on Saturday — it being their Sunday. Oh, well, if I get relieved maybe they will also send me over to the 15th Army and I will be under Gen Patton again.

You know, I like the Hungarian people that are here very much. They really are good people, clean, honest, never make any trouble and very grateful for all that is done for them. I really feel sorry for them as they are not a warlike people at all and just got tricked into this war. Somehow our colony of Hungarians heard that they could join the American Army and go and occupy Japan for us, so I had a delegation today with an interpreter and found out that the whole works wanted to volunteer for the job. They volunteered 100%. They really love our food and are all getting fat as pigs. Baylos is getting so fat I shall have to put him to cutting wood or something.

I hope you go on down to the Bell Ranch this month as planned. It would be a wonderful rest for you and such fun to live in luxury and be waited upon and have no chores or children to care for. Please go. But I am envious and wish I could be with you. I have always wanted to see that place — it sounds so beautiful and lazy and old worldish. So please miss me when you crawl into some great strange bed and when you do new and interesting things in strange surroundings. You know how strange beds used to effect us when we went on a trip — it always seemed to increase our love and make us more sensual and passionate toward each other. How I hate to be so remote from your life and your daily doings — I adore you.

> Your own man,
> Jimmy

7 October, 1945
Bavaria
Sunday — 7 p.m.

My adorable Joey,

The rain continues, it is now past the second solid week of it, and I can hear it pouring down outside while I sit here warm and dry. However, the lights have gone out so I am writing by candle light — most romantic and cozy but a bit hard on the eyes. But if you were just here beside me now I wouldn't have a care in the world. I have one of those old fashioned Nurnberg pottery stoves in the room — a huge white crockery affair with a very small enclosed fire box in it. It takes a great while to warm up but once the thing really gets heated, it stays warm for many hours and keeps my room very comfortable — a funny old thing, very quaint but still very efficient. Open fireplaces are too wasteful for these people.

Gen Haines, the ETO Inspector General, was today visitor at the camp. He didn't give me any trouble and seemed pleased with the state of affairs. Tomorrow or the next day I was told to expect a Mr. Price, President Truman's personal representative on Jewish affairs, to give it another going over. Boy, we really can't get anything done for the inspections we have.

Gen Haines is Ralph Haines uncle and gave me some high level dope on families coming over. He said that a board is studying the question now — about housing, schools, commissary, transportation, and all that. He thinks that families will come over next summer, at government expense, and probably live in civilian communities near the various army installations. It will be necessary to bring a car along as transportation is a serious problem here. Aside from that, probably all one will need to bring is clothing. It sounds like a good deal as we would live very cheaply, have excellent servants, and the country should be much better organized by then. It would be fun for us and very educational for the children — at their age it wouldn't hurt them a bit.

The 3rd Cav Group Headquarters will probably ship home in November or early December. However, everyone says that my chances of coming home with it are very slim at present. I shall do my utmost to bring them home but don't get your hopes up at all about it, for I repeat that my chance of doing so is extremely slim. I will definitely not take a 30 day leave at home if it is offered to me in the near future as I want to stay in command until the outfit ships — for to take a leave is to say you will come back. However, as soon as my outfit is alerted to ship, if I get pulled out I shall immediately try to get my thirty days at home. So that is the way it stands — and perhaps I will be home Xmas, either with the outfit or on a 30 day leave.

I really feel rather desperate about the Xmas thing, having missed being with my family for the last two, I am determined to make it for this coming one. If I don't get to one soon, my children will both be past this Santy Claus idea — and with Jody going to school, she won't be a believer for very much longer. It was really just about two years ago that we were really a family, all together in our little house in Leavenworth, and Jamie was just a baby then. To think that he will soon be three years old and that we will have been married nine years. It really doesn't seem possible that we can be growing old at such a rapid rate — old father time moves more rapidly than we realize. But the trouble is that we are not growing old together — oh, but we must be reunited soon, we simply must be.

I got a letter from Dan, telling me that the shotgun arrived and thanking me for it. However, what really made me feel good was that he said you were more beautiful than ever, so good, so true, so fine. Of course I know that, know it completely and without a doubt, but it is so wonderful to hear it from others. The way to my heart is to praise my wife or my children — anyone that does that is my favorite person forever. Oh, my blessed dear adorable wife, I am so proud of you and all you have done, so proud of our children that you are raising for me. And I shall make it up to you when once we are together again. I love every precious inch of you, every hair on your head and body, every mole and tiny speck of you — I just love you.

Jimmy

9 October, 1945
Bavaria

Dearly beloved,

Well, things are still popping about the place in great shape — yesterday Gen Truscott, the new Army commander, came down to see my place — just one day after he assumed command of Third Army. That is how hot the place is. However, he did seem pleased with what he saw and said that he thought everything possible was being done for my fine feathered friends, the Jewish DPs.

However, I am just about to have a riot on my hands as my Field Artillery Battalion was ordered to move out of their billets and find new homes — so the DPs could move in. Boy, I bet more letters to Congressmen go whistling off to the States on that one. The Battalion is really enraged about this move, it is too bad really for another 500 men are so upset about this whole business that words won't express it. I have had a chronic case of indigestion for the past week, I have been in such a temper. I just have to pop off to someone, so you have to suffer. Believe me, I wouldn't dare express such sentiments in public or even in private.

Oh, man, I am really sick of this country, its filth, poverty, venality, underhand meanness. Everyone seems crooked, everything has its price, every civilian can be bribed — yet they fawn and cringe to an American. It is disgusting. Everyone here has been left by this awful war in a horrible state with no self respect, no honesty, no pride — no nothing.

I guess I feel badly because I haven't heard from you in so long also. But at last, today we had a beautiful, clear, sun shiny day — our first in two weeks. So tomorrow the air mail ought to come in with a rush and I shall have beaucoup letters from you. You don't know how I look forward to those little messages of joy — they mean so much to me — sort of change my outlook on the whole world — oh, to come home and renew my faith in human beings — that is what I really need — I really need you now, and long for you and miss you more than you can ever know. Will this separation never end. It goes on for ever.

I love you,
Jimmy

11 October, 1945
Bavaria
9:30 p.m.

My darling one,

Got a couple of cute letters from you today and it did cheer me up — to hear of you running around with just my cotton robe on and working for the rummage sale and going on a picnic and just being your normal happy self. I do so want to share the every day part of your life — and letters are such a poor substitute, better than none but still leaving so much to be desired. And now Harry is home and apparently Tom is coming home shortly — and here I sit. I am of course damn happy for them — but it does make me furious every time I hear of some short-timer getting back ahead of me — it certainly ought to be my turn soon.

My DP camp continues to improve — not through added efforts of my own but because now all I have to do to get anything is ask — blankets, shoes, suits, food — all are pouring in and in my opinion it is an awful crime — as the plight of other DPs, prisoners of war, and German civilians is desperate—but not the chosen people, they still aren't lifting a finger to help themselves but are living in clover and selling half their supplies on the black market as well. They are all going to leave here rich!

Got a nice letter from Freddy Devereux, it seems he is out of the army and working for an advertising firm in N.Y. — seems a shame that the army is loosing all its good men. He said Wort and Patty are still at W.P. and will remain another year — the bums should be sent over here.

I took a physical exam yesterday — my first in several years — and weighed 151 pounds which is good for me. All was OK except for these cavities in my teeth which I shall hasten to have repaired. I do feel a bit sneezy tonight so shall now take an aspirin and go to bed. Maybe I can break it up before it gets started. I guess these last three days of good weather were too much for me, I am now used to continual rain. Bless you, my lovely wife, I live for the day of our reunion, so keep in good shape, for that first month will be terrific and strenuous — mostly exercise in bed. I love you with all my heart.

Jimmy

14 October, 1945
Sunday — 8:30 p.m.

My darling one,

Today the weather has been simply beautiful, one of those bracing autumn days like we used to have at West Point. All the leaves are now turning golden and beginning to fall and this countryside is really lovely. I put in part of my morning at the camp as we had another general there to inspect — he seemed satisfied so after lunch we were all trying to figure out something to do. Anyway, about that time a classmate of mine named Stan Lonning drove up — he was at the Camp looking for a job and I had seen him at the Riviera — and suggest we go to a football game in Munich. We did and it was an altogether lousy game — soldier football — but it was fun driving about in his snappy open Mercedes. I enjoyed his company as I have so few friends about. He left for his division after a supper here but I hope he gets a job at XX Corps — you would like him. He is also a bit glum about getting stateside — his division goes home next month, without him!

Aside from the little outing mentioned above, my life has been very dull — I haven't even been over to the Frick house in over a week. However, I felt pretty rotten until today with a head cold but it is about over now. However, will you send me one of those "Benzedrine inhalers" for my next head cold — I missed it in this last go around and of course they are unobtainable over here. I think I told you that it wasn't necessary to send cigars anymore — I can now get good U.S. over here.

I haven't heard from you since your letter of September 29th and have been wondering if you have gone down to the Bell Ranch in the meanwhile. I hope you have as you certainly deserve a vacation by this time. You have been on the job ever since I left, it seems. Everyone here simply raves about the Switzerland leave deal, seven days tour through the country. It is very well run, by the American Express Co. I think, and the service, accommodations, and food are said to be superb. Several of my soldiers have come home with handsome watches that cost as little as $12.50. Also a telephone call home to El Paso would only cost about $15.00 — wouldn't that be exciting, would it make you happy? I know it would be wonderful to hear your voice, even if you cried when you heard me. They tell me that you, on that end, would get four hours warning to stand by and be ready for the call. That would give you time to think what to say. One soldier who talked to his wife in Kansas City said the connection was so good that it sounded as if his wife was in the next room.

That really is my main reason for wanting to take the tour — to telephone you. When things cool down at the DP camp, perhaps some time in November, I think I will try it. It really would be heaven just to hear your voice again — write me your mother's telephone number as I can't remember it — and who knows, maybe one of these days a call will come through, from me to you. I shall be in a very private spot when I call you, so I can say very private things, but I don't imagine you can be — and I shall want to hear Jody and particularly Jamie as I have never heard him say a word. If it is in the middle of the night you must awaken them — now don't forget that part.

It has been more than twenty months since I last saw you — what did you once write me, that Hutch said the first twenty months are the hardest. I am damned if I believe that, for me it has seemed so much harder of late to be away from you. I am completely fed up with living this bachelor existence. I really have been miserable of late, just living among men. And everyone over here is so restless, so anxious to be home, so tired of redeployment and talk of point scores, no one seems settled or sure of what the future means.

It is easy to live in the present when the present is full of happenings, even if they are exciting and dangerous. But when one's duty is dull and distasteful it is different — I feel like I am stagnating, I need your confidence and companionship and good sense. And more than that I need your love, the love that shows in your voice and your eyes and your actions, the love that your beautiful pliant passionate body gives me when you surrender to my caresses — I do love you so, my adorable one.

Thy Jimmy

15 October, 1945
Bavaria

My dearest,

Here are some pictures taken on 17 September when Gen Ike and Co. visited my DP camp at Feldafing. The negatives were good but the printing paper over here is very poor so they didn't turn out so well.

No letter from you since yours of 19 September — it makes me unhappy as the mail service was so wonderful for awhile. No news today, life is so dull — I want company, your company to be exact. I love you, yet.

Buenos Noches,
Jimmy

16 October, 1945
I have been all mixed up on
the date — this is right
8:30 p.m.

My dearest one,

Still no mail and it makes me furious, not even any "Stars and Stripes" and we can't figure out what is the matter. Today was lovely, so three of us took a couple of hours off and went sailing — it was fun as there was a stiff breeze and a warm sun, but we still kept on plenty of clothes. It really is a lovely lake with the snow covered mountains as a back drop — would be worth plenty transplanted to Texas.

We were marooned for awhile. As the big boat draws about eight feet of water, we keep it tied to a buoy out about 100 feet in the lake. When we came back and tied up to the buoy, someone had stolen the little row boat we get back to shore with. There was much calling and yelling to get someone to come out and pick us up — we had just about decided to swim for it in the icy water when someone appeared and saved the day. And now it turns out that some DP stole the row boat, isn't that gratitude for you.

We got some bad news today. Our Hungarians are to be sent back to their native land about the 1st of November, whether they want to go or not. It is terrible and I don't know how I shall ever get along without Baylos. The best workers and least troublesome of all the captured people we have — and they have to go and send them home. They wait on tables, take care of the horses, keep the place clean, and are generally indispensable.

Darling, if you knew how I wanted pictures of my family, you would make more of an effort to get them for me. I haven't received any snapshots in several months now — and you mentioned that you would have some family group pictures taken in a studio. What has happened to that project?

I of course carry my photo case in my right breast pocket all the time and very often show it to people. But in my room I only have the two pictures taken at West Point — the one of the two kids is cute but so out of date — and I hate that one of you, I am sick of looking at it as you look so stern and forbidding — it is not at all characteristic of you — it doesn't look loving or affectionate or anything.

So right now, today, you go downtown and order me an enlargement of the small picture you sent last winter — the posed one of you with a right earring and no left one — about 5" by 8" so I can frame it and put it in my room — I love it, because it does look loving and affectionate. Now do this! Also while you are in the studio, make an appointment for pictures of all the family. And don't wait until Xmas to send them — send them as soon as possible. Please, darling.

I get more homesick for you and the kids with each day that passes, but don't worry, I haven't gotten to the point of feeling sorry for myself — but it may be soon. I really am fed up. I've had it. Life is dull and drab and uninteresting and I am loosing all my zip and personality. I need you to revitalize me — and love me — Good night, my love.

Jimmy

21 October, 1945
Bavaria

My own darling one,

The mail has been good, a letter from you yesterday and another today, both very interesting and so full of the you that I love. I like your advice about talking to newsmen and shall heed it. You never know what part of a conversation those bums will report so I guess the answer is to say practically nothing and answer in monosyllables or act dumb. They asked me a thousand questions as we walked around the camp, it was in no sense a press conference or anything like that. However, I have certainly learned my lesson and only hope that the remarks of mine that were quoted did not hurt Gen Patton. The enclosed clippings from the Stars and Stripes shows now that public opinion is turning the other way at last.

To show you how some of these people are, the head DP of the Camp, their elected leader, resigned yesterday. The reason he resigned is that we got him in a squeeze — we found out that he had been shaking down the other DPs and charging them a nice price to move into the homes we had moved the Krauts out of. Boy, we are really going to salt him away for a good long time.

I am distressed that the pictures did not turn out well of the family, really, you don't know how distressed I am and I hope and pray that you will try some other place else. Or hasn't someone got a good Leica or Contax that they can take a bunch of candid camera shots of you all — I have read in the papers that film is now easy to obtain at home. Have a picture taken of you sitting on a rail and showing lots of your pretty legs — because you never have sent me a pin up picture and all the other guys wives have.

Today the weather was beautiful, so after lunch Johnny Logan and I got out the Mercedes, put down the top, and went for a drive. We went south, through Bad Tolz to Mittenwald, deep in the mountains, then to Garmish-Partenkirchen, then back past Wildheim to Tutzing. It took us about four hours but was one of the most beautiful rides I have ever taken — all the trees golden, the snow capped peaks, the rushing mountain streams and water falls. I thought of you all the way and much of it reminded me of around West Point in the fall. You would have loved it and if you had been along with me, we could have stopped and gone walking in the woods. It would be just like our holiday in Ruidoso — almost exactly two years ago — and we could have sat on a rock in the sun — hidden from all prying eyes. I would have snuggled you and kissed you and all sorts of things could have happened. And I know damn well they would have happened if you had been along today. My need of you is really terrific these days, I know we both feel the same way and this separation has seemed harder to us both of late — I guess because everyone else is coming home. I met a man who had been over here 3-1/2 years without going home — it really gave me the shudders. I hope and pray that your intuition is right and that I will be home soon — but I can't see it as yet from here — I love you and adore you, my precious.

Jimmy

25 October, 1945
Bavaria

My adorable wife,

Happy Wedding Anniversary! It breaks my heart that I should be writing this to you instead of being there to say it in person and present you with a gift to mark our nine years of happiness. Think of it, nine years, yet really it ought to be seven, for we have only lived together for seven. Yet you have been so close to me these last two years, close beside me in everything I do, so I know it is proper to call it nine. And those nine years certainly overshadow all the rest of my life —so much that you have always seemed a part of me, I can't conceive of ever living and not being married to you.

It was indeed a happy day when we married and just thinking of it fills me with memories of those days — of my courtship of you, of our doubts about the wiseness of it and our suitability for each other. I suppose all sensible people have such doubts. And memories of our funny honeymoon, so mixed and full of great happiness and young passion, of funny little quarrels and arguments, of learning to live as a couple — our funny awkward loving, so full of desire. Our first years together were lovely, full of happiness and pride for me — yet I think we were young and sometimes foolish and sometimes quarreled foolishly. But our love became deeper all the time — deeper and more meaningful and more important.

On looking back over our years together, I don't believe we were really, deeply, truly in love as we know the meaning of the word now until our little Jody came along. I think since the day I saw you suffer in the Junction City, Kansas hospital, the day our little pumpkin was born, and you were afraid to go to sleep for fear that you might not awaken — since that day I have loved you as completely as it is possible for a man to love a woman, since that day I have been all yours and only yours — without thought, word, or deed to the contrary. Nothing can ever part us, not time or distance nor hell and highwater. My wife, my lover, my companion, my all is Josephine Leavell Polk — no other human can do or will do — I just have to have you.

Before that day, June 2, 1939, I loved you, of course I loved you very much — but I didn't know just how much I did love you, I didn't know what a truly wonderful person you were, I didn't know how important you were to me. Since that day, the knowledge of my love — of our love for each other — has been like a bright, steady flame in my heart — it gives a sort of inner warmth to my body, and must show in my face when I am with you or when you are in the fore front of my thoughts.

And you must know how you have sustained me these last two years — what I have done, I have done for you. So that I could come home to you with my head high and tell you that I had done my duty and done it well and that you could be proud of me — and more, that you are the only woman in the world for me and I have been a true and faithful husband to you, my adorable one.

I bless the day we were married and I bless each day of these last nine years — for they have been ours, to live together as man and wife — beautiful years because of you, my perfect, adorable, wonderful, lovely woman.

Your husband,
Jimmy

27 October, 1945

My dearest one,

Just received your long and understanding letter — written in answer to mine where I was so low and downcast about the Army and the DPs and life in general — and Gen. Patton's relief in particular. You are a sweet and understanding and smart wife and you really said it right when you said all the men need their wives over here. It is the truth, we need balance and companionship and we need to come home in the evening and forget it all and play with the kids.

I feel much better about it all now — I think one reason for my blues was that I had a simply rotten cold, now over. Also I do feel better about my job, particularly since I know I am doing a hell of a lot of good — there are times when I really have a sort of affection for these crazy Jewish DPs — and we shall shortly have the banner camp in the ETO. Some of them are starting to do a bit of work now and we are going to have our first dance tomorrow — some one said it would be just like a "race track" with the dancers going around and around.

To show you how we have progressed, we now have a school, a carpenter shop, shoe shop, plumbing shop, tailor shop, orchestra, dramatic society, and a fine jail. However, the people still continue to throw the garbage out the window, go to the "john" in the hallways, and steal the toilet paper for sale on the black market. Cigarettes are worth $20 a carton, shoes $80.00 a pair, and nickel candy bars sell for the equivalent of a dollar.

Here is a list of some of the things you can send me:

    A good shaving brush
    Some dental floss
    Chili sauce
    Worchester sauce
    A-1 steak sauce
    A good automatic pencil
    2 pair of Colonel's eagles (or more)
    Benzedrine inhaler
    Books

And in one of your recent letters you said you were afraid that I might walk in on you without any warning and try and surprise you. Darling, believe me, you don't need to worry about any such happening — for I won't do it. I shall wire you from this side when and if I get any orders, secondly, I shall wire you when I get to the POE and am about to cross the big water, and finally I shall phone you just as soon as I reach those blessed shores. So don't worry, my darling, I couldn't keep my excitement from you in the first place and in the second, I want you to be all ready for me. I want you all dressed in your trousseau, fresh out of the beauty parlor, looking your loveliest, and all ready for your man. The anticipation is half the fun anyway and I wouldn't deprive you of that. My big worry is not trying to surprise you, my big worry is just plain getting back to you, that is all I want and all I live for — Oh, happy day — will it ever come? I pray it will be soon — I love you, my dearest one.

Your Jimmy

29 October, 1945
10 p.m.

My dearest one,

A raft of mail came in today — from you, mother, and Phil Davidson, all full of news and I am most happy. I am glad the package arrived, why don't you give the little pair of leather pants to Bubba if they are too small for Jody as I thought they would be. The books are from Dr. Frick's house. You asked about him. He goes on trial in Nuremberg very shortly with the other high war criminals and has been indicted on all four counts. I think he will be convicted and executed. Also all his property will be forfeited, leaving his wife a pauper unless she has some property in her own name. I don't know what will happen to the house — I imagine it will be sold at auction. We can stay in it as long as we want to however.

Paul Harkins and Hap Gay have both left Third Army Headquarters and have gone over to 15th Army with Gen Patton — all the rest of the headquarters is unchanged. I have only seen Gen Truscott once, when he visited my camp and I haven't been over to 3rd A since he took command.

I had some rather exciting news from Phil Davidson — he said the 3rd Squadron was moving from Bragg to Bowie — so both the 3rd and 43rd will be together again. They have both been notified that they (the outfits) will remain as part of the regular army — so it does seem logical that they would want the group headquarters to come back to Bowie to command them. Doesn't that seem logical to you? And I should certainly go along to command. Now I just hope the army acts in a logical fashion. But no indication of any orders along that line as yet.

You asked about me going to church. I haven't been in about three months but will get back in the swing of it when I get home and promise to go often with you. We have a Catholic Chaplain — a very devout and good man and we have had many talks on religion. I know I upset him very much because I was once a Catholic and he has tried very hard to reconvert me. However, the experiences of the past two years and my talks with him all go to convince me that I am NOT a Catholic — but certainly I am also a Christian and live by Christian standards. Therefore I want you to continue to be a good Episcopalian and to raise the children the same way. Perhaps some day I can become a good one also.

Yesterday I went to a cocktail party — can you believe it? The General's aide called up Saturday and invited me to a "cocktail buffet" from 4 to 6, just like the old days. The Army is really getting settled over here. It was a lot of fun though, all the Corps officers above the rank of Major, some Red Cross girls, and three frauleins who turned out to be the Corps telephone operators. I certainly didn't like that angle of it a bit and didn't go near that part of the room. The R.C. girls were a bit insulted but are getting used to it. However, we are certainly lowering ourselves and our prestige with the Germans when our high ranking officers are associating with telephone operators. It certainly is high time that the families were allowed over here — as I think it would put a stop to such foolishness or at least slow it down.

The weather continues lovely but I think we are living on borrowed time. Everyone is frantically cutting wood, including my D.P.'s at last. We got in a bunch of German skis and also I got ahold of a gorgeous fur parka, intended for the Air Corps, with a fur hood and collar and all lined in sheep skin. So I know I shall be warm this winter. Also I think I have located a nice gun to send to Chas — don't tell him as I am not sure yet.

I too am living for my return. As I told you earlier, I could probably get a 30 day leave (not 45 from the ETO) but haven't put in for it yet as I am sweating out the return of the 3ed Cav to the states — As soon as I know anything definite I will let you know. We ought to know fairly soon. All my love, my precious one. I adore you —

Jimmy

Editor's Note: On 30 October, 1945 Col. Polk received orders to return immediately to the U.S. with one month's leave of absence and to report thereafter to Fort Riley, Kansas to assume duties as Chief of Tactics at the Ground General School. He arrived in El Paso, Texas on 7 November 1945 in time for his ninth wedding anniversary with his beloved wife and children.

APPENDIX

GENERAL JAMES H. POLK
DECORATIONS AND AWARDS:

UNITED STATES

Distinguished Service Medal (1st Oak Leaf Cluster)
Silver Star (1st Oak Leaf Cluster)
Legion of Merit (2d Oak Leaf Cluster)
Bronze Star
Air Medal
American Defense Service Medal
American Campaign Medal
European African Middle Eastern Medal
World War II Victory Medal
Army of Occupation Medal (with clasp for Germany and Japan)
National Defense Service Medal (1st Oak Leaf Cluster) .
Korean Service Medal
Armed Forces Expeditionary Medal
United Nations Service Medal

FOREIGN

Croix de Guerre (with Palm) (France)
Republic of Korea Presidential Unit Citation
Grand Cross (with Star and Sash) (Germany)
Legion of Honor (Commander) (France)

GENERAL JAMES H. POLK, USA
MILITARY CAREER BIOGRAPHY

James Hilliard Polk was born at Camp McGraw, Batangas, Philippine Islands, on December 13, 1911, of Army parents. He was graduated from the United States Military Academy in 1933 and commissioned a 2d Lieutenant of Cavalry. Prior to World War II, he served as a unit officer in two cavalry regiments, and attended the regular and advanced courses at the Cavalry School.

At the outbreak of World War II, General Polk was a Company Tactical Officer with the Corps of Cadets at West Point. In 1943, General Polk attended the short general staff course at Fort Leavenworth and then joined the 106th Mechanized Cavalry Group at Fort Hood, Texas, serving as Squadron Commander and later as Regimental Executive Officer. The 106th Cavalry Group joined the Normandy beachhead forces and participated in the hedgerow fighting, the St. Lo breakout, and Third Army's drive across France.

In early September 1944, General Polk assumed command of the 3d Cavalry Group, then in combat near Metz, France, and continued to command this mechanized reconnaissance regiment for the balance of the war. The 3d Cavalry remained assigned continuously to General Walton H. Walker's Twentieth Corps of Third Army and frequently spearheaded its advances into central Europe. In these campaigns the regiment was cited frequently for bold and aggressive action and General Polk was decorated three times for gallantry, once by General Patton personally. General Patton authorized the regiment's own patch, which General Polk always wore on his right shoulder.

After brief occupation duty in Germany at the end of World War II, Polk returned to the United States and became Chief of Tactics at the Ground General School, Fort Riley, Kansas, and later attended the Armed Forces Staff College. In 1948, he was ordered to Tokyo, Japan, and served in the G2 Section of the U.S. Far East Command under General Douglas MacArthur for the next three years.

Early in the Korean War, General Polk became Assistant Chief of Staff, G2 of the Tenth Corps and participated in three campaigns. In August 1951, he returned to attend the National War College and was later assigned as an instructor at the Army War College at Carlisle Barracks, Pennsylvania. He was then made Chief of Staff of the 3d Armored Division at Fort Knox, Kentucky and participated in the gyroscope shipment of the division to West Germany. In July 1956, Polk was promoted to Brigadier General and served as Assistant Division Commander for one year.

Following this tour, General Polk's career began to broaden into the field of soldier-diplomat assignments. For two years he served as Assistant Chief of Staff for Plans and Operations, Land Forces Central Europe, at NATO Headquarters at Fontainebleau, France, under General Dr. Hans Speidel.

In July 1959, he returned to Washington D.C. and became the Director of the Policy Planning Staff in the Office of the Assistant Secretary of Defense for International Security Affairs in the Pentagon.

His assignments in the international field were temporarily halted in June 1961 when he was promoted to Major General and ordered back to Western Germany to take command of the 4th Armored Division. However, he returned to soldier-diplomat status when he was assigned as US Commander, Berlin, on January 2, 1963, most notably hosting President John F. Kennedy's historic visit there on June 26, 1963.

General Polk became Commanding General of V Corps on 1 September 1964 and was promoted to Lieutenant General on 4 September 1964. He remained Commanding General of V Corps until February 1966 and then returned to the United States to become the Assistant Chief of Staff for Force Development, United States Army, Washington, D.C. In November 1966, General Polk was assigned as the Deputy Commander in Chief, United States Army Europe, and in June 1967 he was promoted to the grade of General and made Commander in Chief, United States Army Europe and Seventh Army, and Commander, Central Army Group, NATO.

General Polk left the active ranks in March, 1971 after more than 37 years of commissioned military service.

INDEX

CPSIA information can be obtained
at www.ICGtesting.com
Printed in the USA
LVHW031139200319
611264LV00001B/321/P

9 781932 762198